Setting the Agenda

For Betsy and my children,
Molly, Leslie, Max and Sam

Setting the Agenda
The Mass Media and Public Opinion

Maxwell McCombs

polity

First published in 2004 by Polity Press

Polity Press
65 Bridge Street
Cambridge CB2 1UR, UK.

Published in the United States and Canada by
Blackwell Publishing Inc.
350 Main Street
Malden, MA 02148, USA

ISBN: 0-7456-2312-3
ISBN: 0-7456-2313-1 (paperback)

A catalogue record for this book is available from the British Library and has been applied for from the Library of Congress.

Typeset in 10.5 on 12 pt Plantin
by Kolam Information Services Pvt. Ltd, Pondicherry, India
Printed and bound in Great Britain by MPG Books, Bodmin, Cornwall

For further information on Polity, visit our website: www.polity.co.uk

Contents

List of Boxes

Preface

Setting the agenda is now a common phrase in discussions of politics and public opinion. This phrase summarizes the continuing dialogue and debate in every community, from local neighbourhoods to the international arena, over what should be at the centre of public attention and action. In most of these dialogues the mass media have a significant and sometimes controversial role. Noting this role of the media in setting the national agenda during a critical phase of his country's political transition, the editor of South Africa's largest daily, *The Sowetan*, remarked, 'It is our contention that in a country like South Africa, it simply cannot be right that, because of its dominance in the media, a minority should continue to set the public agenda.'[1] In the United Kingdom, *The Guardian* made a similar comment: 'The profoundly dysfunctional British press, over 75% controlled by three rightwing men, has the bit between its teeth, setting the agenda for the nation's political discourse.'[2]

Should there be any doubt about this longstanding and widespread role of the news media, note the *New York Times*'s description of twentieth-century British press baron Lord Beaverbrook as a man 'who dined with prime ministers and set the nation's agenda'.[3] Or former *New York Times* executive Max Frankel's description of his own newspaper:

> It is the 'house organ' of the smartest, most talented, and most influential Americans at the height of American power. And while its editorial opinions or the views of individual columnists and critics can be despised or dismissed, the paper's daily package of news cannot. It frames the intellectual and emotional agenda of serious Americans.[4]

The enormous growth and expansion of these mass media institutions that are now such a compelling feature of contemporary society was a central aspect of the last century. To the host of newspapers and magazines spawned in the nineteenth century, the twentieth century added ubiquitous layers of film, radio, television and cable television. In its closing years came the internet and a kaleidoscopic mix of communication technologies that continue to blur the traditional boundaries between the various media and their content.

Although everyone talks about the impact of these emerging technologies in the new millennium, the enormous social influence of mass communication was already apparent decades before the latest waves of technology spread across the world. In *The Making of the President, 1972*, American journalist Theodore White described the power of mass communication to set the agenda of public attention as 'an authority that in other nations is reserved for tyrants, priests, parties and mandarins'.[5] In the years since White's cogent observation, social scientists across the world have elaborated the ability of the mass media to influence many aspects of our political, social and cultural agendas.

One of the most prominent and best-documented intellectual maps of this influence, the theory of the agenda-setting role of mass communication, is the subject of this book. Theories seldom emerge full-blown. They typically begin with a succinct insight and are subsequently elaborated and explicated over many years by various explorers and surveyors of their intellectual terrain. This has been the case for agenda-setting theory. From a parsimonious hypothesis about the effects of mass communication on the public's attention to social and political issues, this theory has expanded to include propositions about the contingent conditions for these effects, the influences that shape the media's agenda, the impact of specific elements in the media's messages, and a variety of consequences of this agenda-setting process. Agenda-setting theory has become a highly detailed map of the mass media agenda and its effects.

The immediate origins of this idea in its contemporary form began with a casual observation about the play of news stories on the front page of the *Los Angeles Times* one day in early 1967. There were three big stories that day: internationally, the unexpected shift from Labour to Conservative in the British county council elections; nationally, a budding scandal in Washington; and locally, the firing of the Los Angeles metropolitan area director of a large federally funded programme that was a keystone in the national 'War on Poverty'. Not surprisingly, the *Los Angeles Times* put the local story in the lead position on page 1. With its conservative page design, this relegated the other two stories to single-column headlines elsewhere on the front page. Any one of these stories – in the absence of the other two – easily would have been the page 1 lead, a situation that led to a speculative conversation over drinks among several young UCLA faculty members at their Friday afternoon 'junior faculty meeting' in the lobby of the Century Plaza Hotel. Is the impact of an event diminished when a news story receives less prominent play, we wondered? Those speculations grounded in a scattered variety of ideas and empirical findings about the influence of mass media on the public were the seeds for the theory of agenda-setting.

While there are now more than 400 published empirical investigations worldwide, the formal explication of the idea of agenda-setting began with my move that fall to the University of North Carolina at Chapel Hill, where I met Don Shaw and began what is now a 35-year plus friendship and professional partnership. Our initial attempt at formal research on this idea built literally on those speculations in Los Angeles about the play of news stories. We attempted to construct an experiment based on actual newspapers that played the same story in radically different ways. The *Charlotte Observer* was a widely respected newspaper in North Carolina that produced a series of editions during the day, early ones for points distant from Charlotte, the final edition for the city itself. One result of these multiple editions was that some stories would begin the day prominently played on the front page and then move down in prominence in subsequent editions, sometimes moving entirely off the front page. Our original plan was to use these differences from edition to edition as the basis of an experiment. However, the shifts in news play from day to day proved too erratic – in terms both of the subjects of the stories and in the way that their play in the newspaper changed – for any systematic comparison of their impact upon the public's perceptions.

Despite this setback, the theoretical idea was intriguing, and we decided to try another methodological tack, a small survey of undecided voters during the 1968 US presidential election in tandem with a systematic content analysis of how the news media used by these voters played the major issues of the election. Undecided voters were selected for study on the assumption that, among the public at large, this group who were interested in the election, but undecided about their vote, would be the most open to media influence. This was the Chapel Hill study,[6] now known as the origin of agenda-setting theory. A fundamental contribution of the Chapel Hill study was the term itself, 'agenda-setting', which gave this concept of media influence immediate currency among scholars. Steve Chaffee recalls that, when I saw him at the 1968 annual meeting of the Association for Education in Journalism and told him about our study of agenda-setting, the term was new and unfamiliar, but he immediately understood the focus of our research.

Since Don Shaw trained in history, you might expect us to have exact records on the creation of the term 'agenda-setting' – the 'One Tuesday afternoon in early August . . . ' kind of sentence – but, ironically, neither Don nor I recall exactly when we came up with that name. We didn't mention 'agenda-setting' in our 1967 application to the National Association of Broadcasters for the small grant used in partial support of the research, but our 1969 report to the NAB on the results of the Chapel Hill study uses the term as if it had been around forever. Sometime during 1968 the name 'agenda-setting' appeared,[7] and Steve Chaffee undoubtedly was one of the first 'referees' to acknowledge its utility – perhaps the very first outside the immediate Chapel Hill circle involved in the project. Chapter 1 presents the details of that investigation as well as some of the key intellectual antecedents of this idea predating both Chapel Hill and Los Angeles. Additional links with other longstanding communication concepts are reviewed in the discussion in chapter 6 of agenda-setting theory's continuing evolution.

To paraphrase Sherlock Holmes, with the success of the 1968 Chapel Hill investigation the game clearly was afoot. There were promising leads in hand for the solution to at least a portion of the mystery about the precise effects of mass communication upon public opinion. Subsequently, many detectives began to pursue these clues about how public attention and perception are influenced by the media and how various characteristics of the media, their content and their audiences mediate these effects. Much like the adventures of Sherlock Holmes, whose cases fill nine lengthy volumes, a wide variety of links in this vast intellectual web have been chronicled. However, it has been a disjointed series of contributions. Because the marketplace of ideas in communication research is very much one of laissez-faire, elaboration of the agenda-setting role of the mass media has not proceeded in any orderly or systematic fashion. There have been many detectives working on many cases in a variety of geographical and cultural settings, adding a bit of evidence here and another bit there over the years. New theoretical concepts explicating the idea of agenda-setting emerged in one part of this intellectual web, then at another.

Until very recently, the primary emphasis was always an agenda of public issues. Especially in its popular manifestation of polls in the news media, public opinion is frequently regarded in these terms. Agenda-setting theory evolved from a description and explanation of the influence that mass communication has on public opinion about the issues of the day. An open-ended question used by the Gallup Poll since the 1930s, 'What is the most important problem facing this country today?', is frequently used for this research because polls based on this question document the hundreds of issues that have engaged the attention of the public and pollsters over the past five or six decades.[8]

More recently, agenda-setting theory has encompassed public opinion about political candidates and other public figures, specifically the images that the public holds of these individuals and the contributions of the mass media to those public images. This larger agenda of topics – public figures as well as public issues – marks an important theoretical expansion from the beginning of the communication process, what topics the media and public are paying attention to and regard as important, to a subsequent stage, how the media and public perceive and understand the details of these topics. In turn, this second stage is the opening gambit for mapping the consequences of the media's agenda-setting role for attitudes, opinions and behaviour. All of these significant media effects upon the public are presented in this volume, not just theoretically, but in terms of the empirical evidence on these effects worldwide.

In contrast to the piecemeal historical evolution of our knowledge about agenda-setting since the seminal 1968 Chapel Hill study, the chapters of this book strive for an orderly and systematic presentation of what we have learned over those years, an attempt to integrate the vast diversity of this evidence – diverse in its historical and geographical settings, mix of mass media and specific public issues, and research methods. Presenting this integrated picture – in the words of John Pavlik, a *Gray's Anatomy* of agenda-setting theory[9] – is the central purpose of the book. Much of the evidence forming this picture is from an American setting because the 'founding fathers' of agenda-setting, Don Shaw, David Weaver,[10] and me, are American academics, and the majority of the empirical research has been conducted in the United States. However, the reader will encounter considerable evidence from Britain, Spain, Japan, Taiwan and other countries around the world. One of the great strengths of agenda-setting theory is this geographical and cultural diversity in the evidence replicating the major aspects of this mass communication influence on society.

Beyond the immense gratitude to my best friends and long-time research partners, Don Shaw and David Weaver, this book owes a great debt to that host of scholars worldwide who created the accumulated literature that is catalogued here. With the risk of being an absent-minded professor and omitting significant contributors, I especially acknowledge my personal enjoyment of working over extended periods of time with Esteban Lopez-Escobar, Dixie Evatt, Salma Ghanem, Spiro Kiousis, Dominic Lasorsa, Federico Rey Lennon, Juan Pablo Llamas, Paula Poindexter, Toshio Takeshita, Wayne Wanta and Jian-Hua Zhu. Special recognition is due James Dearing and Everett Rogers for their book *Agenda Setting*, a 'must read' on the history and basic ideas of agenda-setting,[11] and special thanks to John Thompson of Polity Press for his long patience in waiting for this book. There also is a personal debt to my professors, Walter Wilcox at Tulane University, who guided me to graduate study at Stanford University, where Chilton Bush, Richard Carter, Nathan Maccoby and Wilbur Schramm started me down this theoretical trail. More recently, my thanks to Issa Luna at Universidad Nacional Autonoma de Mexico and to colleagues at the University of Navarra in Pamplona, Spain, and Catholic University and Diego Portales University in Santiago, Chile, who have been instrumental in the diffusion of agenda-setting theory in Latin America.

The theory of agenda-setting is a complex intellectual map still in the process of evolving. Although the emphasis in this book is on an empirically grounded media-centric map of what we now know about the role of the mass media in the formation of public opinion, there is considerable discussion in the later chapters of the larger context in which this media influence occurs. This agenda-setting role of the mass media has been a rich lode for scholars to mine for more than thirty-five years, and yet much of its wealth remains untapped. However, even the existing theoretical map already identifies exciting new areas to explore, and the flux in our contemporary public communication system creates a plethora of new opportunities for elaborating the map presented here. Reviewing this new age of political communication that is upon us, British scholars Jay G. Blumler and Dennis Kavanagh observed:

> Such a situation is highly promising for research, but demands imagination in tailoring it to these tensions and the new conditions.... Among the field's master paradigms, agenda setting may be most worth pursuing. Are media agendas diversifying across the many different outlets of political communication, and, if so, how are they being received by the audiences of those outlets?[12]

The goal of this book is to present some basic ideas about the role of the mass media in the shaping of public opinion and to catalogue a representative sample of the supporting empirical evidence. This knowledge can guide future map-makers' explorations of mass communication and open the way to understanding the larger social context of mass communication.

Even within the original domain of public opinion, there is more to consider than just the descriptions and explanations of how the mass media influence our views of public affairs. For journalists this phenomenon that we now talk about as the agenda-setting role of the news media is an awesome, overarching ethical question about what agenda the media are advancing. 'What the public needs to know' is a recurring phrase in the rhetorical repertoire of professional journalism. Does the media agenda really represent what the public needs to know?[13] In a moment of doubt, the executive producer of ABC News's *Nightline* once asked: 'Who are we to think we should set an agenda for the nation? What made us any smarter than the next guy?'[14] To a considerable degree, journalism is grounded in the tradition of storytelling. However, good journalism is more than just telling a good story. It is about telling stories that contain significant civic utility.[15] The agenda-setting role of the mass media links journalism and its tradition of storytelling to the arena of public opinion, a relationship with considerable consequences for society.

1 Influencing Public Opinion

The American humorist Will Rogers was fond of prefacing his sardonic political observations with the comment, 'All I know is just what I read in the newspapers.' This comment is a succinct summary about most of the knowledge and information that each of us possesses about public affairs because most of the issues and concerns that engage our attention are not amenable to direct personal experience. As Walter Lippmann long ago noted in *Public Opinion*, 'The world that we have to deal with politically is out of reach, out of sight, out of mind.'[1] In Will Rogers's and Walter Lippmann's day, the daily newspaper was the principal source of information about public affairs. Today we also have television and an expanding panoply of new communication technologies, but the central point is the same. For nearly all of the concerns on the public agenda, citizens deal with a second-hand reality, a reality that is structured by journalists' reports about these events and situations.

A similar, parsimonious description of our situation vis-à-vis the news media is captured in sociologist Robert Park's venerable phrase, the signal function of the news.[2] The daily news alerts us to the latest events and changes in the larger environment beyond our immediate experience. But newspapers and television news, even the tightly edited pages of a tabloid newspaper or internet web site, do considerably more than signal the existence of major events and issues. Through their day-by-day selection and display of the news, editors and news directors focus our attention and influence our perceptions of what are the most important issues of the day. This ability to influence the salience of topics on the public agenda has come to be called the agenda-setting role of the news media.

Newspapers communicate a host of cues about the relative salience of the topics on their daily agenda. The lead story on page 1, front page versus inside page, the size of the headline, and even the length of a story all communicate the salience of topics on the news agenda. There are analogous cues on web sites. The television news agenda has a more limited capacity, so even a mention on the evening television news is a strong signal about the high salience of a topic. Additional cues are provided by its placement in the broadcast and by the amount of time spent on the story. For all the news media, the repetition of a topic day after day is the most powerful message of all about its importance.

The public uses these salience cues from the media to organize their own agendas and decide which issues are most important. Over time, the issues emphasized in news reports become the issues regarded as most important among the public. The agenda of the news media becomes, to a considerable degree, the agenda of the public. In other words, the news media set the public agenda. Establishing this salience among the public, placing an issue or topic on the public agenda so that it becomes the focus of public attention and thought – and, possibly, action – is the initial stage in the formation of public opinion.

Discussion of public opinion usually centres on the distribution of opinions, how many are for, how many are against, and how many are undecided. That is why the news media and many in their audiences are so fascinated with public opinion polls, especially during political campaigns. But before we consider the distribution of opinions, we need to know which topics are at the centre of public opinion. People have opinions on many things, but only a few topics really matter to them. The agenda-setting role of the news media is their influence on the salience of an issue, an influence on whether any significant number of people really regard it as worthwhile to hold an opinion about that issue. While many issues compete for public attention, only a few are successful in doing so, and the news media exert significant influence on our perceptions of what are the most important issues of the day. This is not a deliberate, premeditated influence – as in the expression 'to have an agenda' – but rather an inadvertent influence resulting from the necessity of the news media to select and highlight a few topics in their reports as the most salient news of the moment.

This distinction between the influence of the news media on the salience of issues and on specific opinions about these issues is summed up in Bernard Cohen's observation that the news media may not be successful in telling people what to think, but they are stunningly successful in telling their audiences what to think about.[3] In other words, the news media can set the agenda for public thought and discussion. Sometimes the media do more than this, and we will find it necessary in later chapters to expand on Cohen's cogent observation. But first let us consider in some detail the initial step in the formation of public opinion, capturing public attention.

Our pictures of the world

Walter Lippmann is the intellectual father of the idea now called, for short, agenda-setting. The opening chapter of his 1922 classic, *Public Opinion*, is titled 'The World Outside and the Pictures in our Heads' and summarizes the agenda-setting idea even though Lippmann did not use that phrase. His thesis is that the news media, our windows to the vast world beyond direct experience, determine our cognitive maps of that world. Public opinion, argued Lippmann, responds not to the environment, but to the pseudo-environment constructed by the news media.

Still in print more than eighty years after its original publication, *Public Opinion* presents an intriguing array of anecdotal evidence to support its thesis. Lippmann, for example, describes a discussion in the United States Senate in which a tentative newspaper report of a military incursion on the Dalmatian coast becomes a factual crisis.[4] He begins the book with a compelling story of 'an island in the ocean where in 1914 a few Englishmen, Frenchmen, and Germans lived'. Only the arrival of the mail steamer more than six weeks after the outbreak of World War I alerted these friends that they were enemies.[5] For Lippmann, who was writing in the 1920s, these are contemporary updates of Plato's Allegory of the Cave with which he prefaces the book. Paraphrasing Socrates, he noted 'how indirectly we know the environment in which nevertheless we live ... but that whatever we believe to be a true picture, we treat as if it were the environment itself.'[6]

Contemporary empirical evidence

Empirical evidence about the agenda-setting role of the mass media now confirms and elaborates Lippmann's broad-brush observations. But this detailed picture about the formation of public opinion came much later. When *Public Opinion* was published in 1922, the first scientific investigations of mass communication influence on public opinion were still more than a decade in the future. Publication of the first explicit investigation of the agenda-setting role of mass communication was exactly fifty years away.

Systematic analysis of mass communication's effects on public opinion, empirical research grounded in the precepts of scientific investigation, dates from the 1940 US presidential election, when sociologist Paul Lazarsfeld and his colleagues at Columbia University, in collaboration with pollster Elmo Roper, conducted seven rounds of interviews with voters in Erie County, Ohio.[7] Contrary to both popular and scholarly expectations, these surveys and many subsequent investigations in other settings over the next twenty years found little evidence of mass communication effects on attitudes and opinions. Two decades after Erie County, Joseph Klapper's *The Effects of Mass Communication* declared that the law of minimal consequences prevailed.[8]

However, these early social science investigations during the 1940s and 1950s did find considerable evidence that people acquired information from the mass media even if they did not change their opinions. Voters did learn from the news. And from a journalistic perspective, questions about learning are more central than questions about persuasion. Phrases such as 'what people need to know' and 'the people's right to know' are rhetorical standards in journalism. Most journalists are concerned with informing. Persuasion is relegated to the editorial page, and, even there, informing remains central. Furthermore, even after the law of minimal consequences became the accepted conventional wisdom, there was a lingering suspicion among many social scientists that there were major media effects not yet explored or measured. The time was ripe for a paradigm shift in the examination of media effects, a shift from persuasion to an earlier point in the communication process, informing.

Against this background, two young professors at the University of North Carolina's School of Journalism launched a small investigation in Chapel Hill, North Carolina, during the 1968 US presidential campaign. Their central hypothesis was that the mass media set the agenda of issues for a political campaign by influencing the salience of issues among voters. These two professors, Don Shaw and I, also coined a name for this hypothesized influence of mass communication. We called it 'agenda-setting'.[9]

Testing this agenda-setting hypothesis required the comparison of two sets of evidence: a description of the public agenda, the set of issues that were of the greatest concern to Chapel Hill voters; and a description of the issue agenda in the news media used by those voters. Illustrated in box 1.1, the central assertion of agenda-setting

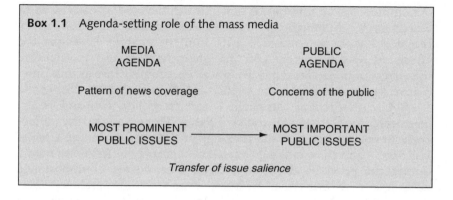

theory is that those issues emphasized in the news come to be regarded over time as important by the public. In other words, the media agenda sets the public agenda. Contrary to the law of minimal consequences, this is a statement about a strong causal effect of mass communication on the public – the transfer of salience from the media agenda to the public agenda.

To determine the public agenda in Chapel Hill during the 1968 presidential election a survey was conducted among a sample of randomly selected undecided voters. Only undecided voters were interviewed because this new agenda-setting hypothesis went against the prevailing view of mass media effects. If this test in Chapel Hill failed to find agenda-setting effects under rather optimum conditions, voters who had not yet decided how to cast their presidential vote, there would be little reason to pursue the matter among the general public where longstanding psychological identification with a political party and the process of selective perception often blunted the effects of mass communication during election campaigns.

In the survey, these undecided voters were asked to name the key issues of the day as they saw matters, regardless of what the candidates might be saying. The issues named in the survey were ranked according to the percentage of voters naming each one to yield a description of the public agenda. Note that this rank ordering of the issues is considerably more precise than simply grouping sets of issues into those receiving high, moderate or low attention among the public.

The nine major news sources used by these voters were also collected and content analysed. This mix of media included five local and national newspapers, two television networks and two news magazines. The rank order of issues on the media agenda was determined by the number of news stories devoted to each issue in recent weeks. Although this was not the very first time that survey research had been combined with content analysis to assess the effects of specific media content, their tandem use to measure the effects of mass communication was exceedingly rare at that time.

Five issues dominated the media and public agendas during the 1968 US presidential campaign – foreign policy, law and order, economics, public welfare, and civil rights. There was a nearly perfect correspondence between the rankings of these issues by the Chapel Hill voters and their rankings based on their play in the news media during the previous twenty-five days. The degree of importance accorded these five issues by these voters closely paralleled their degree of prominence in the news. In other words, the salience of five key campaign issues among these undecided voters was virtually identical to the salience of these issues in the news coverage of recent weeks.

Moreover, the idea of powerful media effects expressed in the concept of agenda-setting was a better explanation for the salience of issues on the public agenda than was the concept of selective perception, which is a keystone in the idea of minimal mass media consequences.[10] Since agenda-setting challenged the prevailing view at that time about mass media effects, the evidence for this statement needs to be examined in some detail.

Agenda-setting is not a return to a bullet theory or hypodermic theory of all-powerful media effects. Nor are members of the audience regarded as automatons waiting to be programmed by the news media. But agenda-setting does assign a central role to the news media in initiating items for the public agenda. Or, to paraphrase Lippmann, the information provided by the news media plays a key role in the construction of our pictures of reality. And, moreover, it is the total set of information provided by the news media that influences these pictures.

In contrast, the concept of selective perception locates the central influence within the individual and stratifies media content according to its compatibility with an individual's existing attitudes and opinions. From this perspective, it is assumed that individuals minimize their exposure to non-supportive information and maximize their exposure to supportive information. During an election, voters are expected to pay the most attention to those issues emphasized by their preferred political party.

Which does the public agenda more closely reflect? The total agenda of issues in the news, which is the outcome hypothesized by agenda-setting theory? Or the agenda of issues advanced by a voter's preferred party, which is the outcome hypothesized by the theory of selective perception?

To answer these questions, those undecided voters who had a preference (albeit not yet a firm commitment to vote for a candidate) were separated into three groups, Democrats, Republicans, and supporters of George Wallace, a third party candidate in that election. For each of these three groups of voters, a pair of comparisons were made with the news coverage on the CBS television network: the issue agenda of that voter group compared with all the news coverage on CBS, and the issue agenda of the group compared with only the news on CBS originating with the group's preferred party and candidate. These pairs of comparisons for CBS were repeated for NBC, the *New York Times*, and a local daily newspaper. In sum, there were a dozen pairs of correlations to compare: three groups of voters times four news media. Which was the stronger correlation in each pair? The agenda-setting correlation comparing voters with all the news coverage, or the selective perception correlation comparing voters with only the news of their preferred party and candidate?

Box 1.2   The power of the press

The power of the press in America is a primordial one. It sets the agenda of public discussion; and this sweeping political power is unrestrained by any law. It determines what people will talk and think about – an authority that in other nations is reserved for tyrants, priests, parties and mandarins.

No major act of the American Congress, no foreign adventure, no act of diplomacy, no great social reform can succeed in the United States unless the press prepares the public mind. And when the press seizes a great issue to thrust onto the agenda of talk, it moves action on its own – the cause of the environment, the cause of civil rights, the liquidations of the war in Vietnam, and, as climax, the Watergate affair were all set on the agenda, in first instance, by the press.

Theodore White, *The Making of the President*

In the stream of the nation's capital, the *Washington Post* is very much like a whale; its smallest splashes rarely go unnoticed. No other newspaper dominates a city the way the *Post* dominates Washington. . . . There are complaints that the paper has lost energy since Benjamin C. Bradley retired as editor, in September of 1991, but nothing seems to have diminished the influence that the *Post* holds over the nation's political agenda; and nothing has diminished the paper's almost mystical importance to the city's permanent population of malcontents, leaders, and strivers.

The New Yorker (21 & 28 October 1996)

Eight of the twelve comparisons favoured the agenda-setting hypothesis. There was no difference in one case, and only three comparisons favoured the selective perception hypothesis. A new perspective on powerful media effects had established a foothold.

The accumulated evidence

Since that modest beginning in Chapel Hill during the 1968 presidential election, there have been hundreds of empirical investigations of the agenda-setting influence of the news media.[11] The accumulated evidence for this influence on the general public in many different geographical and historical settings worldwide includes all the news media and dozens of public issues. This evidence also documents the time-order and causal links between the media and public agendas in finer detail. Here is a sampling of that evidence.

The 1972 US presidential election in Charlotte

To extend the evidence for agenda-setting beyond the narrow focus on undecided 1968 voters in Chapel Hill and their media sources during the early part of the fall election campaign, a representative sample of all voters in Charlotte, North Carolina, and their news media were examined three times during the summer and fall of 1972.[12] Two distinct phases were identified in election year agenda-setting by the news media. During the summer and early fall, the daily newspaper was the prime mover. With its greater capacity – scores of pages compared to half an hour for network television news – the *Charlotte Observer* influenced the public agenda during the early months. Television news did not. But in the final month of the campaign, there was little evidence of agenda-setting by either the local newspaper or the television networks.

In addition to documenting the agenda-setting influence of the local newspaper on the public, these observations across the summer and fall of that election campaign eliminated the rival hypothesis that the public agenda influenced the newspaper agenda. Whenever there are observations of the media agenda and the public agenda at two or more points over time, it is possible simultaneously to compare the cross-lag correlations measuring the strength of these two competing causal hypotheses. For example, the influence of the newspaper agenda at time one on the public agenda at time two can be compared with the influence of the public agenda at time one on the newspaper agenda at time two. In Charlotte, the agenda-setting hypothesis prevailed.

The agenda of issues during the 1972 presidential campaign included three very personal concerns – the economy, drugs, and bussing to achieve racial integration of the public schools – and four issues that were more remote – the Watergate scandal, US relations with Russia and Red China, the environment, and Vietnam. The salience of all seven issues among the public was influenced by the pattern of news coverage in the local newspaper.

The 1976 US presidential election in three communities

An intensive look at an entire presidential election year followed in 1976 and again highlighted variations in the agenda-setting influence of the news media during different seasons of the year.[13] To capture these variations, panels of voters were interviewed nine times from February through December in three very different settings: Lebanon, New Hampshire, a small town in the state where the first presidential primary to select the Democrat and Republican candidates for president is held each election year; Indianapolis, Indiana, a typical mid-sized American city; and Evanston, Illinois, a largely upscale suburb of Chicago. Simultaneously, the election coverage of the three national television networks and the local newspapers in these three sites was content analysed.

In all three communities the agenda-setting influence of both television and newspapers was greatest during the spring primaries, when voters were just beginning to tune in to the presidential campaign. A declining trend of media influence on the public agenda during the remainder of the year was particularly clear for the salience of seven relatively remote issues – foreign affairs, government credibility, crime, social problems, environment and energy, government spending and size, and race relations. The salience of more personal matters, such as economic issues, remained high for voters throughout the campaign regardless of their treatment by newspapers and television. Personal experience can be a more powerful teacher than the mass media when issues have a direct impact on people's lives.

Although these detailed examinations of the issues on the public agenda help us understand the variations in the agenda-setting influence of the news media, the specific issues change from election to election. So it is useful to have some kind of summary statistic that will allow us to compare the degree of agenda-setting taking place in different settings. The most common measure used by scholars exploring the agenda-setting role of the news media is the correlation statistic. This statistic precisely summarizes the degree of correspondence between the ranking of issues on the media agenda – which issue received the most news coverage, which issue the second most coverage, etc. – and the ranking of those same issues on the public agenda – which issue most members of the public regard as most important, which issue ranks second among the public, etc. The possible range of scores for the correlation statistic is from +1.0 (perfect correspondence) through 0 (no relationship at all) to −1.0 (a perfectly inverse relationship). Agenda-setting theory predicts a high positive correlation between the media agenda and the subsequent public agenda.

Using this correlation statistic to summarize a key finding from the intensive year-long look at the 1976 presidential election in three different communities, we find that, during the spring primaries when the agenda-setting influence of both television and newspapers was at its peak, the correlation between the national television agenda and the subsequent voter agenda was +0.63. That is a significant degree of influence. In contrast, the correlation between the agendas of the three local newspapers read by these voters and the voters' agenda of public issues was only +0.34. Nevertheless, this was the peak period for the newspapers. Although it is fashionable to attribute great influence to television in many aspects of life, do not rush to generalize this particular finding about the relative influence of television and newspapers. Chapter 3 will compare these two news media across many settings and find a more cautious picture that, in fact, tilts towards newspapers as the stronger agenda-setters on many occasions.

Finally, these extensive observations of the 1976 presidential campaign across the entire election year provide another opportunity to compare the core hypothesis of agenda-setting theory that the media agenda influences the public agenda with the competing causal hypothesis that the public agenda influences the media agenda. In comparison to the agenda-setting correlation of +0.63 noted above for national television, over the same time period the correlation between the public agenda and the subsequent national television agenda is only +0.22. The difference between the two is further amplified by comparison with the Rozelle–Campbell baseline, a statistic indicating the value to be expected by chance alone. In this instance the Rozelle–Campbell baseline is +0.37. The agenda-setting correlation is far above this baseline. Its rival is below the baseline.

For newspapers, the rather low agenda-setting correlation of +0.34 nevertheless compares quite favourably with the rival correlation of −0.08. The Rozelle–Campbell baseline in this instance is +0.08.

Again the agenda-setting correlation is far above this baseline, and its rival is below the baseline. In both of these instances, the evidence corroborates the causal influence of newspaper and television issue agendas on the public agenda.

These initial empirical efforts to map the agenda-setting role of the mass media encompassed three consecutive US presidential campaigns. Election settings were not selected because of any assumption that agenda-setting effects are limited to elections, but rather because national elections create a natural laboratory for the examination of media effects. During a national election there is a continuing massive barrage of messages on public issues and other aspects of politics. If these messages are to have any significant social effects, the effects must occur by election day.

In addition to these advantages for studying media effects, there is also an enduring tradition of scholarship on the role of mass communication in national elections that began with the seminal studies of Lazarsfeld and his colleagues, first in Erie County during the 1940 US presidential election and then in Elmira, New York, during the 1948 US presidential election. For all these reasons, the initial examinations of agenda-setting were conducted in election settings. But, as we shall see, the agenda-setting role of the mass media is limited neither to elections nor to the United States, nor even to the arena of political communication broadly defined. American presidential elections were just the starting point. The phenomenon of agenda-setting, a continuous and inadvertent by-product of the mass communication process, is found in both election and non-election settings, at both the national and local levels, in a wide array of geographical settings worldwide, and even for a broad array of agendas extending beyond political communication. However, for now we will focus on issue agendas, the best mapped domain of the agenda-setting role of the mass media.

National concern about civil rights

From 1954 to 1976, a 23-year span of time encompassing half a dozen presidential elections and all the years in between, the salience of the civil rights issue in the United States rose and fell with great regularity in response to news coverage.[14] The percentage of Americans naming civil rights as 'the most important problem' facing the country ranged from 0 per cent to 52 per cent in the twenty-seven Gallup polls conducted during those three decades. When this continuously shifting salience of civil rights on the public agenda was compared with the news coverage on the front page of the *New York*

Times for the month preceding each of the twenty-seven polls, the result was a robust correlation of +0.71. Even when the influence of news coverage in earlier months is removed, the correlation remains +0.71.

This is especially compelling evidence of the media's agenda-setting role across a lengthy period of time, a time-span encompassing numerous shifts both up and down in the salience of civil rights. Also note that the salience of the civil rights issue among the public primarily reflects the preceding month of news coverage, a relatively short-term response to the media agenda. Because the media agendas examined over this 23-year period were prior in time to the public agenda, this evidence on time-order further supports agenda-setting's causal assertion that the public agenda results, to a considerable degree, from the media agenda.

British and American concern about foreign affairs

Obviously, the news media are most people's primary source of information about foreign policy issues. In both the United Kingdom and the US, there is major evidence that the salience of foreign affairs regularly rises and falls in response to media attention.[15] The salience of foreign affairs among the British public from 1990 to 2000 was significantly correlated (+0.54) with the number of foreign affairs articles in *The Times*. During an overlapping twenty-year period in the US, 1981–2000, the salience of foreign affairs among the American public was significantly correlated (+0.38) with the number of foreign affairs articles in the *New York Times*. Beyond the sheer number of articles in each newspaper, there is an additional impact on the public agenda by news stories reporting home country involvement.

Public opinion in Germany

Weekly comparisons of the public agenda and media agenda in Germany across the entire year of 1986 revealed that television news coverage had a significant impact on public concern about five diverse issues: an adequate energy supply, East–West relations, European politics, environmental protection, and defence.[16]

The energy-supply issue illustrates these agenda-setting effects. Early in 1986 this issue had low salience on both the news agenda and the public agenda. But a rapid rise in May on the news agenda was followed within a week by a similar rise on the public agenda. News coverage catapulted from fewer than a dozen mentions per week to over a hundred per week. Concern among the public about an adequate supply of energy, which had been around 15 per cent of the population, suddenly moved into the 25 to 30 per cent range. When news coverage subsequently declined, so did the size of the constituency expressing concern about Germany's energy supply.

During this same year there were no agenda-setting effects on eleven other issues. As noted previously, the public is not a collective automaton passively waiting to be programmed by the media. The pattern of media coverage for some issues resonates with the public. For other issues, there is no resonance.

Replication with other issues

Similar evidence about the variable impact of news coverage on the trends in public opinion comes from the individual analysis of eleven different issues in the United States during a 41-month period in the 1980s.[17] In each of these eleven analyses, the media agenda is based on a rich mix of television, newspapers and news magazines. The public agenda is based on thirteen Gallup polls that asked Americans to name the most important problem facing the country. Two patterns are immediately evident in box 1.3. First, all except one of the correlations summarizing the match between the media agenda and the public agenda are positive. The median correspondence between these agendas is +0.45. The negative match for morality is easy to

---

Box 1.3 Comparisons of the trends in news coverage and concerns of the American public for eleven issues, 1983–6

Government performance	+0.87
Unemployment	+0.77
Inflation/cost of living	+0.71
Fear of war/nuclear disaster	+0.68
International problems	+0.48
Poverty	+0.45
Crime	+0.32
Economy	+0.25
Budget deficit	+0.20
Budget cuts	+0.14
Morality	−0.44

Source: Howard Eaton Jr, 'Agenda setting with bi-weekly data on content of three national media', *Journalism Quarterly*, 66 (1989), p. 946.

explain because morality is a topic seldom broached in the news media.

For the other ten public issues during this period in the 1980s, all the correlations are positive. This suggests some degree of agenda-setting influence. However, a pattern of considerable variability in the strength of the association between the two agendas is also apparent. This calls our attention to factors other than media coverage that influence the public's perception of what are the most important issues of the day. The public mind is not a *tabula rasa* waiting to be written upon by the mass media, and chapters 3 and 4 will discuss a variety of psychological and sociological factors that are significant in the public's daily transactions with the mass media and the issues of the day. These factors can enhance or constrain the degree of mass media influence.

Public opinion in Louisville

All our examples of the agenda-setting influence of the news media examined to this point have been grounded in presidential elections or national portraits of public opinion. But there are also agenda-setting effects on local public issues. We begin with the long-term public opinion trends in an American city, trends that are analysed for the aggregate agenda as well as separately for the eight individual issues on that agenda.[18] When the trends in public opinion from 1974 through 1981 in Louisville, Kentucky, were compared to the news coverage of the *Louisville Times*, the overall correlation between the public agenda and the news agenda was +0.65. Further analysis examined the ebb and flow of concern across these eight years for each of the eight issues. Significant agenda-setting effects were found for the top four issues on the news agenda: education, crime, the local environment, and local economic development.

Despite their influence on many issues, the news media are not all-powerful dictators of public opinion nor do they determine their own agenda with total professional detachment from the world about them. The issues ranking fifth and sixth on the *Louisville Times*'s agenda – public recreation and health care, respectively – are examples of reverse agenda-setting, a situation where public concern sets the media agenda.

The lack of media omnipotence is also detailed in two other instances. Public concern about local government was independent of the trends in news coverage despite the fact that local government is one of the traditional staples of daily newspaper coverage. Perhaps heavy continuing coverage of local government – or any other topic, for that matter – becomes a blur of white noise rather than a stream of information. Not only was public concern about local government immune to any agenda-setting influence of the press, the trend in news coverage was also immune to any reverse agenda-setting even though local government ranked sixth on the public agenda during those years.

Similarly, road maintenance, which ranked third on the public agenda, was all but ignored by the *Louisville Times*. Only twenty articles appeared in the newspaper during eight years, an average of one article about every four or five months. Again, there was no evidence of any agenda-setting influence in either direction.

Local public opinion in Spain

Unemployment and urban congestion, especially in the old quarter of the city during the weekends, topped the public agenda in Pamplona, Spain, during the spring of 1995.[19] Comparisons of all six major concerns on the public agenda with local news coverage in the preceding fortnight found high degrees of correspondence. The match with the dominant local daily newspaper was +0.90; with the second Pamplona daily, +0.72; and with television news, +0.66.

A local election in Japan

Agenda-setting at the community level also occurred in a 1986 Japanese mayoral election.[20] Voters in Machida City, a municipality of 320,000 residents in the Tokyo metropolitan area, regarded welfare policies, urban facilities and local taxes as the three most important issues in the election. Comparison of the public agenda, which had seven issues in all, with the coverage of the four major newspapers serving Machida City yielded a modest, but significant, correlation of +0.39. Although there were no significant variations in the strength of this relationship among persons differing in age, sex or level of education, chapter 4 will take up a factor that does provide an explanation for this relatively low correlation.

Local elections in Argentina

This local focus was replicated in the 1997 legislative elections in the Buenos Aires metropolitan area.[21] Corruption was prominent on both the public and media agendas throughout the fall, always ranking first or second. But in September the correlation for the top four issues of the day was −0.20 between the public agenda and the combined issue agenda of five major Buenos Aires newspapers. However, as election day approached in October, the correspondence between these agendas for the top four issues soared to +0.80, an increase that suggests considerable learning from the news media in the closing weeks of the election campaign.[22]

Additional evidence of significant agenda-setting effects in Argentina was found during the 1998 primary election held to select the presidential candidate for a major political coalition. For the six major issues of the day, the correspondence between the public agenda at the time of the election and the newspaper agenda of the previous month was +0.60. For television news, the correspondence was even higher, +0.71.[23]

Cause and effect

The evidence reviewed here, plus many other field studies conducted around the world, corroborate a cause-and-effect relationship between the media agenda and the public agenda. The initial necessary condition for demonstrating causality is a significant degree of correlation between the presumed cause and its effect. In line with this evidentiary requirement, there are substantial correlations between the media and public agendas in all of the analyses just reviewed as well as in hundreds of others.

A second necessary condition for demonstrating causality is time-order. The cause must precede the effect in time. Even the initial Chapel Hill study was careful to juxtapose the results of the public opinion poll measuring public concern about the issues of the day with the content of the news media in the weeks *preceding* the interviewing as well as with the days concurrent with the interviewing.[24] Evidence of the agenda-setting effects of the news media in the two subsequent US presidential elections was based on panel studies. There were two waves of interviewing and content analysis during June and October in Charlotte during the 1972 presidential election, plus a third wave of interviews immediately following the election.[25] During the 1976 presidential election there were nine waves of interviewing from February to December and content analyses of local newspapers and national television news across the entire year in three different communities.[26] As we have seen, both of these panel designs allowed detailed, sophisticated tests of the time-order involved in the relationship between the media and public agendas.

Other evidence of agenda-setting effects reviewed here from a variety of non-election settings also involves longitudinal research designs that allowed detailed, sophisticated tests of the time-order involved in the relationship between the media and public agendas. The examination of the civil rights issue in the US spanned twenty-three years.[27] There are eleven replications of this type of single-issue analysis based on a 41-month period during the 1980s,[28] and an intensive week-by-week examination of five individual issues in Germany during 1986.[29] Eight local issues were analysed, both in the aggregate and individually, in Louisville during an eight-year period.[30] There are many other longitudinal studies corroborating the time-order of the agenda-setting role of the media.

All of this evidence about agenda-setting effects is grounded in the 'real world' – public opinion surveys based on random samples of the public and content analyses of actual news media. This evidence illustrates agenda-setting effects in a wide variety of situations, and it is compelling for the very reason that it portrays public opinion in the real world. But these *réalité* portraits of public opinion are not the best evidence for the core proposition of agenda-setting theory that the media agenda influences – that is, has a causal influence on – the public agenda, because these measures of the media and public agendas are linked with numerous uncontrolled factors.

The best, most unequivocal evidence that the news media are the cause of these kinds of effects comes from controlled experiments in the laboratory, a setting where the theorized cause can be systematically manipulated, subjects randomly assigned to various versions of this manipulation, and systematic comparisons made among the outcomes. Evidence from laboratory experiments provides the third and final link in the chain of causal evidence that the media agenda influences the public agenda, demonstration of a direct functional relationship between the content of the media agenda and the response of the public to that agenda.

Changes in the salience of defence preparedness, pollution, arms control, civil rights, unemployment, and a number of other issues were produced in the laboratory among subjects who viewed versions of TV news programmes that had been edited to emphasize a particular public issue.[31] A variety of controls ascertained that changes in the salience of the manipulated issue were, in fact, due to exposure to the news agenda. For example, in one experiment, subjects who viewed TV news programmes emphasizing defence preparedness were compared to subjects in a control group whose news programmes did not include defence preparedness. The change in the salience of this issue was significantly higher for the test subjects than for the subjects in the control group. In contrast, there were no significance differences between the two groups from before to after viewing the newscasts for seven other issues.

Bringing the cause-and-effect evidence of the laboratory up to date in terms of simulating actual media experience, two recent experiments documented the agenda-setting effects of online newspapers on personal agendas. One experiment found that the salience of racism as a public issue was significantly higher among all three groups of subjects exposed to various versions of an online newspaper discussing racism than among those subjects whose online newspaper did not contain a news report on racism.[32] Another experiment compared the salience of international issues among readers of the print and online versions of the *New York Times*. Although there were stronger effects for the print version of the newspaper, subjects exposed to both versions were significantly different from a control group with no exposure to the *New York Times*. Opening the door to further exploration of the agenda-setting process, these experimenters also argued that 'contemporary incarnations of Internet news are subtly, but consequentially, altering the way that the news media set the public's agenda.'[33]

While laboratory experiments like these are sometimes criticized as artificial situations, they provide vital complementary evidence for the agenda-setting role of the news media. A complete set of evidence for agenda-setting effects requires both the internal validity of experiments where the media and public agendas are tightly controlled and measured and the external validity of content analysis and survey research whose designs assure us that the findings can be generalized beyond the immediate observations at hand to larger settings in the real world.

Methodologically, the agenda-setting role of the mass media is well supported:

> Methodological skill . . . has increased rapidly over the years. Initially tied to procedures involving rank-order correlations, it has expanded to include the most sophisticated structural equations modeling, as well as cross-sectional data and multi-wave panels. Researchers also have used time series analysis of aggregated public opinion measures, naturalistic experimental designs, and in-depth case studies to study agenda setting. Given the amount of activity surrounding agenda-setting research, we can conclude that it is one of the most vigorously pursued models in the field.[34]

There is also methodological strength in the wide variety of substantive measures used to ascertain the agenda-setting effects of the media. The early research – and even most of the research today – focuses on the cognitive effects of the mass media. Frequently, these effects are measured by responses to the question used by the Gallup Poll since the 1930s and now widely imitated by academic researchers and pollsters worldwide: 'What do you think is the most important problem facing this country today?'[35] As we shall see in subsequent chapters, this measure of agenda-setting effects among the public has been supplemented with questions that probe a wide range of behaviours, including conversations, holding opinions, voting, and taking a variety of other actions.

In terms of the media agenda, which is the cause of these effects, a major contribution of agenda-setting theory is that it makes an explicit connection between *specific* media content and its effects among the public. Explicating the basic assumption of quantitative content analysis,[36] agenda-setting theory specifies that the salience of this content can parsimoniously be measured in terms of its frequency of appearance.[37]

Summing up

This is far from all the accumulated evidence that the news media can exercise an agenda-setting influence on the public, but it is a wide-ranging sample of that evidence. The examples presented here describe agenda-setting effects on a wide array of national and local issues, during elections and more quiescent political times, in a variety of national and local settings in the United States, Spain, Germany, Japan and Argentina, and from 1968 to the present.[38]

There are, of course, a number of other significant influences that shape individual attitudes and public opinion. How we feel about a particular issue may be rooted in our personal experience, the general culture or our exposure to the mass media.[39] Trends in public opinion on an issue are shaped over time by new generations, external events and the mass media.[40] None the less, the general proposition supported by this accumulation of evidence about agenda-setting effects is that journalists do significantly influence their audience's picture of the world.

For the most part, this agenda-setting influence is an inadvertent by-product of the necessity to focus on a few topics in the news each day. Television newscasters have a very limited capacity, and even newspapers with their dozens of pages have room for only a fraction of the news that is available each day. Even web sites with their huge capacity must organize their contents into a useful agenda, and each page of the site is highly constrained.

Regardless of the medium, a tight focus on a handful of issues conveys a strong message to the audience about what are the most important topics of the moment. Agenda-setting directs our attention to the early formative stages of public opinion when issues emerge and first engage public attention, a situation that confronts journalists with a strong ethical responsibility to select carefully the issues on their agenda.

In abstract theoretical terms, this chapter's examples of agenda-setting illustrate the transmission of issue salience from the media agenda to the public agenda. As we shall see in subsequent chapters, agenda-setting as a theory about the transmission of salience is not limited to the influence of the mass media agenda on the public agenda or to an agenda of public issues. There are many agendas in contemporary society. Chapter 7, for example, reviews the transmission of salience between the president's agenda and the media agenda. In turn, the president's agenda is only one instance of what has come to be called the policy agenda. Beyond the various agendas that define the context in which public opinion takes shape, this idea about the transmission of salience has been applied to a variety of other settings. Chapter 9 discusses a few of these new, broader applications that extend agenda-setting theory beyond political communication. But first we will add further detail to our theoretical map of the causal influence that the media agenda has on the public agenda.

2 Reality and the News

Some journalists disclaim any agenda-setting influence on the public. 'We just report the news about what is happening in the world', they say. Making a similar assumption, some critics of the idea of agenda-setting have asserted that public and media alike are just responding to their surrounding environment. However, in his discussion of the role of the news media as a bridge between 'the world outside and the pictures in our heads', Walter Lippmann introduced the idea of the pseudo-environment, the view of the world that exists in our mind – a view that is always incomplete vis-à-vis reality and frequently inaccurate. Our behaviour is a response to this pseudo-environment, not the actual environment, asserted Lippmann. Now the accumulated evidence from decades of social science research on the agenda-setting role of the mass media further underscores the importance of Lippmann's distinction between the environment and the pseudo-environment.

This is not to assert that the news is made from whole cloth. Far from it. Journalism is an empirical activity grounded in verifiable observations, and the failure to observe this professional ethic has been the basis of prominent scandals in American and European journalism in recent years. But when the events and situations of each day are refracted through the professional lens of news organizations, the result often is a picture of the world, a pseudo-environment, that is far from isomorphic with more systematic assessments of that environment. There are many events and situations vying for the attention of journalists. Because there is the capacity neither to gather information about all these events nor to tell the audience about them, journalists rely upon a traditional set of professional norms to guide their daily sampling of the environment. The result is that the news media present a limited view of the larger environment, something like the highly limited view of the outside world available through the narrow slit windows of some contemporary buildings. This metaphor is even more apt if the windowpane is a bit opaque and has an uneven surface.

Idiosyncratic pictures

There is a famous *New Yorker* magazine cover parodying Manhattan residents' view of the United States. This drawing is dominated by a very large New York City and a rather large California on the other side of the country. All the states in between are squeezed tightly together and barely exist. There is a similar drawing of the Texan's view of the United States, which, of course, is dominated by a huge Texas with forty-seven tiny states squeezed around the edges. Neither of these psychological maps of the United States bears much resemblance to the geographer's map that you studied in school, but both – albeit exaggerated – are viable psychological maps of the United States. At this point, we shall consider several empirical examples in which the news media's 'maps' of the world – and subsequent perspectives among the public – resemble those famous drawings that satirize New Yorkers and Texans.

A decade of American public opinion

Repeating a pattern with which we are now very familiar, national public opinion in the United States on a wide variety of issues evidenced major agenda-setting effects by the news media across the entire decade of the turbulent 1960s.[1] When the Gallup Poll, in its surveys during that decade, asked Americans to name 'the most important problem' facing the country, Vietnam, race relations and urban riots, campus unrest, and inflation topped the public agenda. Comparing the salience of all fourteen major issues on the public agenda during the 1960s with the coverage of those same issues in *Time*, *Newsweek* and *U.S. News & World Report* revealed a high degree of correspondence. The correlation between the news agenda and the public agenda was +0.78.

To counter the criticism that this strong correlation between the media agenda and the public agenda is spurious because both the media and the public were simply responding to 'the world outside', Ray Funkhouser also constructed an historical agenda, primarily from *Statistical Abstracts of the United States*. For example, the salience of Vietnam was measured by the highly variable number of American troops committed during the 1960s to the war there. This 'control for reality' introduced into the analysis dramatically underscores the strength and social importance of the agenda-setting process. Coverage of the Vietnam War, campus unrest and urban riots peaked a year or two earlier than those events reached their historical climaxes. For all the issues, peaks in coverage frequently appeared during years in which the situation was no different from other years. In some cases, coverage increased while the problem showed improvement or dropped while the problem increased. Funkhouser noted that 'the patterns of media coverage did not have a one-to-one relationship to the realities of any of the issues.'[2] In short, at the same time that the media agenda and the public agenda of the 1960s were strongly related to each other, both maintained an arm's length relationship and minimal correlation with historical trends of the period.

The inclusion of 'reality' here is a particularly significant contribution to the causal evidence of an agenda-setting effect upon the public by the media because it rebuts the contention of some critics of agenda-setting theory that both news coverage and audience concerns are simply reflections of events in the real world. In statistical terms, these critics argue that the significant correlations found between the media agenda and the public agenda are only an artefact of the strong correlations that exist between each of these agendas and real-world situations. There is no support for that view in this comprehensive analysis of the 1960s. The media are far more than a conduit for the major events of the day. The media construct and present to the public a pseudo-environment that significantly shapes how the public views the world.

Additional evidence to be presented next from Germany and the US further rebuts this criticism. These examples of agenda-setting effects by the media involve situations where the problem that is of rising concern among the public is, in reality, either ongoing at a relatively constant level or actually improving.

Creating a crisis

Idiosyncratic pictures of the larger environment beyond personal experience were present in the German press during the fall of 1973.[3] In every week from early September until late December, negative statements in West German newspapers outnumbered positive statements about the available supply of petroleum in the country. Moreover, during October and November the description of the situation as a 'crisis' steadily increased. This news reporting about a crisis was particularly stimulated in November by a federal government prohibition on Sunday driving for four subsequent weeks and by the lowering of highway speed limits. Only in January and February of 1974 did discussion of a crisis abate and the news coverage reflect a balance between positive and negative assessments of the situation.

Was there really an energy crisis in Germany that fall and winter? The impetus for this news coverage was a series of Arab price increases and boycotts in the early fall directed primarily at the United States and the Netherlands. In reality, German oil imports during September and October were significantly higher than in those months the previous year, and in November imports were about the same. Although there was little factual basis for asserting the existence of an energy crisis, five major German newspapers – three national quality papers covering the political spectrum and two tabloids – published more than 1400 articles about the availability of petroleum and petroleum products from September through February, definitely enough to place this situation on the public agenda.

In a series of polls taken during November, more than two-thirds of the vehicle owners interviewed feared that there would be serious shortages of fuel. In December, as the number of negative statements about the situation began to diminish, the percentage who feared shortages dropped to about half of the vehicle owners and then to about one-third.

The salience of the energy situation – as depicted in the newspapers – produced a strong behavioural reaction among the German public. Purchases of petroleum products in October skyrocketed. Sales of petrol and diesel fuel increased 7 per cent over the previous year, heavy fuel oil by 15 per cent and light fuel oil by 31 per cent. Even though the October petroleum imports exceeded those of the previous year and the November imports were about the same, scattered spot shortages did occur because of the unusually high demand. Needless to say, sales were sharply lower in subsequent months due in large measure to the considerable reserves already held by consumers.

This 1973 oil 'crisis' in West Germany resulted from a sharp rise in demand stimulated by intense press coverage, not from any critical decrease in supply. In this instance, the agenda-setting effects of the newspapers extended beyond the creation of salience and concern among the public – the usual cognitive effect demonstrated in hundreds of studies – to include a behavioural effect, the individual reactions of consumers to their picture of the situation at hand.

Agenda-setting effects created by the news media can have significant consequences.

National concern about drugs

A similar situation arose during the 1980s in the United States. Public concern about drugs began to build after the *New York Times* 'discovered' the drug problem in late 1985 and published the first of more than 100 stories.[4] Following the *Times*'s lead on this issue, the next year there was a *Newsweek* cover story, specials on two of the national television networks, a surge in coverage of drugs in newspapers across the US, and, predictably, a rise in public concern about the drug problem.

This agenda-setting influence of the *Times* – on other news media, on the public and on the federal government – was sustained by the drug-related deaths in mid-1986 of All-American basketball player Len Bias and professional football player Don Rogers. But these dramatic events did no more than sustain a media agenda that was already in place. The increasing salience of the drug issue in the news media and subsequently among the public is a dramatic case of 'pure' agenda-setting because there was no change at all in the actual incidence of drug use across all those months. Putting drugs on the national agenda resulted from the intellectual discovery of a situation by journalists, not from any response to a change in the reality of the situation.

But national attention is volatile. Both the *New York Times*'s coverage and public opinion peaked during 1989 in response to a major media campaign by the Bush administration. In September 1989, an astronomical 63 per cent of the public considered drugs the most important problem facing the country. A year later, 9 per cent regarded it so. The agenda-setting triad composed of the news media, the president and the general public is a complex and continually changing set of relationships.[5] This triad's relationship with the world outside is frequently tenuous and its attention span for public issues uncertain.[6]

Fear of crime

In the 1990s there was another occasion on which the agenda-setting process for a public issue operated with extreme independence of any underlying reality. In 1992, when the Texas Poll asked what was the most important problem facing the country, we see in box 2.1 that only 2 per cent named crime. By the fall of 1993, 15 per cent named

Box 2.1   Newspaper coverage and public concern about crime

Time period	Texas Poll*	Crime articles in Dallas and Houston newspapers	
		Total number	Excluding Simpson and Salena
Summer 1992	2%	173	173
Fall 1993	15%	228	228
Winter 1994	37%	292	292
Spring 1994	36%	246	246
Summer 1994	29%	242	216
Fall 1994	22%	220	205
Winter 1995	24%	233	207
Spring 1995	21%	248	211
Summer 1995	19%	212	200
Fall 1995	15%	236	126

*This is the percentage of Texas Poll respondents citing crime as the most important problem facing the country.
Source: Salma Ghanem, 'Media coverage of crime and public opinion: an exploration of the second level of agenda setting', unpublished doctoral dissertation, University of Texas at Austin, 1996.

crime, and in two subsequent polls during the first six months of 1994 more than one-third of the Texas Poll respondents named crime. This is an unusually high level of concern. Although this question originated by the Gallup Poll in the 1930s has been asked dozens and dozens of times since then, few polls have found these levels of concern about any problem. Concern about crime abated somewhat during 1995 and early 1996, but even then about 20 per cent of Texans still designated crime as the most important problem.

Ironically, during that same time period, when public concern over crime rose to unusually high levels, statistical measures of the reality of crime indicated that the rate of crime was actually declining. Of course, a likely source of rising public concern in the face of these declining crime rates was crime coverage in the news media. Box 2.1 also documents a pattern of intense crime coverage during late 1993, 1994 and 1995 in two major Texas newspapers, the *Dallas Morning News* and the *Houston Chronicle*. In all nine periods of time there are more crime stories than during the summer of 1992, when few members of the public expressed concern about crime.

Detailed analysis of these trends in box 2.1 documented that a pattern of increased crime coverage in major Texas newspapers was mirrored in subsequent public opinion.[7] Across two and a half years the match between the trend in public concern about crime as a major social problem and the pattern of crime coverage was +0.70. This high degree of correspondence between news coverage and the public's concern about crime persists even when two sensational crimes occurring during this period are taken into account. During the summer of 1994 the news media began to flood the public worldwide with coverage of the O. J. Simpson murder case. Simpson, a popular football hero and subsequent sports commentator, was accused of stabbing his wife and a friend to death on a Los Angeles sidewalk. In the spring of 1995 a popular Hispanic singer in Texas, Salena, was murdered. Altogether these two murder cases account for nearly one-sixth of the crime coverage from the summer of 1994 through the fall of the next year. One could argue that the coverage of these two spectacular murder cases, one actually occurring in Texas, accounts for much of the concern about crime among the Texas public. However, even when all the news stories about the Simpson and Salena murder cases are excluded from the analysis, the high degree of correspondence between the media agenda and the public agenda remains unchanged, at +0.73.

This same pattern of public response to newspaper crime coverage has also been found among daily newspaper readers in Chicago, Philadelphia and San Francisco.[8] In each of these cities the competing newspapers had very different styles and approaches to crime, one fairly conservative, the other more flamboyant. One measure of this difference is the percentage of the newshole[9] filled with crime stories. When these differences in the amount of space devoted to crime stories were juxtaposed with the fear of crime among readers of each newspaper, the pattern was striking. In all three cities, readers of the newspaper that devoted the largest proportion of its newshole to stories about crime exhibited higher levels of fear about crime than did the readers of the other newspaper.

Newspapers are not the only culprit here. Television, perhaps even more through entertainment programming than through news stories, can foster a fear of crime and violence among its viewers. George Gerbner and his colleagues, who named this worldview 'the mean world syndrome', concluded on the basis of extensive examination of television audiences over many years that 'long-term exposure to television, in which frequent violence is virtually inescapable, tends to cultivate the image of a relatively mean and dangerous world.'[10] This is an assertion, backed by considerable evidence, about entertainment television setting a long-term agenda.

A comprehensive look at the effects of local television crime news in Washington, DC,[11] complements both the investigations of crime news in local US newspapers and the cultivation effects of crime and violence in entertainment television. Outcomes commonly associated with agenda-setting theory – naming crime as the most important problem – and cultivation analysis – the risk of being a crime victim and fear of walking alone at night – were all measured simultaneously. In addition to exposure to local TV news with its heavy diet of crime, three sets of reality measures were examined as predictors of these outcomes – direct experience as a victim of crime, local neighbourhood crime rates, and being the friend, neighbour or relative of a crime victim. Exposure to local TV news was strongly linked with naming crime as an important problem facing the Washington metropolitan area, but only one of the reality measures – neighbourhood violent crime rates – impacted the salience of crime in Washington. In contrast, exposure to local TV news was not linked to any of the outcomes predicted by cultivation analysis, but nearly half of the reality measures were significantly linked with the fear of crime.

Long before contemporary mass media stimulated concern over crime in the minds of the public, an axiom of early twentieth-century tabloid journalism was 'Give me thirty minutes at the police station to browse the crime reports, and I'll give you a crime wave.' In short, the public's fear of crime and concerns about crime as a social problem have far more to do with the media agenda than with the realities of crime in the local neighbourhood, the metropolitan area, or the country at large.

Moreover, observed a *New York Times* editorial, 'A simple truth of human existence is that it is vastly easier to amplify fear than it is to assuage it.'[12] In this case, the object of the observation was a flurry of news reports during the summer of 2001, including a dramatic *Time* magazine cover, about shark attacks on humans. But marine scientists quickly pointed out there was nothing unusual at all in the number of attacks that summer other than concerted media attention to scattered incidents. In comparison, the *Times* editorial noted that twenty-eight children in the United States were killed by falling television sets between 1990 and 1997, four times as many people as were killed by great white shark attacks in the entire twentieth century. Watching the movie *Jaws* on TV may be even more dangerous than swimming in the ocean.

Discovering the environment

Finally, an extensive examination of US public opinion about environmental problems from 1970 to 1990[13] found no relationship between the salience of these problems on the public agenda and the statistical trends for three different 'reality' measures of air and water pollution. In contrast, there was a substantial relationship between the public agenda – measured by MIP questions from sixty-six Gallup polls – and both the length and the prominence of environmental stories in the *New York Times*. With the reality measures partialled out, the correlations with the public concern were +0.93 with the average length of the stories and +0.92 with their prominence in the *Times*. Both the length and prominence of these stories increased substantially from 1970 to 1990, while statistical measures of 'reality' indicated a downward trend in total pollution. These results again demonstrate the influential and independent role of the news media in the formation of public opinion.

Alarmed discovery

Collectively, these portraits of public opinion – the major issues of the 1960s, the German oil 'crisis' in the 1970s, drugs in the 1980s, crime in the 1990s and spring of 2001, fear of shark attacks in the summer of 2001, and concern about the environment from 1970 to 1990 – tell us a great deal about both the discretion of journalists and the discrepancies that are sometimes found in mass media portrayals of reality. These examples cover a diversity of situations. From 1970 to 1990, the public responded to the increasing coverage of environmental problems in the face of decreasing air and water pollution. In the 1990s there was a similar response to an increase in news coverage of crime at a time when there was a decreasing trend in the reality of crime. In the 1980s the public responded to the increasing news coverage of drugs at a time that there was no change at all in the reality of the drug problem. This was also true for the news coverage of shark attacks and the availability of petroleum in Germany. In the 1960s there was no correlation at all between the trends in news coverage of major issues and the reality of these issues.

The public's response in all these situations is reminiscent of the phenomenon of 'alarmed discovery', the initial stage of public response to a new issue on the agenda that is described in Anthony Downs's theory of the 'issue attention cycle'.[14] By extension, the media's presentation of the issues just discussed can also be characterized as 'alarmed discovery' because the news began to emphasize each of these issues at a time that nothing out of the ordinary was occurring in the real world. In effect, these were natural experiments in a real-world setting that yield especially compelling causal evidence of the agenda-setting influence of the news media on the public.[15]

Another sophisticated natural experiment exploring the stages of the 'issue attention cycle' with daily tracking surveys across a five-month period during 1998 found that front-page stories in the *Atlanta Journal and Constitution* significantly influenced the salience of air quality among the public.[16] This evidence about the impact of news coverage on issue salience is especially compelling because it involves an 'invisible' issue, air quality. Ground-level ozone, the harmful component of visible smog, is invisible and odourless. Furthermore, daily measures of four pertinent weather conditions – the reality of the situation – were unrelated to levels of issue salience among the Atlanta public. Again we see that the media agenda involves considerably more than a conduit for the events and situations of the real world.

Perspectives on agenda-setting effects

Explorations of agenda-setting effects around the world have observed this mass communication phenomenon from a variety of perspectives. A four-part typology describing these perspectives is frequently referred to as the Acapulco typology because it was initially presented in Acapulco, Mexico, at the invitation of International Communication Association president Everett Rogers. This typology is defined by two dichotomous dimensions. The first dimension distinguishes between two ways of looking at agendas. The focus of attention can either be on the entire set of items that define the agenda or be narrowed to a single, particular item on the agenda. The second dimension distinguishes between two ways of measuring the public salience of items on the agenda, aggregate measures describing an entire group or population versus measures that describe individual responses. The combination of these two dimensions describes the four distinct perspectives on agenda-setting outlined in box 2.2.

Perspective I encompasses the entire agenda and uses aggregate measures of the population to establish the salience of these items. The original Chapel Hill study of agenda-setting took this perspective. Recall that the media and public agendas consisted of the five major issues in that US presidential election. The relative salience of those issues was determined by two aggregate measures of the election setting. For the media agenda, the salience of the issues was determined by the percentage of news articles on each issue; and for the public agenda, by the percentage of voters who thought the government should do something about each issue. This perspective

Box 2.2 The Acapulco typology: four perspectives on agenda-setting

	Measure of public salience	
	Aggregate data	Individual data
Focus of attention		
Entire agenda	Perspective I	Perspective II
	Competition	*Automaton*
Single item on agenda	Perspective III	Perspective IV
	Natural history	*Cognitive portrait*

is named *competition* because it examines an array of issues competing for positions on the agenda. Another way of thinking about this perspective is in terms of the ability of news coverage to mobilize a constituency among the public for an issue. Other examples of agenda-setting where the full array of competing issues has been examined include the two subsequent US presidential elections, local public opinion in Japan and Spain, and the trend in US public opinion across the entire decade of the 1960s.

Perspective II is similar to the early agenda-setting studies with their focus on the entire agenda of issues, but shifts the focus to the agenda of each individual. Whereas perspective I is at the system level, perspective II is at the individual level. However, when individuals are asked to rank order a series of issues, there is little evidence of any correspondence between those individual rankings and the emphasis on those issues in the news media.[17] This perspective is called *automaton* because of its unflattering view of human behaviour, essentially a return to the hypodermic theory of mass media effects. For agenda-setting to occur in this situation, there must be individuals who are susceptible to being significantly programmed by the mass media. There is no doubt that the media can influence the views of individuals regarding the salience of some issues, but the entire agenda of the media is seldom, if ever, reproduced to any substantial degree by an individual.

Perspective III narrows the focus to a single issue on the agenda, but like perspective I uses aggregate measures to establish the salience of this item. Commonly, the measures of salience are the total number of news stories about the issue and the percentage of the public citing an issue as the most important problem facing the country. This perspective is named *natural history* because its focus is on the history of a single issue on the media and public agendas. In other words, the focus is on the degree of correspondence between the media agenda and the public agenda in the shifting salience of a single issue *over time*. Examples of this perspective already discussed include a 23-year look at the civil rights issue in the US, an eight-year look at eight different issues in the city of Louisville, and an intensive year-long look at sixteen individual issues in Germany.

Perspective IV again focuses on the individual, but narrows its observations to the salience of a single agenda item. This perspective, called *cognitive portrait*, is illustrated by the experimental studies of agenda-setting in which the salience of a single issue for an individual is measured before and after exposure to news programmes where the amount of exposure to various issues is controlled.

The existence of these varied perspectives on the agenda-setting phenomenon, especially an abundance of evidence based on perspectives I and III, strengthens the degree of confidence that we can have in our knowledge about this media effect. Perspective I provides useful, comprehensive descriptions of the rich, ever changing mix of mass media content and public opinion at particular points in time. This perspective strives to describe the world as it is. Perspective III provides useful descriptions of the natural history of a single issue, but at the expense of the larger social context in which this issue exists. Nevertheless, knowledge about the dynamics of a single issue over an extended period of time is highly useful for understanding how the process of agenda-setting works. Perspective IV also makes a valuable contribution to our understanding of the dynamics of agenda-setting. From a theoretical viewpoint, evidence generated by perspectives III and IV is absolutely necessary to the detailed explication of agenda-setting theory that will explain how and why this phenomenon occurs. But the ultimate goal of agenda-setting theory returns us to perspective I, a comprehensive view of mass communication and public opinion in the life of each community and nation.

Agenda-setting in past centuries

Although the term 'agenda-setting' was not coined until 1968, there is historical evidence of this phenomenon in much earlier times. In the British colonies that became the United States, the focus of geographical attention and the salience of place names in the American colonial press changed dramatically in the forty years preceding the Declaration of Independence in 1776.[18] About a third of the place names in the earliest of these decades, the period 1735 to 1744, referred to a location in the larger Anglo-American community, that is either Great Britain or North America. But in the decade immediately prior to the Declaration of Independence a third of the names referred to North America alone. In the final two years, 1774 and 1775, fully half of the place names referred to North America alone. Even more pertinent to the idea of an agenda-setting role of the press in achieving political consensus, symbols referring to the American colonies as a single unit increased significantly after 1763. After that date, about a fourth of all the American symbols in the newspapers referred to the colonies as a single, common unit. The geographical agenda of the eighteenth-century colonial press built the cultural and political identity of a new nation.

Moving to the late nineteenth century, the strong belief of progressive-era reformers in this role of the news media has also been noted.

> Setting the public agenda, it seems, is an exercise of power that lies at the heart of democratic politics. Municipal reformers learned this lesson in the 1890s, not only in Chicago and St. Louis, but in other large cities as well.[19]

In Chicago, for example, all the public issues that exploded in the late 1890s had been prominent on the newspapers' agendas for much of the decade. The intense and continuing coverage of one issue, street railway regulation, resulted in that issue dominating local elections for years, so much so that by 1899 all the candidates for mayor felt compelled to make street railway regulation the chief issue of their campaigns.[20]

Elsewhere in turn-of-the-century American politics, the famous Kansas editor William Allen White used his newspaper, the *Emporia Gazette*, to articulate an anti-populist agenda. Although it is difficult to ascertain the precise effects of this newspaper's agenda on the local public agenda of that time, Jean Lange Folkerts concluded that:

> White set an agenda for his readers that denied the economic hardship of farmers from 1895–1900 because he disliked the institutional remedies they proposed, and he feared loss of control by businessmen and loss of Eastern capital.[21]

At the beginning of this chapter, the evidence of news media influence on the focus of public opinion included a look at the entire decade of the turbulent 1960s.[22] Chapter 1 reviewed the evolution of the civil rights issue in the United States from 1954 to 1976.[23] Although these two twentieth-century examples are attenuated bits of history, they are useful benchmarks because they have the advantage of comparing the content of the news media with a systematic assessment of public opinion over a substantial period of time. Most historical research, which is to say, all research on periods of time prior to the development of public opinion polling in the 1930s, does not have this advantage. But drawing upon the vast array of contemporary evidence that defines agenda-setting theory, Edward Caudill concluded: 'the historical ramification is that the press agenda might be a reasonable guide to opinion beyond the immediate audience of the newspaper or magazine.'[24] Of course, he noted, there are limits and constraints, notably the requirement that widespread mass communication existed and enjoyed meaningful links to the populace whose opinions are of interest.[25]

Summing up

The pictures in our heads have many origins. Among the various sources of our knowledge about the world around us, the mass media are especially prominent. Chapter 1 reviewed a considerable body of evidence demonstrating a high degree of correspondence between the priorities of the media agenda and the subsequent priorities of the public agenda. To remove any doubt about this causal relationship between the media agenda and the public agenda, the idea of agenda-setting was taken into the experimental laboratory. Further solidifying the proposition that the media agenda sets the public agenda, this chapter reviewed additional evidence demonstrating a considerable degree of independence between the events of the world and the portrayal of those events in the news media. For a wide array of issues in the 1960s, for the availability of petroleum in the 1970s, for drugs in the 1980s, for environmental problems from the 1970s to the 1990s, for crime in the 1990s, and for both crime and shark attacks at the beginning of this century, the media agenda bore little resemblance to the historical agenda of events.[26] Nevertheless, in all these situations, there is strong evidence that it is the media and its portrayals of the world that set the public agenda.

The knowledge that we have gained in recent times about the agenda-setting role of the mass media has been used, in turn, to organize our understanding of the historical past. Assuming that the contemporary dynamics of public opinion described by agenda-setting theory can be extrapolated to the past, scholars have used content analyses of newspapers and magazines to write the history of past public opinion.

This merger of historical analysis with contemporary explications of public opinion offers rich theoretical promise for understanding the rapid evolution of new political practices for campaigning and governing, practices that are linked with new communication technologies and global media.[27] Important conceptual adjuncts of this theoretical promise are two of the perspectives identified by the Acapulco typology, the *natural history* perspective at the system level and the *cognitive portrait* perspective at the individual level. Both offer a close-up view of how the agenda-setting process works. Insights gleaned from these perspectives can be incorporated into a more finely tuned theoretical picture of the complex interactions of media and public for a continuously changing mix of issues. This broader perspective with its focus on an array of issues is labelled *competition* in the Acapulco typology. Agenda-setting research began in Chapel Hill with this 'real-world' situation, which remains the ultimate perspective for both scholars and citizens seeking to understand the evolution of public opinion in society.

Finally, echoing Lippmann's idea of the pseudo-environment in this new century, *New York Times* columnist William Safire provided this succinct summary of reality and the news: 'And in politics, what is widely perceived by the press and public is what *is*.'[28]

3 How Agenda-Setting Works

The agenda-setting effects of mass communication are widespread. Observations have found agenda-setting effects all across the United States in a variety of small towns and large cities. These effects also have been found abroad in cities as diverse as Tokyo, Japan, and Pamplona, Spain, and in countries as different as Argentina and Germany. Altogether, there are now more than 400 empirical studies of agenda-setting, many following the original Chapel Hill example and conducted during political campaigns, others monitoring public opinion in non-election periods. There is considerable diversity in the public issues that have been examined over the past thirty-five years, a diversity encompassing the economy, civil rights, drugs, the environment, crime, a wide variety of foreign policy questions, and dozens of other public issues. Agenda-setting is a robust and widespread effect of mass communication, an effect that results from specific content in the mass media.

For many persons, one of the most surprising aspects of these wide-ranging effects is the tremendous variability of the geographical and cultural settings in which agenda-setting by the media occurs. The culture and politics of the United States are exceedingly different from the cultural and political setting of Pamplona and the province of Navarra in northern Spain, where numerous agenda-setting effects have been measured in recent years. There is even more of a cultural and political contrast when we shift from Western countries to the young democracies of East Asia, where agenda-setting effects also have been observed.

A few years ago, a seminar in Taipei discussed this widespread international replication of media effects originally found in the United States and came to the conclusion that agenda-setting effects

– the successful transfer of salience from the media agenda to the public agenda – occur wherever there is a reasonably open political system *and* a reasonably open media system. Arguably, there is no perfectly open political system in any country in the world today, no system where the principle of one person, one vote, fully applies to every adult in the population. But the political systems of the United States, Spain and Taiwan – to cite some countries previously mentioned – are reasonably open in that elections really matter and actually determine the course of political history. Moreover, the vast majority of adults are eligible to participate in these elections. The media systems of these countries – or at least significant portions of them – are also open in that they are independent sources of news and political expression free from the domination of the government and major political parties. Where both of these conditions of openness exist, the public accepts considerable portions of the issue agenda put forward by the news media.

Observations made during the 1994 Taipei mayoral election in Taiwan[1] underscore the validity of this axiom that explains the widespread occurrence of agenda-setting. At the time of that election, there were three television stations serving Taipei, and all three in one way or another were controlled by the government and the long-dominant KMT political party. At the extreme, the Department of the Navy held 40 per cent of the shares in one of these television stations. Not surprisingly, no agenda-setting effects were found for television news. To echo a signature expression of American political scientist V. O. Key, albeit in a vastly different cultural setting, 'The voters are not fools!' In contrast, significant agenda-setting effects were found for the two dominant daily newspapers in Taipei. Although these newspapers, like most newspapers around the world, favour a particular political perspective, they are independent businesses free of any direct control by the Taiwan government or the KMT. This Taipei example is a useful comparison of the influence of open and closed media systems where all the other political and cultural factors are essentially held constant.

Evolution of issue agendas

An ongoing stream of public opinion evolves in these civic arenas around the world that are defined by open political and mass media systems. Over time, the salience of individual issues rises and falls as the attention of the mass media and the public shifts. Here we will outline major aspects of this public opinion process as issues appear on the media agenda and then move to the public agenda. We shall consider the capacity of the public agenda and competition among issues for a place on this agenda, the time-span that is involved in the evolution of the public agenda, and the comparative roles of newspapers and television news in the agenda-setting process.

The intense competition among issues for a place on the agenda is the most important aspect of this process. At any moment there are dozens of issues contending for public attention. But no society and its institutions can attend to more than a few issues at a time. The resource of attention in the news media, among the public, and in our various public institutions is a very scarce one. One of the earliest insights about agenda-setting was the limited size of the public agenda. For many years, a statement that the public agenda typically included no more than five to seven issues at any moment was accepted as an empirical generalization and regarded as another instance of what the psychologist George Miller called the 'magic number seven plus or minus two', a sweeping empirical generalization that describes the limits of a wide variety of sensory processes.[2]

The accumulation of evidence over subsequent years suggests an even smaller limit. Only a few problems demonstrate any sizeable constituency among the public when the Gallup Poll asks a national sample of Americans, 'What is the most important problem facing this country today?'. Across the ten Gallup polls asking this most important problem (MIP) question from 1997 to 2000, only half found a public agenda on which as many as five issues had a constituency of 10 per cent or more. Ten per cent is the level of concern among the public that has been identified as the threshold for significant public attention.[3] Five issues, of course, is the bottom of the range for Miller's axiom. Across all ten polls, the public agenda ranged from two to six issues.

This tight constraint on the size of the public agenda is explained by the limits of the public's resources, limits that include both time and psychological capacity. Limits on the size of most media agendas are even more obvious, a limited amount of space in the newspaper and a limited amount of time for broadcast news. Even in the case of internet web sites, with their seemingly unlimited capacity to add pages, the public's attention span and available time impose severe constraints.

All these constraints on the agendas of public issues within a society at any moment are summed up in the idea of the agenda-setting process as a zero-sum game, a perspective that underscores the intense competition among issues for attention by the media and the public. Explicit evidence that the public agenda is a zero-sum game was found in an analysis of three issues that dominated the US public agenda in the early 1990s.[4] The salience on the public agenda for each of the dominant issues at that time – the Gulf War, economic recession and federal budget deficit – resulted from two factors. One factor, the one emphasized by agenda-setting theory, of course, is the pattern of news coverage. The second factor is the relative salience of the two competing issues on the agenda.

Historically, one result of this limited agenda capacity and intense competition among issues is that a few perennial concerns have held centre stage in US public opinion. In the years immediately following World War II, foreign affairs and economics occupied centre stage, with foreign affairs nearly always in the leading role. Although other issues were able to garner a constituency from time to time, this pair of issues dominated the US public agenda.[5]

Updating this portrait, another analysis of trends from 1954 to 1994 – based on responses to the 'most important problem' question in 140 Gallup polls – found no change in the capacity of the American public agenda despite major increases in the level of formal education among the American public. During those years the proportion of the population with a high school education increased from 34 per cent to 78 per cent, and the proportion with a college degree rose from 6 per cent to over 21 per cent. Despite the lack of change in the capacity of the public agenda during this time, there is evidence that rising levels of education impacted another aspect of these trends in American public opinion, the diversity of issues on the public agenda.[6]

In *The Reasoning Voter*, Samuel Popkin observes:

> Education affects politics not by 'deepening' but by *broadening* the electorate – by increasing the number of issues that citizens see as politically relevant, and by increasing the number of connections they make between their own lives and national and international events.[7]

His observation acknowledges the widely documented situation that most people, even highly educated persons, rarely possess detailed, in-depth knowledge of public issues. Persons with higher levels of education do read newspapers and discuss the news more frequently with their family, friends and co-workers. The principal outcome of this activity, notes Popkin, is that educated persons 'will have limited information about a wider range of subjects, including national and international events, that are further from daily-life experience.'[8]

This broadening effect of education on the public agenda is readily apparent in the growing diversity of issues found on the public agenda.[9] As previously noted, at the time of World War II and in the post-war years up to 1960, a single category, international affairs, largely dominated the public agenda. But in the next two decades, the 1960s and 1970s, a larger array of issues were prominent. International issues were still on the agenda, principally Vietnam and the Cold War, but there also were large constituencies for economic issues as well as for civil rights. In the final two decades of the twentieth century, the public agenda continued to broaden and diversify. Four major issues each claimed more than 10 per cent – jobs, personal economic issues, law and order, and international affairs. Another four minor issues concerned with other aspects of the economy and domestic issues each claimed a 5 to 10 per cent share. The American public agenda reflected a growing sensitivity to a broader array of issues.

How can this increasing diversity of the public agenda be reconciled with the evidence that its capacity remained constant? The answer is that some issues now move on and off the public agenda faster than in previous decades. In other words, the explanation that reconciles these aspects of the agenda-setting process is that a collision between the expansive influence of education and the restrictive influence of limited agenda capacity has resulted in a more volatile public agenda. At mid-century, one category, international affairs, dominated centre stage. But the cast of issues began to grow in the 1960s, and this trend for major issues to share the stage with minor issues, at least for brief intervals, has continued. As we see in box 3.1, the long-reigning divas of public affairs continue to get starring roles on the public agenda, and the duration of their time on stage is lengthy, often exceeding two years or more. But now they share the limelight from time to time with an array of minor issues. These minor issues, such as the environment, education and health, do not appear nearly as often, nor is their duration on stage nearly as lengthy. But they do appear despite the limited capacity of the public agenda, the result of education's broadening influence on public perspectives about the issues of the day.

Further insight into the role of formal education in the agenda-setting process comes from a comparison of five demographic characteristics that appear time and again in public opinion polls: age, education, income, sex and race. Using a mix of issues that received either very high or very low coverage in the local newspapers, their salience was examined among nearly a thousand Americans in three communities stretching diagonally across the United States from Florida to the Pacific Northwest.[10] Only a single demographic characteristic was related to the pattern of salience for these issues.

Box 3.1 Duration of major issues on the public agenda

	Average duration per cycle (in months)*	Number of cycles, 1954–94*
Personal economic issues	47.4	7
Politics and government	40.8	8
Asia	27.8	4
General foreign policy issues	25.2	13
Government spending	21.8	5
Russia and Eastern Europe	19.3	4
Jobs	15.1	14
General economic issues	14.0	5
Law and order	10.3	12
Technology	8.7	3

*A cycle is the period of time beginning when 10% or more of the responses to the MIP question first name this issue and continuing until this issue is named in less than 10% of the responses.

Source: Maxwell McCombs and Jian-Hua Zhu, 'Capacity, diversity, and volatility of the public agenda: trends from 1954 to 1994', Public Opinion Quarterly, 59 (1995), pp. 495–525. Details of the specific issues mentioned over time that fall in these ten categories are in Appendix A of the article.

Citizens with more years of formal education more closely mirrored the media agenda.

This primacy of the educational experience is striking throughout the realm of politics and public affairs.

> Whether one is dealing with cognitive matters such as level of factual information about politics or conceptual sophistication in assessment; or such motivational matters as degree of attention paid to politics and emotional involvement in political affairs; or questions of actual behavior, such as engagement in any of a variety of political activities from party work to vote turnout itself; education is everywhere the universal solvent.[11]

Education has the conjoint effect of increasing individuals' attention to the news media and sensitizing them to a wider range of issues appearing in the news. On the other hand, higher levels of education do not appear to increase individuals' defensive responses to the pattern of emphasis in the news. Well-educated persons do not show any greater tendency than less-educated persons to argue against or erect psychological barriers to acceptance of the media agenda.[12]

However, one must be careful not to overstate the role of education and individual differences in the agenda-setting process. To define further the role of education vis-à-vis the messages of the media in determining the public agenda, the salience of four issues among the American public between 1977 and 1986 – inflation, unemployment, international problems and government spending – was compared to the pattern of coverage on national television during the same ten-year period.[13] Shifts in the salience for each of these four issues was examined separately for population subgroups that were simultaneously defined by both education and family income. The salience of all four issues was expected to be higher among the more educated. Family income was also used as a measure of issue sensitivity to these four issues because inflation and unemployment were assumed to be less relevant and international problems and government spending more relevant to higher income families.

There were massive shifts in the salience of these issues between 1977 and 1986. Each issue displays a pattern of peaks and valleys, rising and falling sharply both on the media agenda and among all the income and education subgroups. In contrast, the differences among the demographic subgroups themselves are minimal. Specifically in terms of the fit between the salience of each issue on the media agenda and its salience among the public, for three of the issues – inflation, unemployment and international problems – all the demographic subgroups followed a similar trajectory over time that paralleled the number of TV news stories. There are significant demographic differences, but, in statistical terms, individual differences defined by education and family income accounted for only 2 per cent of the variance in salience while the wide swings from year to year accounted for 37 per cent. 'In other words, media agenda-setting effects are not manifested in creating different levels of salience among individuals, but are evident at driving the salience of *all* individuals up and down over time.'[14]

Finally, there is an important footnote on the lack of agenda-setting effects for the fourth issue, government spending. In the final three years of the decade that was examined, the salience of government spending rose sharply and remained at high levels among most sectors of the public despite a low level of attention in television news. Part of the explanation for the high salience of this issue among the public may come from what we know about the limited capacity of the public agenda and about the recurring appearance of some issues. During those final three years, 1984 through 1986, the salience of two other aspects of the economy, unemployment and inflation, were low on both the media and the public agenda. Recall that unemployment was one of the reigning divas on the public agenda during the last half of the twentieth century and that inflation also made frequent appearances. Government spending is best described as one of the minor issues that make an occasional appearance on the stage of public opinion. Its move to centre stage during 1984–6 may well have occurred because both unemployment and inflation were offstage during much of this period. This again calls attention to the powerful constraints on the size of the public agenda.

Timeframe for effects

The old hypodermic theory viewed media effects as essentially immediate. In that view, media messages were injected into the audience much as medical injections are administered to patients and typically achieve rather quick effects. Support for that view essentially disappeared with the accumulation of empirical evidence in the 1940s and 1950s, a body of evidence summarized in Klapper's *The Effects of Mass Communication* as the Law of Minimal Consequences. In response, scholars such as Wilbur Schramm asserted that the truly significant effects of mass communication were likely to be very long term, much as awesome formations of stalactites and stalagmites in caves are created drop by drop over eons of time. Against that background, how long does it take for media attention to an issue to translate into high salience for that issue on the public agenda? Does it really take the psychological equivalent of eons? Or could it be that the shift from attitude and opinion change to earlier points in the communication process, such as focus of attention and perceived importance, yields evidence of relatively short-term media effects?

Recall that the rise and fall of public concern about civil rights in the United States across a 23-year span of time reflected primarily the pattern of media attention to this issue in the preceding month.[15] Further examination of that evidence adds a few details, but yields the same conclusion: agenda-setting effects are far from instantaneous, but they are relatively short-term.

Comparing the salience of civil rights on the public agenda across twenty-three years with the number of civil rights stories on the front pages of the *New York Times* in each of the six months preceding those Gallup polls reveals a monotonic pattern of declining correlations across those prior six months. The strongest correlation was +0.71 for the month of news coverage immediately preceding the polls. For the second month prior to the polls, the correlation was +0.70. Continuing back through the third, fourth, fifth and sixth months, the values continued to decline, reaching a low of $+0.38$ for the sixth month. This pattern might suggest some significant accumulation of influence and contribution by the news coverage in each of the preceding months. But when partial correlations were calculated in which the influence of each month on the public salience of civil rights was determined with the influence of the other five months eliminated, the results clearly indicated the primacy of the first month of news coverage preceding the public opinion polls. The correlation of $+0.71$ for the first month preceding the polls remained unchanged while all the other correlations substantially declined. The highest value for any of the other partial correlations was $+0.48$.

Taking the analysis one step further, use of all six months together to predict the salience of civil rights on the public agenda produced a correlation of $+0.89$, but the first two months alone produced a correlation of $+0.84$. The difference is not statistically significant.

The conclusion from this long statistical journey is that, although the strongest relationship between the public agenda and the media coverage of civil rights was found for the single month immediately preceding the measurement of public opinion, addition of the second month preceding the polls did result in a modest increase in the correlation. Adding the other months did not increase the strength of the relationship at all. In short, the accumulation of news coverage over a two-month period accounted for the trend over these twenty-three years in the salience of the civil rights issue among the American public. Within that two-month period, the month of news coverage immediately prior to the polls exerted the most influence.

There is, of course, the question of how generalizable this picture is of the agenda-setting process. We already know that the strength of agenda-setting effects can vary from issue to issue. However, two other investigations of the timeframe for agenda-setting effects also suggest that the span of time involved in the transfer of issue salience from the media agenda to the public agenda is generally in the range of four to eight weeks. A longitudinal analysis of the public opinion trends for each of three major issues during the 1960s and 1970s – pollution, drug abuse and energy – found a median correlation of $+0.66$ between the public agenda and the national television news agenda of the preceding month.[16] A three-wave panel study found a median correlation of $+0.77$ between the salience of the environment among the public and the agenda of three local newspapers during the preceding two months.[17] Our confidence that the public agenda typically reflects the media agenda of the preceding one to two months is enhanced by both the strength and the high degree of convergence among the correlations in all three investigations, which included both newspapers and television news and a variety of issues.

Under conditions of high personal involvement in the news, the timeframe for agenda-setting effects may be even shorter.[18] A particularly lively aspect of the internet, electronic bulletin boards where individuals discuss public issues, was monitored during the 1996 US presidential election. The frequency of discussion from September until a week after the November election for four issues – immigration, health care, taxes and abortion – was compared with the pattern of news coverage on these issues in the *New York Times*, Reuters, Associated Press, CNN and *Time* magazine. Discussion of immigration responded immediately to news coverage. Discussions of health care and taxes had longer timeframes, but still the effects were evident within a week. Among the four issues examined, only the discussions of abortion were not linked to the pattern of news coverage, an outcome most likely linked to the highly controversial and emotional nature of this issue. For the three issues where the pattern of media coverage did influence the salience, the timeframe was much shorter than for the agenda-setting effects of traditional news media. This outcome is not surprising because electronic bulletin boards are an outcropping of the public agenda where persons with high interest in an issue respond behaviourally.

All this evidence about the timeframe for agenda-setting effects is based on analyses tracing the salience of individual issues on the public agenda across time, analyses that are designated in the Acapulco typology as the *natural history* perspective. Obviously, there are other perspectives to consider, notably the *competition* perspective that takes into account the full array of issues competing for positions on the agenda. While it is useful analytically to examine a single issue in order to understand the process underlying its natural history, the *competition* perspective provides a portrait of the real world where there is always a mélange of issues in flux. From this perspective, what timeframe links the media and public agendas?

The comprehensive body of evidence summarized in box 3.2 is based on an agenda of eleven public issues and a range of news media from local TV news and the local newspaper to national TV news and the weekly news magazines.[19] Although there are variations across these five news media in which weeks of news coverage show the best fit with the public agenda, the variation is relatively small and falls in essentially the same range observed for individual issues. The range of time-spans producing the optimum match between the media and public agendas is one to eight weeks, with a median span of three weeks. In every case, the agenda-setting effects are sizeable.

Box 3.2 Time-spans for appearance and disappearance of agenda-setting effects

News medium	Time lag (in weeks)*	Maximum correlation	Decay of effect (in weeks)**
National TV news	1	+0.92	8
Local TV news	2	+0.91	12
Regional newspaper	3	+0.88	26
Local newspaper	4	+0.60	26
News magazine	8	+0.58	26

*Number of accumulated weeks producing the maximum correlation between the media agenda and the public agenda.
**Number of weeks before the disappearance of a significant correlation between the media agenda and the public agenda.
Source: Wayne Wanta and Y. Hu, 'Time-lag differences in the agenda setting process: an examination of five news media', International Journal of Public Opinion Research, 6 (1994), pp. 225–40. Reproduced by permission of the World Association for Public Opinion Research and Oxford University Press.

If our benchmark is the four to eight weeks typically found for the natural history of issues, the distribution in box 3.2 based on a *competition* perspective falls towards the shorter end of that range. However, another look at issue competition under two very different sets of circumstances – the agenda of issues during a US national election that included the highly salient issue of Watergate and another agenda that included the Egypt-Israeli War among college students during a non-election period – found time-spans falling at the other end of the distribution, eight weeks or more.[20] Nevertheless, considering the complexity of the situation here – the full array of issues on the media and public agendas – the time-span for the appearance of significant agenda-setting effects is still rather short.

Over the course of a relatively few weeks, the salience of topics featured in the news media is absorbed by significant numbers of the public. This continuous and virtually invisible learning process is an important civic instance of a larger phenomenon, incidental learning from the mass media. Long ago, Paul Lazarsfeld described mass communication as an informal classroom where the students continuously come and go and, much like some students in more formal classrooms, do not always pay full attention even when they are present. But people do learn from the mass media. They learn a panoply of facts, many of which they incorporate into their images and attitudes about a variety of objects. They also learn about the most important issues of the moment, incorporating the agenda of the mass media into their own agenda of the key issues facing society.

The circumstances of this incidental learning differ from the learning that commonly takes place in school, but the outcomes can be just as powerful and influential. After all, if incidental learning did not yield significant outcomes, the vast advertising industry would not exist.

The mass media are teachers whose principal strategy of communication is redundancy. Over and over again, our mass media teachers repeat topics, at times with great emphasis, at other times just in passing. It is primarily the accumulation of these lessons over the period of one to eight weeks that is reflected in the responses of citizen students when we inquire about the most important issues facing the nation. Of course, in most cases the lessons did not begin abruptly eight weeks previously, but it is the pattern of coverage in the most recent weeks that has by far the greatest impact on the public.

There is also empirical evidence about the reverse side of the learning coin, the decay of information and the forgetting that takes place for any pattern of learning. Without delving into this aspect of learning in as much detail as we have spent on the acquisition of information, we see in box 3.2 that the time-span for the decay of learning lacks the tight focus reflected in the evidence about acquisition of current public concerns.[21] The decay of agenda-setting effects, which is defined in box 3.2 as the point in time where significant correlations between the media agenda and the public agenda disappear completely, ranges from eight to twenty-six weeks. Not entirely without surprise, each lesson learned in the mass communication classroom is visible over a considerable expanse of time.

These conclusions about the duration of issues on the public agenda, both the learning process involved in the rise of issues in public attention and the decay of learning as issues disappear from public attention, are essentially empirical generalizations. We know about these timeframes because the logs of various social scientists' exploratory voyages into this realm yield rather consistent data, especially in regard to the rise of issues on the public agenda. But empirical generalizations are less sound than empirical findings that support carefully reasoned hypotheses grounded in an explicit theoretical context.

In this regard, the status of agenda-setting theory differs little from the larger literature on media effects. Examination of the indices of two comprehensive and widely used texts on communication theory reveals scant attention in the field at large to the question of time-frames for various media effects.[22] This is simultaneously a theoretical deficit and an opportunity for advancement.

There are the beginnings of a theoretical framework for agenda-setting effects in an early discussion of time-related concepts.[23] These concepts include the time lag between the appearance of an issue on the media agenda and its appearance on the public agenda as well as the optimal effect span, the length of time yielding the peak association between the two agendas. There is also a larger theoretical framework in the idea of the agenda-setting process as a zero-sum game.[24] However, considerable work remains to be done.

Newspapers versus television news

Longstanding concern with the effects of the mass media has frequently been accompanied by a certain fascination with the relative power of the various mass media to achieve those effects. With the advent and widespread diffusion of television in the latter half of the twentieth century, attention has been directed particularly at comparisons of newspapers and television. Probably the best-known example of this topic on the intellectual agenda is Marshall McLuhan's *The Medium is the Message*.

Examinations of the agenda-setting influence of the mass media have been no exception. Once people understand the basic idea of agenda-setting, they are usually quick to ask which medium is more powerful in setting the public agenda, television or newspapers. The best answer is, 'It depends.' Whether there is any difference at all in the influence of the two media or whether one clearly surpasses the other in impact varies considerably from one situation to another. A moment's reflection will reveal why this is hardly surprising. After all, the evidence on the agenda-setting influence of the mass media covers a wide variety of situations in terms of geography, historical periods, political settings, the array of issues, and news organizations. Furthermore, the evidence that we do possess – despite its considerable breadth – in no way represents any systematic sampling of these varied situations.

To complicate matters further, not every agenda-setting study even affords a comparison of newspapers and television. Many investigations use a single medium as a surrogate for the news agenda, relying upon the well-established assumption of a high degree of redundancy across the news agendas of individual media.[25] In the United States, the *New York Times* has frequently been assigned this surrogate role. At other times, the national television networks have been assigned this role because of the Vanderbilt University Archive's exhaustive abstracts of network news programme content. Yet other investigations merge the agendas of print and electronic media to create a single media agenda. Our measures of the media agenda reflect many variations. Under these circumstances, what can we say about the comparative agenda-setting influence of newspapers and television beyond 'It depends'?

We can begin with a broad generalization grounded in decades of accumulated evidence on agenda-setting effects. Then a variety of evidence will be reviewed that illustrates this empirical generalization. Finally, some theoretical suggestions for solving this intellectual puzzle about the comparative roles of the various mass media will be advanced.

First, as a broad empirical generalization, about half the time there is no discernible difference in the agenda-setting roles of newspapers and television news. The other half of the time, it appears that newspapers have the edge by a ratio of about 2 to 1. This latter pattern is a surprise to many because the conventional wisdom is that television is the dramatic, powerful medium of our time. But if we briefly consider the natural history of most issues, the larger capacity of daily newspapers relative to television news means that audiences often have a longer period of time to learn the newspaper agenda. Television news is more like the front section of the newspaper. Newspaper readers may have considerable exposure to an issue long before it ever reaches the top of the newspaper agenda or appears on the television agenda at all.

In the international setting, there is an additional factor that frequently places newspapers at an advantage over television. In many countries, all or a considerable portion of the television service is controlled to some degree by the government whereas almost universally, newspapers are in private hands. This is a situation that can diminish the credibility of television news.

As we turn to the empirical evidence, another complicating factor must be recognized. In many situations, especially in the United States, which is the setting for much of our evidence on agenda-setting, comparisons of newspapers and television involve a mix of levels. The original Chapel Hill study involved two national television networks, four local newspapers and the *New York Times*, the closest approximation to a national newspaper in the United States until the appearance in the final decades of the twentieth century of *USA Today*. Local television news was not included in that seminal 1968 examination of agenda-setting, but other investigations do take in news agendas based on local television news. As the examples that follow illustrate, just about every possible combination of local newspapers, regional newspapers, the *New York Times*, local TV news, and some mix of the national television networks' evening news can be found.

Beginning with the original Chapel Hill study, the general pattern found is that the agenda-setting influence of the *New York Times* was greater than that of the local newspaper, which, in turn, was greater than that of the national television news.[26] But there are overlaps in the correlations that summarize this media influence on the public agenda. The differences between the various media are not totally distinct. Moving on to the 1972 US presidential campaign, an extensive set of comparisons again favoured the local newspaper over national television news by a wide margin.[27] But in the next presidential election, comparisons of local newspapers in three communities with national television reversed the pattern: national television news was more influential in 1976 than local newspapers.[28] This pattern was also replicated in the 1980 US presidential election.[29]

Outside an election setting, the evidence is equally mixed. Comparisons of local newspapers and local television news in Minneapolis[30] and Louisville[31] favoured newspapers. In Toledo, for the agenda of national issues, both national and local television news had greater influence than the local newspaper.[32] For an agenda of local issues, the local newspaper had greater influence than local television news. Finally, revisiting box 3.2's summary of the findings from three American communities, the local newspaper trailed national television news, local television news and a regional newspaper.[33] Among the latter three, there was no significant difference. As we said, 'It depends.'

A major portion of the answer to the subsequent question, 'Depends on what?', is discussed in the next chapter, which presents a psychological explanation for agenda-setting effects. By way of preface to that discussion, it must be noted that both the frequency and the quality of attention to the news media differ considerably from individual to individual. Some people are exposed to television news and a newspaper nearly every day. Many others are exposed far less frequently. Looking at the public's motivation to attend to the news media, about a fourth of the American population strongly believe it is their civic duty to keep up with the news.[34] The vast majority of these dutiful citizens read a newspaper daily and nearly half view national television news daily. As the strength of this civic belief declines, so does regular exposure to any news medium.

Whatever the pattern of exposure, there are also individual differences in the level of attention. While few students in the media classroom prepare for an election, much less everyday conversation, in the way that graduate students prepare for their comprehensive examinations, some of these citizen students do pay considerable attention to election news and news about the issues of the day. One analysis found that serious newspaper readers, defined as persons who regularly read national and international news, local government news and political news, account for about a fourth of the total newspaper audience. Albeit a minority, it is a sizeable and well-informed minority.[35]

Closer examination of individual differences in why people come to the news may explain differences in frequency of exposure, degree of attention to public affairs news in the media, and the variable pattern of outcomes found in the comparisons of newspapers and television. A theoretical explanation, perhaps grounded in the ideas about audience psychology that are presented in chapter 4, is needed to bring greater meaning to what is at best a vague empirical generalization about the agenda-setting influence of various news channels.

At the societal level, even more important than the relative impact of newspapers and television is the sheer diversity of news sources available to the public. Diversity in the public agenda – measured by the number of different problems mentioned by people when asked to name the most important problem facing the local community or the nation – is significantly related to the number of newspaper, radio and television voices in the community.[36]

Summing up

Citizens are involved in a continuous learning process about public affairs. Their responses to the pollster's quiz about what are the most important issues typically reflects the media's lessons of the past four to eight weeks. Sometimes it is the newspapers' lessons that dominate these responses, but often both newspapers and television news share equally the role of civic teacher. The content of these media lessons also reflects the intense competition among issues for a position on the media and public agendas,[37] a situation in which only a small handful of perennial issues frequently have the spotlight.

The agenda-setting effects that are frequently the outcome of this complex process are shaped to a considerable degree by characteristics of the media's messages and to a far lesser degree by the characteristics of the recipients of those messages. Mass communication is a social process in which the same message, in either printed, audio or audio/visual form, is disseminated to a vast population. Numerous characteristics of these messages influence how many persons pay any attention to the message and apprehend at least some portion of its content. Front-page stories in the newspaper have about twice the readership of stories that appear inside the newspaper. Stories with attractive graphics and large headlines attract more readers. Many other characteristics of the newspaper – and analogous characteristics of television and other mass media – influence the extent to which mass communication is successful in finding an audience.

Ultimately, mass communication is a transaction between a single member of the audience and the media message, a transaction in which individual differences might seem paramount. In a sense, mass communication effects are a large set of overlapping, but not identical, personal experiences. Although, arguably, no two of these experiences are identical, it is fortunate for our goal of a parsimonious theory of mass communication effects that persons with vastly different characteristics frequently have highly similar experiences. Among all these individual differences, the most important ones are the basis of the psychological explanation for the occurrence of agenda-setting that is presented in the next chapter.

4 Why Agenda-Setting Occurs

Sometime back in a high school physics class you probably encountered the scientific principle 'Nature abhors a vacuum.' A similar proposition applies to human psychology. Innate within each of us is a need to understand the surrounding environment.[1] Whenever we find ourselves in a new situation, in a cognitive vacuum, so to speak, there is an uncomfortable feeling until we explore and mentally map that setting. Think back to your freshman year in college when you probably arrived on a new and unfamiliar campus to undertake a new intellectual voyage. Or your experience in moving to a new city – or even visiting a new city, especially one in a foreign country. In those situations newcomers feel a need to orient themselves to the situation at hand. Colleges conduct extensive freshman orientation sessions. Publishers find it profitable to offer tourists guidebooks that contain maps, lists of hotels and restaurants, and a variety of other orienting information.

In the civic arena, there are also many situations where citizens feel a need for orientation. In primary elections to select a party's nominee for office, there are sometimes as many as a dozen candidates. Because it is a primary election, the orienting cue frequently used by voters, party affiliation, is moot. All the candidates belong to the same party. In this circumstance, many voters feel a strong need for orientation. Much the same situation exists in bond elections and other referenda elections, where again party labels are not pertinent, as well as in many elections for lower-level offices that present non-partisan and, often, unfamiliar candidates. In all these circumstances, voters frequently turn to the mass media for orientation, either to the news to garner pertinent information about the situation at hand or directly to the editorial endorsements of newspapers.[2] Not every voter feels this need for orientation to the same degree, of course. Some citizens desire considerable background information before making their voting decision. Others desire no more than a simple orienting cue. Need for orientation is a psychological concept, which means that it describes individual differences in the desire for orienting cues and background information.

These patterns of behaviour frequently exhibited in election settings are one outcropping of psychologist Edward Tolman's general theory of cognitive mapping.[3] Earlier we encountered a similar idea in Lippmann's concept of the pseudo-environment, not the world as it is, but the picture of the world that is in our minds. What is common to both is the idea that we form maps – albeit many times sketchy and highly condensed maps – of the external environment. Emphasizing the purposive nature of this map-making, Robert Lane's *Political Life: Why and How People Get Involved in Politics* reviews 'efforts to extract meaning from the political environment'.[4] Lane attributes the origins of these efforts variously to the innate nature of humans, the process of childhood socialization, and formal education. The psychological concept introduced in this chapter, need for orientation, describes these efforts at meaning and provides a psychological explanation for the transfer of salience from the media agenda to the public agenda.

Relevance and uncertainty

Conceptually, an individual's need for orientation is defined in terms of two lower-order concepts, relevance and uncertainty, whose roles occur sequentially. Relevance is the initial defining condition of need for orientation. Most of us feel no psychological discomfort and no need for orientation whatsoever in numerous situations, especially in the realm of public affairs, because we do not perceive these situations to be personally relevant. The internal politics of Armenia or New Zealand stir little interest among most citizens of Europe or North America. Much the same can be said of many issues of the day even in our own country. There are many issues with little constituency among the public at large. In these situations, where relevance to the individual is low or even non-existent, the need for orientation is low.

The relevance of a topic – feeling that an issue has any personal relevance or relevance to the larger society – springs from many sources. However, there was remarkable consistency in the reasons that people gave for their response to the 'most important problem facing the country' question in a 1992 and a 1996 Texas Poll.[5] The reasons given by respondents for naming a particular problem as 'the most important' were, in order from the most to the least frequently cited, civic duty, emotional arousal, personal interest, peer influence and self-interest. Comparing the pattern of responses in those two years, the median difference in the percentage of Texas Poll respondents citing each of these reasons in 1992 and 1996 was only 3.2 per cent. For example, when these polls asked to what extent it was one's civic duty to be concerned about the problem nominated as most important, 83.3 per cent of the respondents in 1992 and 83.6 per cent in 1996 replied 'very much'. Asked if the problem named was emotionally arousing, 68.4 per cent in 1992 and 64.9 per cent in 1996 replied 'very much'. Although civic duty most likely was over-reported – the results of social desirability bias – the conventional wisdom that self-interest plays a major role in the shaping of public opinion was not supported by this evidence.

Another exploration of issue relevance elicited reasons why any of nine contemporary issues should be moved higher or lower on the public agenda.[6] Reasons for moving issues higher were nearly three times as frequent as moving an issue down. Pollution and AIDS were the issues most often seen as threats at that time, and a third of the responses cited a threat to society as the reason for moving an issue higher on the agenda. Another quarter of the responses cited the social consequences:

> Unemployment and the budget deficit were most often seen this way. For example, unemployment leads to poverty. Threat may be implicit. But, unlike threat, this kind of reason specifies a particular undesirable consequence. Such specification could be of help in addressing the problem.[7]

Among individuals who for whatever reason perceive the relevance of a topic to be high – to keep matters simple, relevance is considered here as either low or high – the *level of uncertainty* about the topic must also be considered. As we see in box 4.1, level of uncertainty is the second and subsequent defining condition of need for orientation. Frequently, individuals already have all the information that they desire about a topic. Their degree of uncertainty is low. This is the case for many public issues where public opinion is highly stable over long periods of time. In this circumstance, people do not usually ignore the news media, but they monitor the news primarily in order to detect any significant changes in the situation at hand.[8] Under these conditions of high relevance and low uncertainty, the need for orientation is moderate.

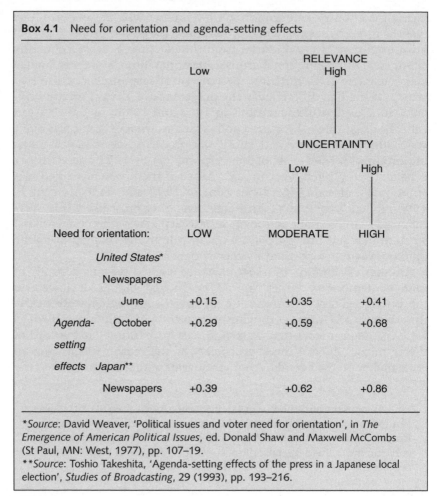

Box 4.1 Need for orientation and agenda-setting effects

	RELEVANCE		
	Low	High	
		UNCERTAINTY	
		Low	High
Need for orientation:	LOW	MODERATE	HIGH
*United States**			
Newspapers			
June	+0.15	+0.35	+0.41
Agenda- October	+0.29	+0.59	+0.68
setting			
effects *Japan***			
Newspapers	+0.39	+0.62	+0.86

Source: David Weaver, 'Political issues and voter need for orientation', in *The Emergence of American Political Issues*, ed. Donald Shaw and Maxwell McCombs (St Paul, MN: West, 1977), pp. 107–19.
**Source*: Toshio Takeshita, 'Agenda-setting effects of the press in a Japanese local election', *Studies of Broadcasting*, 29 (1993), pp. 193–216.

At other times, both relevance and uncertainty are high. This is often the case in party primary elections where there are many unfamiliar candidates and the easy orienting cue of party affiliation is unavailable. This is also the case for what are essentially new issues on the public agenda, such as the extensive debates on health-care reform and free trade during Bill Clinton's presidency in the United States. The complexity and broad implications of these issues resulted in high relevance and high uncertainty for many Americans. In theoretical terms, those citizens had a high need for orientation.

But in President Clinton's second term most Americans felt little need for orientation in regard to the sexual scandal involving the president and Monica Lewinsky. While most perceived the president's personal conduct as reprehensible, a majority also regarded this behaviour as irrelevant to his position as president. Poll after poll reported extraordinarily high job performance ratings for Clinton despite the continuing obsession of the news media with the scandal. Sometimes the public perceives little need for orientation and little need to attend to the media's agenda.[9]

Occurrence of agenda-setting effects

The greater an individual's need for orientation in the realm of public affairs, the more likely they are to attend to the agenda of the mass media.[10] Among voters in Charlotte, North Carolina, during the 1972 US presidential election, for example, 79.8 per cent of those with a high need for orientation were frequent users of newspapers, television and news magazines for political information. In comparison, 62.5 per cent of those with a moderate need for orientation and only 47.4 per cent of those with a low need for orientation were frequent users of the mass media for political information.

This concept also explicates the venerable relationship discussed in the previous chapter between education and exposure to the mass media agenda.[11] Among Texas voters during the 2000 US presidential primaries, level of education was strongly linked both to viewing the candidate debates on cable television and to the existence of need for orientation defined specifically in terms of whether there was any personally relevant issue on the campaign agenda. Detailed analysis of these relationships revealed that need for orientation is an intervening variable that explains the link between education – a broadbrush, background predictor of an individual's cognitive orientation to public affairs – and viewing the candidate debates – a highly specific information-seeking behaviour. With increased education, particularly some college or more, there was more likely to be a need for orientation. In turn, the existence of this need was linked with debate watching.

During an election voters frequently learn a great deal about the candidates and their issue positions from the news media and from political advertising. This learning includes significant adoption of the media agenda in direct relation to the voters' level of need for orientation. Below the conceptual diagram in box 4.1 of need for orientation is a summary of the degree of agenda-setting that occurred among voters in Charlotte during the 1972 US presidential election.[12] During the summer months as the campaign took shape and, later, during the fall campaign, agenda-setting effects increased monotonically with the strength of the need for orientation. The metaphor of an election as an open civic classroom is bolstered by the increased degree of agenda-setting that occurred from June to October. The students were doing their lessons.

This same pattern of agenda-setting effects was found in the Japanese mayoral election previously discussed in chapter 1.[13] When these Japanese voters are stratified according to their level of need for orientation, box 4.1 shows that the strength of the agenda-setting effect increases monotonically with the degree of need for orientation. Recall that the overall result among these voters was a modest, but positive, correlation of +0.39. This is a very low correlation in comparison to those found in the majority of evidence from elsewhere in the world. However, box 4.1 shows a correlation of +0.62 between the media agenda and voters with a moderate need for orientation and an astounding correlation of +0.86 for those voters with a high need for orientation. Further examination of the evidence from that election provides an explanation for the overall modest correlation of +0.39. A majority of the voters interviewed, some 57 per cent, had a low need for orientation. Only 21 per cent had a high need for orientation. In this situation, the concept of need for orientation provides a concise explanation for the low degree of correspondence overall between the media agenda and the public agenda. With a low need for orientation, the majority of voters had little motivation to attend to the media agenda or to adopt that agenda.

The concept of need for orientation also provides an explanation for the near-perfect match between the media agenda and the public agenda in the seminal Chapel Hill study.[14] The overall correlation obtained there was +0.97, a degree of correspondence that greatly encouraged the continued exploration of the agenda-setting phenomenon. Although the concept of need for orientation was not explicated as part of agenda-setting theory until a few years later, it is clear in retrospect that the original Chapel Hill evidence of agenda-setting effects was based exclusively on persons with a high need for orientation. Recall that the persons interviewed in Chapel Hill were selected randomly from the list of registered voters. In other words, the presidential election and its issue agenda were relevant to them. They were registered voters, but registered voters who had not yet made a commitment to a particular presidential candidate. The entire sample consisted of these undecided voters. In theoretical terms, all of these voters had high uncertainty. High relevance and high uncertainty define a high need for orientation, the theoretical condition under which the highest degree of correspondence is predicted between the media agenda and the public agenda. Chapel Hill's correlation of +0.97 is very high, but not astronomically high in comparison with the +0.86 found among those Japanese voters who also had a high need for orientation.

Additional evidence for the validity of the need for orientation concept is found in box 4.2, which indicates that the importance voters attach to knowing the presidential candidates' positions on the issues increases with need for orientation.[15] In other words, this general concept of intellectual curiosity explains differences in the level of voter interest in a specific kind of information. The consistently higher levels of interest in the issue positions of Jimmy Carter, the relatively unknown challenger, compared to the issue positions of Gerald Ford, the incumbent president running for re-election, further validates the idea of need for orientation.

Agenda-setting effects are more than the result of how accessible or available an issue is in the minds of the public. Although the empirical measure most commonly used to predict these effects is the amount of news coverage for an issue on the media agenda, the salience of an issue among the public is not simply a matter of its cognitive availability. If the sheer availability of an issue is the key to agenda-setting effects, then the Monica Lewinsky–Bill Clinton scandal would have soared to the top of the public agenda. With its 'All Monica, all the time' approach, the media inflated the salience of this topic on their own agenda, but it never achieved salience among the public as an important public issue. There are many other, albeit less dramatic, examples of the failure of intense news coverage to influence the public agenda. Citizens are not defenceless, even in the face of continuous massive media barrages about a topic.

Although the frequency of media coverage is usually the best single predictor of salience on the public agenda, the accuracy of this

Box 4.2 Need for orientation and average level of interest in political information			
	Need for orientation		
	Low	Moderate	High
Ford's issue positions	4.8*	5.5	5.7
Carter's issue positions	5.0	5.6	6.3

*Maximum rating = 7
Source: David Weaver and Maxwell McCombs, 'Voters' need for orientation and choice of candidate: mass media and electoral decision making', paper presented at the American Association for Public Opinion Research, Roanoke, VA, 1978.

prediction is significantly honed by knowledge about what degree of need for orientation exists among the public. This is illustrated in the variety of examples already considered in this chapter, especially by return visits to the original Chapel Hill study and the Japanese mayoral election. Frequency of coverage in the news media is part of the explanation for agenda-setting effects, but only in tandem with the psychological relevance of items on the media agenda to members of the public. Public salience is the combined result of availability and personal relevance.[16]

Personal experience with public issues

The mass media are not our only source of orientation to public affairs. Personal experience, which includes conversations with our family, friends and co-workers, also informs us about many issues. The dominant source of influence, of course, will vary from issue to issue. For an economic issue such as inflation, personal experience is almost certainly dominant. If there is significant inflation in the economy, personal experience with routine purchases will reveal its presence. We do not need the mass media to alert us to this problem or to dispel any uncertainty about its significance. In contrast, for economic issues such as national trade deficits or budget deficits, the news media are likely to be our sole source of orientation. There are many other public issues, especially in the realm of foreign affairs, where personal experience is greatly limited, if not non-existent. In theoretical terms, some issues are obtrusive, that is, they obtrude into our daily lives and are directly experienced. Other issues are unobtrusive. We encounter them only in the news, not directly in our daily lives.[17]

Examination of the agenda-setting influence of the news media on the salience of three public issues in Canada found the pattern of results predicted by this distinction between obtrusive and unobtrusive issues.[18] In box 4.3, there is very little correspondence (+0.28) between the pattern of news coverage for inflation and the salience of this issue among the Canadian public over a sixteen-month period of time. But for the abstract, unobtrusive issue of national unity, there is an extraordinary match (+0.96). We shall return shortly to the third issue, unemployment, which *a priori* would seem to be an obtrusive issue, but whose empirical outcome here (+0.67) more closely fits the prediction for unobtrusive issues. But first let us examine some additional evidence from the United States that sustains the validity of this distinction between obtrusive and unobtrusive issues.

Box 4.3 Agenda-setting effects for obtrusive and unobtrusive issues (natural history perspective)

OBTRUSIVE ——————————————————————— UNOBTRUSIVE

Canada*

| Inflation +0.28 | Unemployment +0.67 | National unity +0.96 |

United States**

Crime +0.19	Unemployment +0.60	Pollution +0.79
Cost of living +0.20		Drug abuse +0.80
		Energy +0.71

*Source: James Winter, Chaim Eyal and Ann Rogers, 'Issue-specific agenda setting: the whole as less than the sum of the parts', *Canadian Journal of Communication*, 8, 2 (1982), pp. 1–10.
**Source: Harold Zucker, 'The variable nature of news media influence', in *Communication Yearbook 2*, ed. Brent Ruben (New Brunswick, NJ: Transaction Books, 1978), pp. 225–40.

This same pattern of results – a high degree of correspondence between public opinion and news coverage for unobtrusive issues and little correspondence for obtrusive issues – was found across a decade of public opinion in the US.[19] Box 4.3 displays high correlations for the unobtrusive issues of pollution, drug abuse and energy, but very low correlations for the obtrusive issues of crime and the cost of living. At the local level in the US, the pattern of agenda-setting in Louisville summarized in chapter 1 also indicates a lack of media influence on obtrusive issues. Detailed comparisons of the issue rankings on the media agenda and public agenda, whose overall correlation was +0.65, found that 'the major differences between the two agendas involve issues with which people would likely have personal experience: road maintenance, health care, the courts, drainage, and mass transit.'[20]

All this evidence about the differences between obtrusive and unobtrusive issues is based on the analysis of individual issues. In terms of the Acapulco typology, this evidence is based on the natural history perspective. There also is evidence pointing to the same conclusion that is based on the competition perspective, which considers the entire agenda of issues. Box 4.4 presents a series of comparisons in which the issues on the media and public agendas have been divided into two sets, an agenda of unobtrusive issues and an agenda of obtrusive issues.[21] The agenda of unobtrusive issues

Box 4.4 Agenda-setting effects for agendas of obtrusive and unobtrusive issues (competition perspective)

	Agenda of obtrusive issues	Agenda of unobtrusive issues
New Hampshire		
Newspapers	+0.32	+0.67
Television news	+0.33	+0.74
Indiana		
Newspapers	+0.06	+0.60
Television news	+0.06	+0.59
Illinois		
Newspapers	+0.20	+0.95
Television news	+0.32	+0.95

Source: David Weaver, Doris Graber, Maxwell McCombs and Chaim Eyal, *Media Agenda Setting in a Presidential Election: Issues, Images, and Interest* (Westport, CT: Greenwood, 1981).

consists of seven items: government credibility, government spending, foreign affairs, the environment and energy, crime, race relations and social problems. The four issues on the obtrusive issue agenda are all economic concerns: unemployment, taxes, inflation and the general state of the economy. In box 4.4, all six measures show substantial agenda-setting effects for the agendas defined by unobtrusive issues. The median correlation falls between +0.67 and +0.74. In contrast, there is very little correspondence between the media and public agendas of obtrusive issues. The median correlation falls between +0.20 and +0.32.

A general explanation for these striking differences in the public's response to media coverage of obtrusive and unobtrusive issues is provided by the concept of need for orientation. Because obtrusive issues are defined as issues obtruding into people's everyday lives, personal experience in many instances will sufficiently orient individuals to the situation at hand. The result is a low need for any additional orientation, a circumstance that predicts low correlations between the media agenda and the public agenda. One of the examples of an obtrusive issue cited previously was inflation. On the other hand, personal experience is not a sufficient source of orientation for unobtrusive issues. For these, the theoretical assumption is that the media agenda is commonly the primary source of orientation, the source to which people turn to reduce their uncertainty.

Individual differences, media use and agenda-setting

When the concept of obtrusive and unobtrusive issues was added to the theory of agenda-setting, this distinction was initially treated as a simple dichotomy. Issues were either obtrusive or unobtrusive. The examples in box 4.4 are typical of this research. But box 4.3 already anticipates a more subtle treatment of this concept in which obtrusive and unobtrusive are the polar anchors of a continuum.[22] Examination of the public's encounters with any issue will reveal individual differences in the degree of their personal experience.

The issue of unemployment, which earlier we set aside in our discussion of the evidence in box 4.3, illustrates the importance of treating this concept as a continuum rather than as a simple dichotomy. For persons who are unemployed or who know unemployed persons, this is an obtrusive issue. But for tenured university professors, affluent professionals and many others, unemployment is an abstract, unobtrusive issue. There is a vast range of personal experience in regard to unemployment – and many other issues. In box 4.3 this range of experience with unemployment is reflected by its placement in the middle of the page beneath the line that connects obtrusive and unobtrusive to illustrate a continuum. The values of the two correlations there, which are highly similar even though measured at different times in Canada and the US, suggest that for the majority of North Americans, albeit certainly not for all, the issue of unemployment is essentially an unobtrusive one.[23]

A detailed look at individual differences regarding personal experience with issues is available from a panel study of American voters who were asked to name 'the one most important problem that the national government in Washington should do something about'.[24] This analysis focused on three major issues. For the issue of unemployment, the distinction between obtrusive and unobtrusive was based on survey respondents' personal or household employment situation. For the issue of inflation, each respondent's household financial situation was the basis of this distinction. For the issue of crime, the distinction was based on perceptions about how safe it was to walk around in their neighbourhood at night.

Among persons for whom these were obtrusive issues, the evidence supports the theoretical assumption that need for orientation is satisfied largely through personal encounters with these issues and that the media are not important sources of influence. High media users were no more likely to name any of these three issues than were low media users. Increased exposure to newspapers and television news did not increase the salience of these issues among this group.

However, among persons for whom these were unobtrusive issues, the evidence supports the tandem theoretical assumption that need for orientation is largely satisfied through use of the mass media and that the degree of media influence increases with greater exposure. Among voters for whom these issues are unobtrusive, their salience was higher among high media users than among low media users.

The role of the mass media vis-à-vis personal experience in regard to the salience of public issues is not always so distinct. Evidence for the tandem influence of the frequency of media use *and* personal experience with public issues is found both in public opinion about crime in Syracuse, New York, and in Texans' level of agreement with a thirteen-issue media agenda.[25] In support of the basic agenda-setting hypothesis, the salience of local crime as an issue in Syracuse was greater among those with high exposure to news about local crime, and in Texas frequency of media use was the best predictor of agreement with the media agenda. But personal experience with these issues was also a significant predictor of the salience of crime in Syracuse and of overall agreement with the media agenda in Texas. In both of these geographical settings – a middle-sized city in the northeastern US and a large southwestern state – media use and personal experience combined to produce strong agenda-setting effects. In Syracuse, for example, the salience of crime as a local issue was highest among those with high exposure to news about local crime on television and in the newspapers *and* some personal experience with crime. In Texas, the more that people used the news media *and* the more involved they were personally with those thirteen public issues, the more the public agenda reflected the media agenda.

This positive, tandem relationship of media use and personal experience with agenda-setting effects would seem to contradict the evidence presented in boxes 4.3 and 4.4. More fundamentally, however, this outcome contradicts the assumption of conflicting cues – media versus personal experience – for personal orientation that is implicit in all the early research on obtrusive and unobtrusive issues. However, negative evidence prompts the explication of a more detailed theoretical map. Consider the possibility that personal experience with an issue does not always result in a psychologically satisfactory level of orientation. Parallel to individual differences in media use and personal involvement with issues are considerable individual differences in the amount of information that satisfies each individual's need for orientation. For some individuals, personal experience with an issue rather than satisfying the need for orientation may trigger a search in the mass media for further information and validation of the problem's social significance.[26] Sensitized to the issue, these individuals may become particularly apt students of the media agenda. In conjunction with these individual differences in issue sensitization, also recall Lane's observation at the beginning of this chapter about the influence of formal education upon 'efforts to extract meaning from the political environment'. In this regard, the educational background of the Texans whose surprising behaviour has been noted here was considerably higher than the national average. Explicit measurement in the future of the breadth and depth of need for orientation can clarify the roles of personal experience and media use in the agenda-setting process.

Elaboration of the need for orientation can also assist in explicating channel effects in the agenda-setting process. Earlier we considered the puzzle of when newspaper and television news effects differ and when they are similar. One can hypothesize that persons with a high need for orientation are more likely to turn to newspapers with their wealth of detail – and perhaps now to specialized web sites – while persons with a lower need for orientation are more likely to find the brevity of television news reports satisfactory.

The Texas evidence[27] also introduces personal conversation, a channel of communication that has not been considered in any detail up to this point. Among those Texans, the frequency of talking about public issues was positively linked to the frequency of both media use and personal experience with public issues. Although talking about public issues was a companion of these other behaviours, it did not have an independent role, either positive or negative, in determining people's level of agreement with the media agenda. This lack of a distinct role for talking about public issues represents a rough average of the accumulated evidence on the role of political conversation in the agenda-setting process.[28] Sometimes, conversation reinforces the impact of media agendas.[29] In the contemporary setting of the internet, examination of electronic bulletin board postings on four issues – immigration, health care, taxes and abortion – during the fall 1996 US presidential campaign found evidence that traditional news media set the agenda of discussion for all these issues except abortion with time lags of one to seven days.[30] At other times, conversation is a conflicting source of orientation that reduces the influence of the media.[31]

Again, consideration of an individual's level of need for orientation has the potential to identify the circumstances in which interpersonal communication either reinforces or conflicts with the agenda-setting role of the mass media. For some persons, conversations may lead to a search for more information in the mass media, resulting in sub-stantial acquisition of the media agenda.[32] In contrast, for others whose personal agenda has been shaped by conversations with family or friends, the perceived need for any additional orientation may be low. These persons have little reason to attend to the media agenda.[33]

Summing up

Need for orientation is the cognitive version of the scientific principle 'Nature abhors a vacuum.'[34] In the realm of public affairs, the greater an individual's need for orientation, the more likely he or she is to attend to the agenda of the mass media with their wealth of infor-mation on politics and government.[35] This concept also identifies the issues that are most likely to move from the media agenda to the public agenda, namely, unobtrusive issues where an individual has little or no personal experience. If an unobtrusive issue resonates with the public, need for orientation will be moderate to high. For obtru-sive issues, need for orientation may be satisfied largely by personal experience. However, on occasion personal experience will create a desire for more information and people will turn to the mass media for additional orientation. In addition to clarifying the circumstances under which people are more likely to acquire the agenda of the mass media, need for orientation may assist in the explication of channel effects in the agenda-setting process: how people use newspapers and television news and now the internet; under what circumstances these media effects are distinct; and under what circumstances the mass media and political conversation have competitive or comple-mentary roles.

Need for orientation provides a detailed psychological explanation for why agenda-setting effects occur. As one critic noted:

> to conclusively demonstrate and document the existence of a media effect such as agenda setting, researchers must assemble a variety of evidence – including content, exposure, effect and conditions.[36]

The initial large-scale panel studies of agenda-setting reviewed in chapter 1 – Charlotte during the 1972 US presidential election[37] and three diverse US communities during the 1976 US presidential election[38] – documented all four of these elements and, most import-antly, introduced need for orientation as a psychological explanation for the occurrence of agenda-setting effects.

In the evolution of agenda-setting theory, the concept of need for orientation is the most prominent of the contingent conditions for agenda-setting effects, those factors that enhance or constrain the strength of these effects. These contingent conditions can be sorted into two groups, audience characteristics – such as need for orientation – and media characteristics – such as the comparisons of newspapers and television.[39]

Contingent conditions were introduced as the second phase of agenda-setting theory during the early 1970s. The first phase, of course, was the basic relationship between the media agenda and the public agenda. These phases of agenda-setting research are not successive eras marked by the closing of one line of inquiry and the opening of another. Rather they are continuing lines of inquiry that parallel each other in time. The initial phase of agenda-setting research, inaugurated by the exploration of basic agenda-setting effects in Chapel Hill, continues to this day in new settings, such as the internet and online newspapers,[40] as does the second phase, elaboration of the contingent conditions that modify agenda-setting effects.[41] Subsequent chapters will introduce additional phases of the theory's evolution.

5 The Pictures in our Heads

Walter Lippmann's eloquently argued thesis that the news media are a primary source of the pictures in our heads[1] has produced a hardy intellectual offspring, agenda-setting, a social science theory that maps in considerable detail the contribution of mass communication to our pictures of politics and public affairs. Specifically, agenda-setting is a theory about the transfer of salience from the mass media's pictures of the world to the pictures in our heads. The core theoretical idea is that elements prominent in the media picture become prominent in the audience's picture. Those elements emphasized on the media agenda come to be regarded as important by the public.

This is a more general description of the agenda-setting role of the mass media than is found in the previous chapters. There, similar to most discussions of agenda-setting, the focus is on agendas of public issues. Theoretically, however, these agendas can be composed of any set of elements, a set of issues, political candidates, competing institutions, or whatever. But, in practice, just like the examples of agenda-setting discussed in the previous chapters, the primary focus of the vast majority of the 400 or so studies around the world to date has been on an agenda composed of public issues. In these investigations of agenda-setting, the core finding is that the degree of emphasis placed on issues in the news influences the priority accorded those issues by the public. But even the original agenda-setting study in Chapel Hill during the 1968 US presidential election found that only about one-third of the news coverage concerned issues. The remainder emphasized the events and political strategies of the campaign and information about the candidates.[2]

Nevertheless, there are compelling reasons why public issues have prevailed as the major focus of agenda-setting theory. First, the easy fit of the metaphor to an agenda composed of public issues provided a strong, explicit theoretical link between mass communication and public opinion, a link that is obvious to anyone interested in journalism, politics and public opinion. Second, there exists a strong normative tradition in social science research on elections that places great emphasis on the importance of issues to informed public opinion. Finally, the well-established practices of public opinion polling, with its emphasis on public issues, provided the methodology that has most commonly been used to measure the public agenda.

> Although agenda-setting is concerned with the salience of issues rather than the distribution of pro and con opinions, which has been the traditional focus of public opinion research, the core domain is the same – the public issues of the moment. Walter Lippmann's quest in *Public Opinion* to link the world outside to the pictures in our heads via the news media was brought to quantitative, empirical fruition by agenda-setting research.[3]

When the key term of this theoretical metaphor, the agenda, is considered in totally abstract terms, the potential for expanding beyond an agenda of issues becomes clear. In most discussions of the agenda-setting role of the mass media the unit of analysis on each agenda is an *object*, a public issue. However, public issues are not the only objects that can be analysed from the agenda-setting perspective. In the party primaries that precede the national election in the United States, the objects of interest are the candidates vying for the presidential nomination of their political party. In that situation, the agenda is an agenda of candidates whose prominence on both the news agenda and the public agenda varies considerably during the political season. In the Israeli parliament another agenda, the agenda of questions posed to government ministers by Knesset members, also reflects the agenda-setting influence of the newspapers.[4] Historically, the number of questions grounded in news reports steadily increased from 8 per cent in the inaugural 1949–51 Knesset to 55 per cent in the 1969–73 seventh session. There are many objects that can define an agenda. Communication is a process, which can include any set of objects – or a single object – competing for attention among journalists and various audiences.

In all these instances, public issues, political candidates, or other items defining an agenda, the term *object* is used in the same sense that social psychologists use the term *attitude object*. The object is that thing towards which our attention is directed or the thing about which we have an attitude or opinion. To repeat, traditionally in discussions of agenda-setting that object has been a public issue. But the kinds of objects that can define an agenda in the media and among the public are virtually limitless.

Beyond the agenda of objects there is another level of agenda-setting to consider. Each of these objects on the agenda has numerous *attributes*, those characteristics and properties that fill out the picture of each object. Just as objects vary in salience, so do the attributes of each object. These attributes, of course, can vary widely in their scope, from such narrow descriptions as 'left-handed' to such broad descriptions as 'literary genius'. In agenda-setting theory, attribute is a generic term encompassing the entire range of properties and traits that characterize an object.

Both the selection of objects for attention and the selection of attributes for picturing those objects are powerful agenda-setting roles. An important part of the news agenda and its set of objects are the attributes that journalists and, subsequently, members of the public have in mind when they think and talk about each object.

How these news agendas of attributes influence the public agenda is the second level of agenda-setting. The first level is, of course, the transmission of object salience. The second level is the transmission of attribute salience. These two aspects of the agenda-setting role of the mass media are shown in box 5.1. In the theoretical context of the larger communication process traditional agenda-setting is focused on a key early step in communication, gaining attention.[5] The appearance of an issue, political candidate or other topic on the public agenda means that it has gained substantial public exposure and attention. Attribute agenda-setting is focused on a subsequent step in the communication process, comprehension, the step that Lippmann described as the pictures in our heads. The focus here is on which aspects of the issue, political candidate or topic are salient for members of the public. This theoretical distinction between attention and comprehension is important. Although media messages usually contain information that is simultaneously relevant to both the first and the second level of the agenda-setting process, the nature of the influence is distinct – the salience of objects versus the salience of specific attributes. Furthermore, these two aspects of agenda-setting influence are not always coincidental. Commenting on the candidacy of veteran politician H. Carl McCall in the 2002 New York governor's race, the *New York Times* observed:

But despite 30 years on the political scene, Mr. McCall, 67, the Democratic candidate, is barely known by voters, who, according

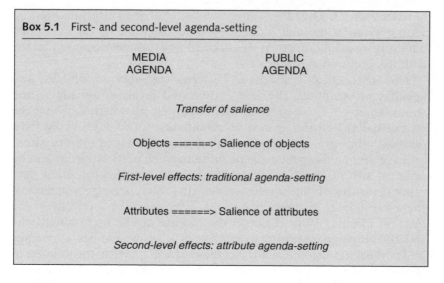

Box 5.1   First- and second-level agenda-setting

to polls, may recognize his name but do not have an impression of him.[6]

With this expanded perspective on agenda-setting, it is necessary to revise Bernard Cohen's famous dictum about the influence of mass communication. Recall that in a succinct summary statement distinguishing agenda-setting from earlier research on media effects, Cohen noted that, while the media may not tell us *what to think*, they are stunningly successful in telling us *what to think about.*[7] Explicit attention to the second level of agenda-setting further suggests that the media not only tell us what to think about, but that they also tell us *how to think* about some objects. Could the consequences of this be that the media sometimes do tell us *what to think*?

Pictures of political candidates

Although popular images of science centre on dramatic discoveries, most social science is better described as an evolutionary process in which the *implicit* gradually becomes *explicit*. This evolutionary process is illustrated particularly well by the gradual translation and expansion of Walter Lippmann's phrase 'the pictures in our heads' into a social science theory backed by precise, rigorous evidence. Beginning with the 1968 Chapel Hill study, the vast majority of this evidence concerns which public issues are on the agenda. In Lippmann's language, this evidence focuses on what these pictures in our heads are about. Over time, attention has shifted to attribute agenda-setting as an additional influence where the focus is on the actual details of these pictures. At this second level, the concern is literally with the pictures in our heads.

This theoretical distinction between agendas of objects and agendas of attributes, the first and second levels of agenda-setting shown in box 5.1, is especially clear in an election setting where the official ballot lists the agenda of candidates. Candidates vying for a political office are – in agenda-setting terms – a set of objects whose salience among the public can be influenced by news coverage and by political advertising. Campaign research on 'name recognition' and other measures of object salience describe the relative prominence of these candidates in the public mind. Who is at the forefront of the election picture? Who is not in the picture at all? Increasingly, the task of campaign managers worldwide is to secure the news coverage and to design the political advertising that will increase the salience of their candidates among the voters.[8] However, the goals of these mass media campaigns extend considerably beyond object salience and usually include building an image of the candidate in which specific attributes are particularly salient.

Several of these pictures in our heads about political candidates – and their origins in the news media – were sketched by scholars during the 1970s. However, they remained isolated, idiosyncratic pieces of evidence about agenda-setting until renewed theoretical discussions at the end of the last century prompted a new look at those sketches as well as the production of new sketches.[9]

Candidate images in national elections

The pictures in voters' heads of the 1976 US presidential candidates concisely illustrate this second level of agenda-setting and its attention to an agenda of attributes. The Republicans had an incumbent president, Gerald Ford, to head their ticket that year, while the Democrats had eleven aspiring presidential candidates competing for their party's presidential nomination during the spring primaries. This was an extraordinarily large group of candidates to learn about and, because most American voters are not avid students of politics, raises an obvious question about the extent to which voters' images of them were shaped by the news coverage. Comparison of descriptions of the candidates by upstate New York Democrats with the agenda of attributes presented in *Newsweek*'s early January sketches of the eleven contenders found significant evidence of media influence.[10]

Especially compelling in this evidence is the increased correspondence between the news agenda of attributes and the voter agenda of
attributes from +0.64 in mid-February to +0.83 in late March.
Voters not only learned the media's agenda, but with some additional
exposure over the weeks of the primaries they learned it even better.

Jimmy Carter emerged from those primaries as the Democrat
challenger to incumbent Republican president Gerald Ford, and
there is additional evidence of voter learning from the news media
about these two men among a general sample of Illinois voters.[11] A
striking degree of correspondence was found between the agenda of
attributes presented in the election coverage of the *Chicago Tribune*
and the agenda of attributes in those Illinois voters' descriptions of
Carter and Ford. Across the entire election year, the median value of
cross-lagged correlations between the media agenda and the subsequent public agenda was +0.70. Defined in terms of fourteen different traits, these attribute agendas included such wide-ranging traits
as competency, compassion and political beliefs. Because these cross-
lagged correlations simultaneously take into account the influence of
the news media on the voters *and* the influence of voters on the news
media, the evidence is especially clear that the direction of influence
was from the media agenda to the public agenda.

As more and more evidence accumulates, it is clear that the attribute agenda-setting influence of the mass media occurs in elections
worldwide wherever both the political system and the mass media are
reasonably open and free. The existence of these media effects in
diverse cultural settings is well illustrated by the extensive evidence
gathered during the 1996 Spanish general election.[12]

In 1996 José María Aznar, the conservative Popular Party's candidate, successfully challenged Spain's twelve-year incumbent Socialist
prime minister, Felipe González. A third candidate, Julio Anguita,
represented a coalition of far-left parties. Among voters in Pamplona,
Spain, there was evidence of significant influence by the major news
and advertising media on the images of these three candidates.

The five substantive attributes in the descriptions of the candidates
by the mass media and by the voters were issue positions and political
ideology; formal qualifications and biographical data; personality;
perceived qualifications and evaluative judgements; and integrity,
which was based on statements explicitly describing a candidate as
'corrupt' or 'not corrupt'. This last attribute was noted in the descriptions of the candidates in order to capture a major issue in the
national election, corruption in the government and the related controversy over whether the incumbent prime minister, Gonzalez, was
personally involved in the corruption.

Going beyond previous examinations of attribute agenda-setting in US elections, the tone of these candidate descriptions, both in the mass media and by voters, was also noted as positive, negative or neutral. Tone, of course, is a particularly important aspect of political communication.

In a demanding test of second-level agenda-setting effects, the substantive categories and the tone of these descriptions were combined to create a rich set of 5 × 3 descriptive matrices (5 substantive categories × 3 categories of tone). First, a descriptive matrix was prepared from a post-election survey of Pamplona voters for each of the three candidates. Twenty-one additional descriptive matrices were prepared from the content analyses of two local newspapers, two national newspapers, two national TV news services and the TV political ads (7 media × 3 candidates). The addition of political ads to the mix of news media is another new feature of this evidence from Spain.

Comparisons of the voters' pictures of the candidates with these twenty-one descriptions of the candidates in the various mass media yielded striking results. First, all twenty-one correlations were positive. The comparisons of the voters with the newspapers, both local and national, are especially impressive. For example, the correlations between the voters' agenda of attributes and the attribute agenda of a local newspaper, *Diario de Navarra*, were +0.87 for Gonzalez, +0.82 for Aznar and +0.60 for Anguita. For *El Pais*, a national newspaper, the correlations were +0.84, +0.83 and +0.86, respectively.

Overall the evidence shows:

- For all six comparisons between the voters and the two local newspapers (3 candidates × 2 newspapers), the median correlation was +0.70.
- For all six comparisons with two national newspapers, the median correlation was +0.81.
- For the six comparisons with the two national TV news services, the median correlation was +0.52. Here it should be noted that all the correlations for the commercial service were higher than for the public television service, findings that recall our discussion and comparison of newspapers and television in chapter 3.
- For the three comparisons with the political ads appearing in the public television service, the median correlation was +0.44.

Additional analyses found that these mass media messages overcame selective perception, the tendency to emphasize the positive attributes of one's preferred candidate and the negative attributes of the competing candidates. With increased exposure to newspapers, television news and political advertising, there were increases both in positive appraisals of other candidates and in negative appraisals of one's preferred candidate.[13] Voters do learn from the media. This evidence for attribute agenda-setting by the mass media is especially impressive because it combines a large, diverse set of mass media with rich substantive and affective descriptions of three national candidates in the political setting of a young democracy.

Moving to this century and the 2000 New Hampshire primary, which marks the formal beginning of the US presidential election, three regional newspapers' coverage of George W. Bush and John McCain was compared with the public's perceptions of these two contenders for the Republican Party nomination for president.[14] Strong similarities were found between the media and the public regarding which candidate was more likely to get things done, had a vision for the country, was more trustworthy, and would cut taxes. The media and the public differed on who had the best chance to win, perhaps as a result of journalistic efforts at balanced coverage.

Candidate images in local elections

Extending our view both to an East Asian setting and to a local election, there is further evidence of attribute agenda-setting from the 1994 mayoral election in Taipei, Taiwan.[15] In this setting the voters' images of the three candidates for mayor were compared with the descriptions of these men by the Taipei newspapers and TV stations. The agenda of attributes consisted of twelve categories representing a wide variety of personal and political attributes. Comparisons of the voters' images with the agenda of attributes in the *China Times* and *United Daily News* ranged from +0.59 to +0.75. The median value of these six comparisons (3 candidates × 2 newspapers) was +0.68. None of the comparisons with the opposition newspaper, *Liberty Times*, was significant, nor were any of the comparisons with TV news significant. In the case of Taipei television, voters were well aware that all three television stations at that time were under the domination of the government and long-ruling KMT political party. In one instance, 40 per cent of the shares in the television station was held by the Department of the Navy. The lack of attribute agenda-setting in these instances further confirms our previous observation that the appearance of these effects requires the existence of a free and open media system.

Returning to the Spanish political setting, the images of five political parties' candidates in the 1995 local elections in Pamplona were examined in terms of substantive attributes and, separately, affective tone.[16] Images among members of the public at three levels of media exposure were compared with descriptions in local television news and news stories in two Pamplona newspapers. Like the earlier evidence from the US on images of the 1976 contenders for the Democrat Party's presidential nomination, each of these comparisons was made for the candidates taken as a group. In box 5.2, for substantive attributes – descriptions of political candidates in terms of ideology, qualifications, personality, etc. – the match between the media agenda and the public agenda increases monotonically with greater exposure to political information both in the newspapers and on television. Although the pattern is perfectly monotonic across the three levels of exposure, the critical distinction is between exposure to none and at least some of the political information in the media. This same pattern is found in box 5.2 for affective descriptions of the candidates. Persons making at least some use of the political information in the newspapers and on TV describe the candidates in a manner very similar to the news media. The match between the affective descriptions of the news media and members of the public making no use of political information in the media is much weaker.

In sum, acquisition of the media agenda increases with greater exposure to mass communication. But, regardless of the level of exposure, there is a significant degree of correspondence between

---

Box 5.2 Attribute agenda-setting in Spanish local elections

Substantive attributes

Level of exposure to political information in each medium	Newspapers	TV news
None	+0.74	+0.81
Some	+0.90	+0.91
All	+0.92	+0.92

Affective attributes

Level of exposure to political information in each medium	Newspapers	TV news
None	+0.49	+0.56
Some	+0.88	+0.86
All	+0.79	+0.83

Source: Esteban Lopez-Escobar, Juan Pablo Llamas and Maxwell McCombs, 'Una dimension social de los efectos do los medios de difusion: agenda-setting y consenso', *Comunicacion y Sociedad* IX (1996), pp. 91–125.

the public and the mass media, testimony at least in part to the widespread diffusion of mass communication content throughout most communities.

Parallel to the accumulated evidence for traditional agenda-setting effects on the salience of public issues, this growing body of evidence about attribute agenda-setting and the images of political candidates among the public is grounded primarily in comparisons of public opinion polls with content analyses of the news media and political advertising. Both the advantages of this kind of evidence in presenting a representative picture of political communication and its limitations in terms of definitively proving a cause-and-effect relationship between the media agenda and the public agenda were noted in chapter 1's discussion of traditional agenda-setting. Also noted was the importance of laboratory experiments as complementary evidence to document the existence of a causal relationship between the media agenda and the public agenda. Fortunately, this experimental evidence on causality also exists for attribute agenda-setting and the images of political candidates among the public.

In a laboratory experiment[17] half of the subjects read a newspaper article in which a fictitious American political candidate was presented as highly corrupt. The other half of the subjects read a newspaper article presenting the candidate as a moral person. Subsequent descriptions of the candidate by individuals exposed to these contrasting characterizations revealed major differences in responses both to an open-ended question and to closed-end rating scales. Even brief exposure to a news article resulted in significant differences between the two groups' responses to the question, 'Suppose that your friend came to see you from another state, and he doesn't know about the candidate. How would you describe the candidate to your friend?'. Similar differences were also found between the two groups of subjects in rating how honest, sincere and trustworthy the candidate was perceived to be. Both the rating scales and the open-ended question documented the appearance of second-level agenda-setting effects under the controlled conditions of the laboratory.

Media influence on candidate images

The influence of the mass media on the public's images of political candidates is a very straightforward instance of attribute agenda-setting. Most of our knowledge about the attributes of political candidates – everything from their political ideology to their personality – comes from the news stories and the advertising content of the mass media. In recent years the existence of this influence, initially documented in the 1970s, was replicated numerous times in a wide variety of geographical and political settings. For national candidates, we have evidence from the United States and Spain. For local candidates, we have additional evidence from Spain and Taiwan. Attribute agenda-setting was found during elections in Asia, Europe and North America. The evidence from actual elections is complemented by an experiment in the United States. The mass media's causal influence on the pictures in our heads about political candidates is well documented.

Attributes of issues

Issue salience, which has been the traditional centre of attention for agenda-setting theory, can also be extended to the second level. Public issues, like all other objects, have attributes. Some aspects of issues, which is to say, some attributes, are emphasized in the news and in how people think and talk about these issues. Moreover, the salient attributes of a particular issue often change over time. As we shall see, this is especially true for the economy, a recurring major issue for many countries in recent decades. Sometimes the prominent attribute of the economy is inflation; at other times it is unemployment or budget deficits. Attribute agenda-setting extends our understanding of how the news media shape public opinion on the issues of the day.

> The media set the agenda when they are successful in riveting attention on a problem. They build the public agenda when they supply the context that determines *how people think about the issue and evaluate its merits.*[18]

Again demonstrating the validity of agenda-setting theory across cultures as well as at two distinct levels of cognition, attention to an object and comprehension of its attributes, both the first and second levels of agenda-setting were simultaneously examined during the 1993 Japanese general election.[19] Beginning with traditional agenda-setting, the impact of intensive news coverage was examined on the salience of political reform, an issue which accounted for more than 80 per cent of the issue coverage in two major national newspapers and three TV networks. Because the issue of political reform had a near-monopoly on the news agenda, the usual comparison of the rank order of issues on the media agenda with their ranking on the public agenda was not feasible in this situation.

Of course, the assumption behind such comparisons is that the high degree of correspondence between these agendas results from exposure to the mass media. In this Japanese election, the behaviour linking these two agendas – exposure to the media – was explicitly measured. Combining measures of exposure and political interest to yield an index of attentiveness to political news, support was found for the proposition that the salience of a prominent media issue among members of the public is positively correlated with their level of attentiveness to political news. For attentiveness to TV news, the correlation with the salience of political reform was +0.24. For attentiveness to newspapers, the correlation was +0.27. Additional analyses, which controlled for voters' party identification, education, age and sex, yielded the same results.

Moving to the second level of agenda-setting, the fact that both TV news and the newspapers mentioned system-related aspects of reform twice as often as ethics-related aspects created counterbalanced expectations about the attribute agenda-setting roles of the news media. First, the salience of system-related aspects of reform on the public agenda should be positively related with attentiveness to political news. This was the aspect of the issue, its attribute, emphasized in the news. In contrast, there was little reason to expect any significant relationship between the salience of the ethics-related aspects of reform on the public agenda and attentiveness to political news. This attribute of political reform received minor attention in the news.

Both hypotheses were supported. For the ethics-related aspect of political reform, the correlations were nearly zero (+0.05 for TV and +0.09 for newspapers). For the system-related aspect of political reform, the correlations were +0.20 for TV news and +0.26 for newspapers. Additional analyses of the system-related aspect of political reform, which controlled for voters' party identification, education, age and sex, yielded correlations only two points lower. Note that all of these correlations are virtually identical for both first- and second-level agenda-setting effects as well as for newspapers and TV news.

Beyond an election setting, news coverage and people's ideas about a complex issue such as the economy can involve many different aspects or attributes. One set of attributes associated with the recurring general topic of the economy consists of the specific problems of the moment, their perceived causes and the proposed solutions to these problems. Another, more narrow, set of attributes consists of the pro and con arguments for the proposed solutions to economic problems. For both of these sets of attributes, agenda-setting effects were found among the general public in Minneapolis for newspapers, but not for television news.[20] For the specific problems, causes and proposed solutions associated with the general topic of the economy, the correspondence between the newspaper agenda and the public agenda was especially high (+0.81). The degree of correspondence was less, but still substantial, for the pro and con arguments for economic solutions (+0.68). The focus of attention on specific aspects of national economic concerns in the newspaper had a major influence on how members of the public thought about this issue.

Attributes of environmental issues

The environment is another contemporary issue that is equal in breadth and complexity to the economy. As a public issue, the environment can range from international to very local concerns and from rather abstract to very concrete concerns.[21]

The influence of news coverage in two major Japanese daily newspapers was apparent in the pattern of concerns among residents of Tokyo about global environmental problems.[22] During the four months leading up to the United Nations Conference on Environment and Development (UNCED), which was held in Rio de Janeiro during June 1992, both *Asahi* and *Yomiuri* steadily increased their coverage on eight aspects of the global environment. These aspects ranged from acid rain and preservation of wildlife to the population explosion and global warming. Four months before UNCED, *Asahi* and *Yomiuri* published a total of ninety-one stories on these aspects of the environment over a four-week period. In April and May, as the conference approached, a total of 162 stories on these eight sub-issues were published in these two newspapers during a four-week period. In the four weeks that included the conference itself, there were 194 stories.

Among Tokyo residents, these media attribute agendas resulted in significant learning. Their agenda of sub-issues about the global environment, ascertained by a survey conducted after UNCED, shows substantial agreement with the emerging agenda of the two newspapers during the months leading up to the conference. As early as February, the match between the newspapers' agenda and the subsequent public agenda was +0.68. By early April, the correspondence had increased to +0.78, its highest point, and it remained there through mid-May. The lower degree of correspondence with the newspapers' agenda in the weeks immediately preceding and the weeks including UNCED reflects the time lag discussed in chapter 3 as part of the learning process involved in agenda-setting. The time lag found in Japan is similar to that found for aspects of the global environment issue in the United States.[23]

Aspects of the environment can also be compelling local issues. In Austin, Texas, there has been a long-running controversy about the pollution of Barton Springs, a local environmental icon that discharges more than 15 million gallons of fresh water each day into a large natural pool in the heart of the city. An issue pitting environmentalists against developers, this controversy has been key in many local elections for mayor and members of the city council. News coverage on this issue in the local newspaper in the early 1990s most frequently identified developers, new housing and shopping malls as the key causes of Barton Springs' pollution. Much lower on the news agenda was the growth of Austin, a city that expanded by more than 50 per cent in the 1980s and 1990s. Barely mentioned in the news coverage was the impact on the environment of population growth per se, not just in Austin, but globally. The news agenda was quite clear. And the pictures in people's heads, which were obtained through a public opinion survey, were equally clear. There was a perfect correspondence (+1.0) between the relative salience of the attributes that define the pictures of this environmental issue in the newspaper and among the public.[24]

For another local environmental issue in the mid-western US, there was also a strong level of correspondence (+0.60) between the pictures in people's minds and local newspaper coverage on six facets of the development of a large, man-made lake.[25] And in line with the patterns found for object salience at the first level of agenda-setting, the degree of correspondence between the newspaper's agenda of attributes and the pictures in people's heads increased with their need for orientation. Among persons with a low need for orientation, the match between their attribute agenda and the newspaper's attribute agenda was only +0.26. Among those with a high need for orientation, the match was +0.77. Again we see that increased need for orientation results in greater acquisition of the media agenda.

Media influence on issue attributes

Evidence continues to accumulate that the ways we think and talk about public issues are influenced by the pictures of those issues presented by the mass media. The attributes of issues that are prominent in media presentations are prominent in the public mind. This was true for the issue of political reform during a Japanese general election and outside an election setting for global environmental problems. In the US, this was true for two local environmental issues as well as national economic problems.

These are significant extensions of the original idea of agenda-setting about the ability of the mass media to shape the agenda of issues that are considered important by the public. It is the agenda of attributes that define an issue and in some instances tilt public opinion towards a particular perspective or preferred solution. In the US, for example, President George W. Bush's definition of the energy issue emphasized the development of new sources for fossil fuels and construction of new power plants and transmission lines while largely ignoring the environmental consequences of these solutions and downplaying conservation as a key aspect of energy policy. Setting the agenda of attributes for an issue is the epitome of political power. Controlling the perspective of the political debate on any issue is the ultimate influence on public opinion.

Diversity of salience measures

The considerable diversity in the empirical measures of these attribute agendas for political candidates and public issues in Europe, Asia and North America counters earlier criticisms that the evidence for the agenda-setting influence is based on too narrow a representation of the public agenda.[26] More generally, both object *and* attribute salience have been measured with a rich variety of open-ended questions and rating scales.

The early investigations of issue salience built on the solid methodological foundation inherited from the Gallup Poll – the rich lode of open-ended questions in the US dating from the 1930s that asked 'What is the most important problem facing this country today?'.[27] Although this MIP question – and similar open-ended questions assessing issue salience – continues to be widely used, there are many creative alternatives for measuring the salience of public issues.

The experimental comparison of the printed and online versions of the *New York Times* supplemented the traditional MIP question with two other measures of salience, recognition and recall of news stories that had appeared in the paper and ranking the importance of various sets of these news stories.[28] In another experimental setting, the salience of racism was measured by three different five-point scales: the importance of the issue, extent of discussion with friends, and need for more government action.[29] A creative series of experiments using eight different issues ranging from global warming to dental health developed a sophisticated set of thirteen bipolar semantic differential scales to measure issue salience.[30] Additional analysis of these scales reveals three underlying dimensions: social salience – measured by such scales as irrelevant/relevant and unimportant/ important; personal salience – e.g., matters to me/doesn't matter to me and of no concern to me/of concern to me; and emotional arousal – e.g., boring/interesting, and exciting/unexciting. These are rich theoretical leads for further explication of the agenda-setting process.

An analysis of public opinion about local crime in Syracuse, New York, used both a traditional rating scale and a behavioural measure to ascertain the salience of this issue:

> Thinking about the issue of crime in the Syracuse area, on a scale from 1 to 10 where 1 is of no importance to you personally and 10 is most important to you personally, how would you rate the issue of crime? How concerned are you about being a victim of crime? Would you say you are not at all concerned, slightly concerned, or very concerned?[31]

To measure the salience of political reform in the 1993 Japanese general election, voters were asked first to select the most important issues from a list of ten. Then to measure attribute salience these voters were asked to select the most important aspects of political reform from a list of eight solutions.[32] The salience of the various attributes of an environmental issue, development of a man-made lake in the mid-western US, was ascertained in three different ways.[33] There were two open-ended questions asking which aspects of this issue were of most interest and which had been discussed the most. The third measure of salience used paired comparisons, a scaling technique in which all possible pairs from a list of attributes are shown to survey respondents. For each pair, the respondent selects the one regarded as most important. These sets of judgements from a group of respondents can then be used to create an interval scale of salience. As we see in box 5.3, all three measures of attribute salience documented very similar attribute agenda-setting effects regarding this mid-western lake development. The similarity of these replications attests to the robustness of these effects.

Returning to an open-ended approach to measuring salience, the investigation of attribute agenda-setting by Minnesota news media for the issue of the economy used content-free questions to ascertain which aspects of this issue were salient among the public.[34] Analyses worldwide of attribute agenda-setting for candidate images have used

Box 5.3 A comparison of attribute agenda-setting effects based on three measures of attribute salience among the public for an environmental issue

Open-ended questions		*Paired-comparison scaling*
'most interesting aspect'	'aspect discussed the most'	
+0.60	+0.61	+0.71

Source: David Cohen, 'A report on a non-election agenda setting study', paper presented to the Association for Education in Journalism, Ottawa, Canada, 1975.

some version of the open-ended question originally devised for the 1976 presidential election study in the US: 'Suppose you had some friends who had been away for a long time and were unfamiliar with the presidential candidates. What would you tell them about [candidate x]?'.[35]

Finally, using what is arguably the most fundamental of all measures of salience, recent investigations of both object and attribute agendas have used non-response as an inverse measure of salience. For example, the smaller the number of persons who have no opinion about a presidential candidate, the greater the salience of that candidate among the public.[36] Or, the greater the number of persons who have no opinion about a particular aspect of a public issue, the lower the salience of that attribute of the issue among the public.[37]

In step with our expanding knowledge of the agenda-setting process across the years, the diversity and sophistication of the evidence about object *and* attribute salience among the public has also undergone considerable methodological growth.

Summing up

Elements prominent in the mass media's presentation of the vast world of public affairs become prominent elements in our individual pictures of that world. Originally, this general proposition of agenda-setting theory was tested in terms of attention to the issues of the day, comparing the issues emphasized on the media agenda with those that became prominent on the public agenda. Time after time, these comparisons showed a high degree of correspondence between the media and the public in the ranking of issues on their agendas. To borrow Lippmann's phrase, there is a high degree of correspondence in what these pictures were about. This is the first level of agenda-setting.

There is also a high degree of correspondence in the actual details of these pictures. Comparing descriptions of political candidates and of public issues in the mass media with descriptions of these same objects by the public reveals a high degree of correspondence in their content. Application of the idea of attribute agenda-setting to the images of political leaders is straightforward and has produced a wealth of supporting evidence worldwide. A similar body of evidence regarding attribute agenda-setting also exists for a variety of public issues around the world. Attributes that are prominent in the mass media are prominent in the public mind. This is the second level of agenda-setting, where specific aspects of media content about public affairs are explicitly linked to the shape of public opinion.

Both traditional agenda-setting and attribute agenda-setting are media effects of considerable magnitude, effects in the early stages of the communication process that encompass both the audience's initial level of attention and its subsequent understanding about a message's subject.[38] In the evolution of agenda-setting theory, attribute agenda-setting is the third phase, a significant expansion beyond the focus of the first phase on the transfer of object salience and that of the second on the contingent conditions that enhance or reduce these agenda-setting effects. In the evidence reviewed here for this third phase of agenda-setting theory, there are glimpses of additional substantial effects in later stages of the communication process, in particular, intriguing implications for media influence on subsequent attitudes and opinions regarding both candidates and public issues. Although the general expectation is that the public's views of candidates are considerably more volatile than their views on most issues,[39] it may be the case that the topics and perspectives in the news affect a wide range of opinions as well as the salience of both candidates and public issues. This will be taken up in chapter 8's discussion of the consequences of agenda-setting.

6 Attribute Agenda-Setting and Framing

Agenda-setting theory has continued to evolve for more than thirty-five years because it complements and is compatible with a variety of other ideas in the social sciences. As scholars have constructed an increasingly detailed intellectual map of mass communication's influence on the public, the theory of agenda-setting has incorporated or converged with a number of other communication concepts and theories.

Incorporated concepts include status conferral, stereotyping, image building and gatekeeping. Status conferral refers to the increased salience of a person who receives intensive media attention.[1] This conceptualization of celebrity identifies an instance of first-level agenda-setting in which the object is a person. Stereotyping and image building, which involve the salience of attributes, are instances of second-level agenda-setting.[2] Gatekeeping, which describes and explains the flow of news from one media organization to another, was linked with agenda-setting theory in the early 1980s when scholars opened a new phase of intellectual map-making by asking 'Who sets the media's agenda?'[3] Responses to this question have identified a web of relationships and influences extending far beyond the news media. Within the matrix of newspapers, magazines, TV news, wire services and, more recently, the internet, exploration of this question has expanded and reconceptualized gatekeeping as intermedia agenda-setting at both the first and second level of agenda-setting. This aspect of agenda-setting theory will be detailed in the next chapter.

Theoretical complements to agenda-setting include cultivation analysis and the spiral of silence. Taking a long-range view of the cognitive effects of mass communication, cultivation analysis examines the salience of various perspectives engendered by the mass media, especially by entertainment programming on television.[4] One of the best-known of these perspectives, 'the mean world syndrome', is a pessimistic picture of the world around us stemming from the abundance of crime shows on television.[5] The theories of agenda-setting and the spiral of silence[6] appear to examine very different kinds of behaviour among mass media audiences, cognitive representations of the world versus a willingness to engage in conversation on public issues. However, there is a common psychological basis for both ideas in an individual's surveillance of his or her social surroundings. One consequence of this surveillance is the public agenda of issues; another consequence is the frequency of conversations with others about the issues of the day.[7]

Explication of a second level of agenda-setting, attribute agenda-setting, also links the theory with a major contemporary concept, framing. Sometimes this concept refers to a particular frame in media content and at other times to the process of framing, the origins of frames or their diffusion from the mass media to the public.[8] Applied to the media agenda, a frame is 'the central organizing idea for news content that supplies a context and suggests what the issue is through the use of *selection, emphasis, exclusion and elaboration*.'[9] Specifically in terms of salience and the process of framing:

> To frame is to *select some aspects of a perceived reality and make them more salient in a communicating text, in such a way as to promote a particular problem definition, causal interpretation, moral evaluation and/or treatment recommendation* for the item described.[10]

To paraphrase this definition in the words of second-level agenda-setting, framing is the selection of – and emphasis upon – particular attributes for the media agenda when talking about an object. In turn, as we know from the evidence on attribute agenda-setting, people also frame objects, placing varying degrees of emphasis on the attributes of persons, public issues or other objects when they think or talk about them.

Both framing and attribute agenda-setting call our attention to the perspectives of communicators and their audiences, how they picture topics in the news. The previous chapter documented the influence of media content on the pictures that the public holds of political candidates and public issues. The convergence of framing and attribute agenda-setting significantly advances the explication of media effects by underscoring the special status held by certain attributes, frames, in the content of a message.

The convergence of agenda-setting with framing for the analysis of media effects stemming from specific message content has been recognized over the years in many scholarly fields. Points of convergence include analyses of news media influence on voters' images of the 1976 US presidential candidates,[11] the impact of the Gulf War news coverage on public opinion[12] and press portrayals of presidential rhetoric subsequent to the demise of Cold War frames.[13] Attribute agenda-setting explicitly merges agenda-setting theory with the concept of framing.[14]

Attributes and frames

Descriptions of people, public issues and other objects in the news range from very simple attributes, such as a person's age or place of birth, to highly complex attributes, such as compassionate conservative or New Labour. This range of attributes along a micro–macro continuum was illustrated by numerous examples in the previous chapter on attribute agenda-setting. The cognitive and affective attributes of political candidates in Spanish elections are arrayed primarily from the middle towards the micro end of this continuum.[15] In contrast, the aspects of two public issues described in that chapter, the economy in the US[16] and political reform in Japan,[17] are complex macro-attributes.

Broad-brush labels for these attributes of issues, political candidates and other objects are the stuff of news headlines. They also can be shorthand labels for frames, the dominant perspectives used to organize both news presentations and personal thoughts about objects. A frame is an attribute of the object under consideration because it describes the object. However, not all attributes are frames. If a frame is defined as a dominant perspective on the object – a pervasive description and characterization of the object – then a frame is usefully delimited as a very special case of attributes.

A frame possesses significant gestalt qualities that set it apart from other attributes of an object. Noting that attributes fall along a micro–macro continuum, McCombs and Ghanem positioned frames at the macro end of this continuum:

> most frames tend toward the complex because they encompass or imply a number of lower level attributes. Another way of putting it is that frames are organizing principles incorporating and emphasizing certain lower level attributes to the exclusion of many others. Frames serve as efficient bundling devices of micro-attributes and, in turn, can be thought of as macro-attributes.[18]

This role of frames in organizing thought, in creating an integrated pattern that is considerably more than the sum of its parts, is the foundation of their gestalt character. A further aspect of this gestalt quality that distinguishes frames from the mass of attributes is their power to structure thought, to shape how we think about public issues, political candidates or other objects in the news.[19] Frames have been described as 'schemata of interpretation'.[20] Attribute agenda-setting focuses on the ability of the media to influence how we picture objects. Frames call our attention to the dominant perspectives in these pictures that not only suggest what is relevant and irrelevant,[21] but that actively *promote a particular problem definition, causal interpretation, moral evaluation and/or treatment recommendation for the item described.*[22] This power role of frames in communication is frequently noted, recently, for example, by the authors of twelve different chapters in *Framing Public Life*, and by Stephen Reese nine times in his comprehensive prologue to the book.[23]

Positioning the concept of framing in the context of agenda-setting theory underscores its subsequent consequences as well as this power to organize and structure thought. Agenda-setting theory emphasizes the dynamics between communicators and their audiences. This emphasis on the consequences of media content for cognitions, opinions and behaviour among the public also suggests a criterion for deciding which specific objects and attributes to study. Although omissions are sometimes significant, a sound general strategy is to focus on the origins and transformations of content that successfully moves from agenda to agenda and to bypass those aspects of messages that become the dross of the communication process. A focus on successful agenda-setting outcomes reiterates the emphasis among framing scholars on the power of frames.

A boundary line

A longstanding difficulty in discussions of framing is the plethora of widely disparate, sometimes contradictory, definitions of the concept. Positioning the concept in the context of agenda-setting theory offers the prospect of sorting out some of these definitions and drawing a distinct and useful boundary between frames and the mass of other attributes – many of which are sometimes also labelled as frames – that can characterize objects. Returning to the previous shorthand definition of a frame as a dominant perspective distinguishes two distinct types of attributes, central themes and aspects, both of which have frequently been called frames.

Research articles with the word 'framing' in their title taken from a variety of communication journals provide examples of this distinction between attributes that are central themes or aspects. Operationally, this distinction is apparent in the way that the media messages are analysed: identifying the attributes defining the major theme of each news story versus a tally of the various attributes that appear throughout the sentences and paragraphs of each news story.

A laboratory experiment demonstrated a variety of effects after subjects were exposed to news stories whose central theme was social protest.[24]

A catalogue of aspects of the women's movement found in news coverage ranged from feminists' appearance (145 times in 499 news stories) to the seldom mentioned goals of the movement (44 times in the 499 news stories).[25]

A comparison of the framing in US and Chinese newspapers of the 1995 United Nations Conference on Women examined the level of attention to key aspects of the conference.[26] Out of 2,924 mentions of aspects of the conference in seven US dailies, only 25 per cent were about the conference's twelve issues of critical concern. Among the 3,219 mentions in the Chinese newspaper, 46 per cent described these critical areas of concern.

Detailed analysis of the attributes of four Republican candidates for their party's 1996 US presidential nomination used computerized content analysis to identify twenty-eight attribute categories in campaign press releases and news stories about the campaign in the *New York Times*, *Washington Post* and *Los Angeles Times*.[27] Although the focus of the study was the attribute agendas of the candidates' press releases and news stories, this focus was described in the article's title as 'framing the candidates', and the published article did not compare the descriptions advanced by the candidates' campaign organizations and the descriptions presented by journalists. Agenda-setting theory suggests taking the additional step of making these comparisons in order to determine the attribute agenda-setting effect of the candidates' press releases on the news agenda. Calculated in a seminar on agenda-setting theory at the University of Texas, the evidence from this framing study for attribute agenda-setting effects was substantial: $+0.74$, $+0.75$ and $+0.78$ for three of the candidates, and a slightly lower, but still robust $+0.62$ for Robert Dole, the front runner and eventual party nominee.

Although an instance of significant attribute agenda-setting effects, this is not the best example of the power of frames because many of the 'frames' were aspects of the candidates' images that ranked very low on the attribute agendas of both their campaigns and the news media. If we emphasize the idea of power, as so many commentators have, it is best to limit the term frame to 'central themes' or 'dominant perspectives', a special class of attributes. This is not to ignore 'aspects' because their influence is identified – and, in fact, precisely measured – at the second level of agenda-setting.

A creative look at the boundary between frames and other attributes comes from an investigation of public opinion about the Japanese economy and its difficulties in recent years.[28] Grounded in the idea that frames are bundling devices for lower-order attributes, this analysis also drew upon the concept of problematic situations, a perspective that translates specific social issues and concerns into a set of broader cognitive categories.[29] A content analysis of the *Mainichi Shimbun* during a 52-week period identified twelve distinct aspects or attributes of the country's economic difficulties in the news coverage. Placing these attributes of Japan's economic difficulties in the context of problematic situations, a survey of the public asked how problematic they regarded each of the twelve aspects. A factor analysis of these items found that four macro-frames previously identified theoretically as problematic situations – breakdowns in institutional values, loss of individual value, ambiguous and confusing situations, and social conflicts – subsumed all twelve items.

The attribute agenda-setting effects of *Mainichi Shimbun*'s coverage of the economy was tested both at the level of lower-order attributes, the twelve aspects of the issue, and at the macro-level of frames, the four problematic situations. At both levels, the degree of correspondence between the newspaper's agenda and the public's agenda increased monotonically with greater exposure to the news. At the level of lower-order attributes, the correlations for low, moderate and high exposure to the news are $+0.54$, $+0.55$ and $+0.64$, respectively. For the frames, the correlations for these three levels of exposure are -1.00, $+0.80$ and $+1.00$. Although the striking differences in the absolute values of the correlations are undoubtedly due to the difference in the number of categories, twelve versus four, the overall pattern is consistent. In this analysis of Japanese public opinion, there are agenda-setting effects for both micro- and macro-attributes.

Compelling arguments

As with the inhabitants of George Orwell's *Animal Farm*, some attributes are more equal than others. There are inherent differences among attributes. Some are more likely than others to be regularly included in media messages, and some are more likely than others to be noticed and remembered by the audience quite apart from their frequency of appearance or dominance in the message.[30] In the interpretation of a message some attributes will also be considered more pertinent than others. Certain characteristics of an object may resonate with the public in such a way that they become especially compelling arguments for the salience of the issue, person or topic under consideration.

The idea that certain attributes of an object function as compelling arguments for their salience adds a new link to the theoretical map of agenda-setting. And, as we shall see, this idea of compelling arguments, explicated as an aspect of agenda-setting theory, further integrates framing and agenda-setting. Compelling arguments are frames, certain ways of organizing and structuring the picture of an object that enjoy high success among the public.

In the previous chapter, box 5.1 illustrated the first and second levels of agenda-setting with two horizontal arrows connecting the media agenda and the public agenda. Object salience on the media agenda influences object salience on the public agenda. Attribute salience on the media agenda influences attribute salience on the public agenda. Box 6.1 adds a further link to this diagram, a diagonal

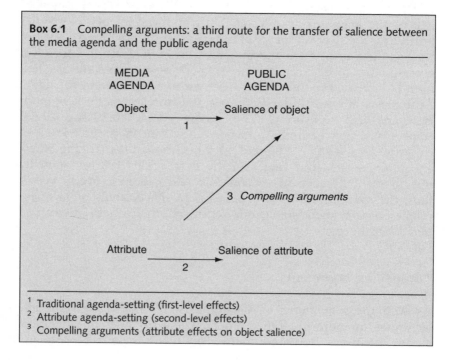

Box 6.1 Compelling arguments: a third route for the transfer of salience between the media agenda and the public agenda

MEDIA
AGENDA

PUBLIC
AGENDA

Object ——————→ Salience of object
                        1

                        3 *Compelling arguments*

Attribute —————→ Salience of attribute
                        2

[1] Traditional agenda-setting (first-level effects)
[2] Attribute agenda-setting (second-level effects)
[3] Compelling arguments (attribute effects on object salience)

arrow connecting attribute salience on the media agenda with object salience on the public agenda. In other words, when a particular attribute of an object is emphasized on the media agenda, there may be a direct impact on the salience of that object among the public. Certain ways of describing an object may be more compelling than other ways in creating object salience among the public. Up to this point, the salience of an object among the public has been explained primarily by how frequently the object appeared on the media agenda. Mentions of the object on the media agenda have not been stratified according to the kinds of attributes ascribed to the object by the media.

But there is now evidence in hand that the diagonal arrow in box 6.1, a relationship called compelling arguments, is an important aspect of the agenda-setting process.[31] Chapter 2 discussed a situation in Texas during the early 1990s when intensive crime coverage in the news generated astoundingly high levels of public concern about crime as the most important problem facing the country. Box 2.1 detailed those parallel trends in news coverage and public concern. Ironically, during this time when public concern about crime rose to unusually high levels, the actual rate of crime in Texas was declining and had been doing so for several years. Is crime simply a 'hot button' issue to which the public responds in a particularly volatile way when it is emphasized in news coverage? Or did the news coverage include especially compelling arguments about the salience of crime as a social issue? Was there more to this situation than traditional agenda-setting effects?

Examination of the various ways in which crime was framed in the news revealed that two perspectives had especially strong links with public concern, links whose strength actually exceeded the total impact (+0.70) of crime coverage on the public.[32] Both of these frames were aspects of crime in which the psychological distance is small between the average person and the criminal activity described in the news story. While Texans were not anxious about distant gang murders and the traditional array of crimes that are a staple of the news, they were anxious about drive-by shootings, robberies of individuals in broad daylight, and local crime. Specifically, the salience of crime among Texans as the most important problem facing the country was strongly related to the frequency of newspaper stories about crime in which the average person would feel personally threatened by that kind of crime (+0.78) or where the crime actually occurred in Texas (+0.73). Each of these frames in the coverage explained the salience of crime as well as or even somewhat better than the total barrage of crime coverage during this time. These two frames were compelling arguments for the salience of crime.

Other compelling arguments

There is other evidence in hand as well about the impact of compelling arguments, specific attributes in the news coverage that have an impact on the salience of an object among the public. An analysis of US public opinion during the 1990s about the salience of the federal budget deficit found substantial agenda-setting effects.[33] The frequency of news coverage in nineteen major daily newspapers across the country explained 85 per cent of the variance in the salience of this issue during an eighteen-month period from 1994 to 1996. Additional analysis of four specific aspects found that two of them (non-confrontational talks among political leaders and political conflicts and clashes over the deficit) were compelling arguments for public concern about the budget deficit. Adding this pair of attributes to the analysis accounted for 92 per cent of the variance in the salience of the federal budget deficit among the US public. Although these compelling arguments, the salience of two aspects of the federal budget deficit, made only a minor contribution to the overall salience of this issue among the American public, this evidence is a rare opportunity to observe simultaneously the distinct effects of first- and second-level agenda-setting. In the messages of the mass media and in the communications of the public, these two components of the agenda-setting process are bundled together and largely inseparable in practice.

A dramatically different result of a compelling argument was found during the 1990 German national election, where the salience of problems in the former East Germany significantly declined among voters despite intensive news coverage.[34] The decline – an agenda-deflating effect – was especially apparent among readers of the large circulation tabloid *Bild*, whose coverage of the integration of East Germany was framed in highly optimistic terms. In this case, the compelling argument was the positive tone of the news coverage on the issue of German integration, an attribute that reduced the salience of the issue on the public agenda.

Extending the concept of framing to the total issue agenda during the 1980 US presidential election, the agenda-setting effects of news coverage on the salience of twelve national issues framed explicitly as campaign issues was compared with the influence of news coverage on the salience of those same issues when they were not explicitly framed as campaign issues.[35] Box 6.2 details substantial effects for the campaign issue agenda on what mid-western voters regarded as the important issues of the campaign when they talked with others. When issues were explicitly identified in the news coverage as campaign issues, there were significant effects for all three national television networks and a modest effect for the local newspaper. For the agenda defined by coverage containing no explicit links between the issues and the presidential campaign, there was only a single modest effect for one television network on what these voters regarded as the most important campaign issues when they talked with others. The ways in which specific issues, political candidates or other objects are framed can be compelling, sometimes early on at the level of attention, sometimes further on in the communication process.

Finally, particular attributes of an issue may be compelling arguments for certain social groups. In other words, a particular way of framing a topic in the news media may result in highly stratified consequences among the public. There is significant evidence that the pattern of attributes in US newspapers' coverage of air pollution – a pattern that was remarkably consistent from the 1970s until the turn of the century – was a compelling argument for middle- and upper-class people to join the Sierra Club and other environmental organizations.[36] Perhaps more importantly, the media's presentation of air pollution as an environmental issue was a compelling argument for working-class people, which is to say, most members of minority groups, to eschew membership in environmental organizations.

Box 6.2   The effects of issue framing by the media on the public's perception of important campaign issues

News media	Campaign* agenda	General** agenda
ABC	+0.60	+0.37
CBS	+0.64	+0.04
NBC	+0.78	−0.12
Local newspaper	+0.22	−0.10

*Issues on the campaign agenda were explicitly linked in the news coverage to the presidential election campaign.
**Issues on the general agenda were not explicitly linked in the news coverage to the presidential election campaign.
Source: Wenmouth Williams Jr., Mitchell Shapiro and Craig Cutbirth, 'The impact of campaign agendas on perceptions of issues', *Journalism Quarterly*, 60 (1983), pp. 226–32.

In the framing of air pollution, industry was consistently suggested as the cause and government was overwhelmingly cited as the primary agent responsible for correcting the situation. In line with considerable evidence that minorities have a high distrust of both industry and government, this framing of the issue arguably served as a negative compelling argument. This lack of participation by minorities has persisted despite abundant evidence that minorities are often disproportionately affected by environmental problems, such as air pollution, and that they are aware of and concerned about these problems.

In short, the agenda of attributes in newspaper coverage of air pollution simultaneously constituted both a set of compelling arguments for middle- and upper-class people to support environmental organizations and a set of compelling arguments for working-class people to ignore these organizations. Even though the Sierra Club, for example, grew from about 15,000 members in 1960 to over 500,000 by 1990, the mainstream environmental movement continues to be overwhelmingly white and middle to upper class. Here we have an instance of media agenda-setting with discernible and disparate behavioural consequences among the public. Certain ways of framing objects are compelling arguments for subsequent responses among the public.[37]

In many instances, these worldviews of journalism substantially influence the pictures of the world held by the public. But not always! Although an extensive examination of how the American media and public frame news about public affairs identified five major frames – conflict, economics, human interest, powerlessness and morality – the level of agreement between media and public regarding the salience of these frames was only +0.20.[38] However, the lack of media agenda-setting in this situation is not nearly as great as this summary index of +0.20 might appear to indicate. When a single frame, conflict, which ranked second in the media but last among the public, is removed from the agenda, the level of agreement between the media and the public on the remaining four frames is +0.80.[39] The news media are the public's major source of information about public affairs, but the public is not an automaton passively waiting to be programmed by the media.

Attention to this impact on the public resulting from an emphasis on various attributes and ways of framing in news stories is the basis of a new approach to media criticism. Traditional criticism of the media examined whether the content of news stories was accurate and balanced. This new approach, grounded theoretically in attribute agenda-setting, examines the patterns of emphasis and tone in media messages and the consequences of these attribute agendas for public thought and behaviour. Chapter 8 will examine these consequences in detail.

Summing up

Taking Lippmann's phrase 'the pictures in our heads' rather literally, the theory of attribute agenda-setting brings additional depth to our knowledge about the influence of the mass media. The convergence of attribute agenda-setting with the concept of framing offers new insights into the influence held by various patterns of attributes found in the news on how the public thinks about public affairs. These influences on the public include broad sets of attributes picturing the various aspects of an object, single attributes that define dominant frames, and single attributes that function as a compelling argument.

Because how the public thinks about these matters typically embraces both cognitive and affective elements, this also involves what the public thinks, their attitudes and opinions. In *Agendas and Instability in American Politics*, Frank Baumgartner and Bryan Jones found that major shifts in public opinion and public policy were frequently preceded by significant shifts in the salient aspects of these issues among the public. Their case studies included nuclear power, tobacco, pesticides and auto safety.[40]

It is ironic that these consequences of attribute agenda-setting and framing bring us back to the influence of the mass media on attitudes and opinions. That is where mass communication theory started in the 1940s and 1950s, and that is the area that was largely abandoned after a generation of scholars reported that there were few significant effects.[41] The theory of agenda-setting emerged as a response to that narrow judgement, and chapter 8 will revisit that judgement in light of recent theoretical developments.

7 Shaping the Media Agenda

As more and more evidence accumulated about the agenda-setting influence of the mass media on the public, scholars in the early 1980s began to ask, 'Who sets the media's agenda?' A new phase of theoretical inquiry began to explore the various factors that shape the agenda presented by the mass media. In this new line of inquiry, the media agenda becomes the dependent variable, the outcome that is to be explained. In our examination of agenda-setting theory up to this point, the media agenda has been an independent variable, a key causal factor in the shaping of public opinion. Box 7.1 illustrates this broader, more comprehensive model of mass communication and the agenda-setting process that includes major antecedents of the media agenda. Thinking about the origins of the media agenda brings to mind many other agendas, such as the agenda of issues and policy questions considered by legislative bodies and other public agencies that are routinely covered by the news media, the competing agendas in political campaigns, or the agenda of topics routinely advanced by public relations professionals. There are many organized agendas in modern societies.

A useful metaphor for understanding the relationships between all these other agendas and the agenda of the mass media is 'peeling an onion'. The concentric layers of the onion represent the numerous influences at play in the shaping of the media agenda, which is the core of the onion. This metaphor also illustrates the sequential nature of this process in which the influence of an outer layer is, in turn, affected by layers more proximate to the core of the onion. A detailed elaboration of this onion contains many, many layers. Pamela Shoemaker and Stephen Reese's *Mediating the Message*, for example, identifies five distinct layers of influence that range from the prevail-

---

Box 7.1   An expanded view of agenda-setting

OTHER	MEDIA	PUBLIC
AGENDAS	AGENDA	AGENDA

Organizations
Interest groups
Public relations
Political campaigns

Objects ======> | *News norms* | Objects ======> Objects

Transfer of salience

Attributes ======> | *News norms* | Attributes ======> Attributes

---

ing social ideology to the psychology of the individual journalist.[1] A number of the intermediate layers in this onion describing the behaviour of news organizations and the professional norms of journalism constitute the sociology of news, an area of scholarship with which agenda-setting theory began to converge in the 1980s.[2]

In this chapter, a response to the question of who sets the media's agenda will be outlined in terms of the three fundamental layers illustrated in box 7.2. At the surface of our theoretical onion are key external news sources, such as the president of the United States, routine public relations activities, and the efforts of political campaigns. Deep inside the onion are the interactions and influence of the various mass media on each other, a phenomenon now commonly referred to as intermedia agenda-setting. To a considerable degree these interactions validate and reinforce the social norms and traditions of journalism. These norms and traditions, which are the layer of the onion immediately surrounding the core, define the ground rules for the ultimate shaping of the media agenda.

The president and the national agenda

One way of describing and evaluating a national political leader, such as the president of the United States, is his role in setting the national agenda. Increasingly, a major task for the US president is to influence the focus of news coverage as a means of shaping supportive public opinion that, in turn, will leverage his influence on the actions of the

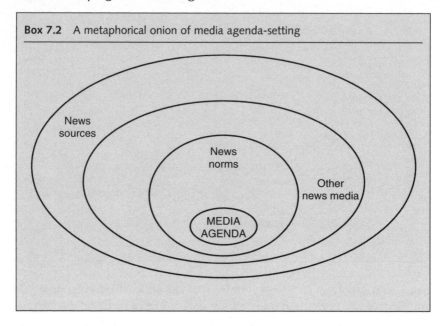

Box 7.2   A metaphorical onion of media agenda-setting

Congress. There is considerable anecdotal evidence that the president is America's number one news-maker. Virtually everything that a president does, from convening international conferences to stopping for a snack during his afternoon jog, is considered newsworthy. Does being at the centre of media attention provide significant opportunities for the president to set the media's agenda?

One rich opportunity for assessing the president's influence is his annual State of the Union address. Required by the US Constitution, for more than a century this report was a written document submitted to the Congress. But in the late twentieth century the annual State of the Union address became a major media event, a public address in the Capitol by the president to a joint evening session of the House of Representatives and Senate that was broadcast live nationally by all the television networks.

The format of this address in our time – essentially a shopping list of issues that the president wants the Congress to address – makes it ideal for assessing the president's agenda-setting influence. Here in a single message – a message that is weeks in the making with considerable input from numerous political and policy advisers – is a list of the president's priorities. Do these priorities reflected in the president's agenda have any significant influence on the subsequent media agenda, any influence on the pattern of news coverage extending beyond those days immediately surrounding the State of the Union address?

Surprisingly, the initial exploration of this question, which examined President Jimmy Carter's 1978 State of the Union address, found no significant impact on the subsequent month's coverage of his eight priority issues in the *New York Times* and the *Washington Post* or on the three national television networks.[3] However, there was evidence that the coverage of these eight issues in the *New York Times* and on the television networks during the month preceding the State of the Union address had influenced the president's agenda.

A replication based on the identical research design examined a very different American president, Richard Nixon.[4] In this instance, the agenda of fifteen issues in President Nixon's 1970 State of the Union address did influence the subsequent month's news coverage in the *New York Times* and the *Washington Post*, and on two of the three national television networks. There was no evidence of any media influence on the president. Enormous differences in presidential personalities is, of course, a major factor to be considered in these kinds of historical analyses. However, even with this factor in mind, there is also evidence of a shifting relationship between a president and the news media over the years of his administration. Analyses of President Franklin Roosevelt's first seven State of the Union addresses, which were delivered from 1934 to 1940, yielded highly mixed evidence about the relationship between the news media and the president.[5] Similar evidence of mixed effects is also found in analyses of President Reagan's 1982 and 1985 State of the Union addresses.[6] Sometimes, the president is able to direct the attention of the news media towards certain issues and to set the agendas of the media and the public. At other times, he follows the media and public opinion.[7]

These examinations of the State of the Union addresses provide considerably more than an answer to the question of who sets the media's agenda. They also illustrate one aspect of policy agenda-setting, the process by which governments make decisions about what social issues will be the focus of their attention.[8] However, there has been considerably less empirical study of the role of the news media in the shaping of public policy than in the shaping of public opinion.[9]

Perhaps the major reason for this situation is that the role of the news media is typically inconsistent for any particular issue over the lengthy periods of time usually required for the evolution of the public policy process. Media agendas are shaped far more by the news values of immediate events and situations than by the social value of deliberation. This is, of course, one of the values of contemporary news media that has been challenged by the emerging philosophy and practice of public journalism.[10] However, there is some evidence that from time to time the media have exerted substantial influence on the policy agenda at both the national and the local level. Examples include a seminal article on child abuse in the *Journal of the American Medical Association* that stimulated considerable mass media attention and subsequent actions by the Congress and many state legislatures;[11] a new year's community agenda on the editorial page of the *San Antonio Light* – supported by subsequent news reporting – that resulted in vastly increased spending for a children's programme by the city government;[12] and two series of investigative reports by a Chicago television station that led to policy changes in the city's police and fire departments.[13] News reports on public issues can also have substantial, albeit more indirect, policy impacts through a shift in the long-term framing of an issue, a change creating a climate that is favourable to new policy approaches.[14]

But in many instances the relationship between news coverage and the evolution of public policy over time is extremely circular, a pattern documented in careful detail for such diverse issues as AIDS,[15] global warming[16] and drugs.[17] Because of both the intermittent and often circular role of the news media, examinations of mass communication and public opinion have less frequently included the third member of the democratic triad, government policy.

Subsidizing the media agenda

All the journalists in the world can observe only a small fraction of each day's situations and events. Even with the routine exclusion of many kinds of events in many places, there are still not enough journalists to cover all aspects of even the major topics in the daily news. Much of what we know, for example, about the workings of government and business, from the international level down to the local level, originates with public information officers and other public relations practitioners who represent important news sources. These communication professionals subsidize the efforts of news organizations to cover the news by providing substantial amounts of organized information, frequently in the form of press releases prepared in the exact style of news stories.[18] Examination of the *New York Times* and *Washington Post* across a twenty-year period found that nearly half of their news stories were substantially based on press releases and other direct information subsidies. Some 17.5 per cent of the total number of news stories appearing in these newspapers were based, at least in part, on press releases. Press conferences and background briefings accounted for another 32 per cent.[19] The *New York Times* and *Washington Post* are major newspapers with large staffs and immense resources. Their substantial reliance on public relations sources underscores the key role that information subsidies play in the daily construction of all media agendas.

News coverage of six state government agencies by Louisiana's major daily newspapers was also substantially based on information provided by those agencies' public information officers.[20] Slightly more than half of the information subsidies provided by these public information officers, primarily written news releases but occasionally personal conversations, appeared in subsequent news stories. The agenda of topics ranged from state finances and the general economy to ceremonial events and celebrations. Specifically, the correspondence during an eight-week period between the agenda originating with the public information officers and the agenda of the news stories using that information was +0.84. The correspondence between the agency-originated agenda and all stories on those state government agencies during that period was +0.57. Inquiries into the reasons for this high level of success underscored the central role of journalistic norms and traditions as the final layer of the onion that sets the ground rules for the shaping of the media agenda. Newsworthiness was the most important consideration 82 per cent of the time.

The reporting of public health issues, such as AIDS or polio, also reflects information subsidies provided by scientists and other expert news sources.[21] The sustained and rising coverage of AIDS during the 1980s was set in motion by the scientific agenda, but sustained by the appearance in the latter half of the decade of new frames for telling the AIDS story. Concomitant with the appearance of these new frames were shifts in the agenda-setting roles of the biomedical community and the news media. Just as with the interaction of presidents, the news media and the public, there is a temporal dynamic to be considered in the natural history of nearly every issue.

Without the subsidies routinely provided by public relations professionals in the public, non-profit and private sectors, the media agenda would be considerably different in scope and content. After all, agenda-setting is a significant part of what public relations is about.[22] Furthermore, public relations influence on the media agenda is sometimes considerably more than a simple information subsidy to augment the routine work of journalists. Examination of professional public relations interventions on behalf of foreign governments, many with highly negative international images, found two measures of success. Their total coverage in the *New York Times* declined as the media spotlight shone less frequently on these governments, and this reduced news coverage was more positive.[23]

Capturing the media agenda

Although the ultimate goal of any political campaign is to win on election day, campaigns increasingly see their immediate purpose as capturing the media agenda.[24] Implicit in this campaign perspective is the idea of public agenda-setting because control of the media agenda implies significant influence on the public agenda. A portion of the mass communication agenda, of course, is under the immediate and direct control of a campaign. Vast amounts of money are spent on political advertising in the mass media, predominantly television in many countries. These messages convey exactly the agenda desired by the campaign. But major efforts are also exerted to influence the issue agenda of the news media because these messages are less obviously self-serving and therefore more credible to the public.[25]

A comparative analysis of the 1983 British general election and the 1984 US presidential election found considerable differences between the two countries in the political parties' influence on the news agenda.[26] In the 1983 British general election, the parties enjoyed considerable success in focusing the attention of the news media on their issues. Extensive comparisons of the Conservative, Labour and Alliance parties' emphases on five key policy issues with the coverage of those issues on the BBC and ITV and in five newspapers, both broadsheets and tabloids, found a median correlation of +0.70. In these twenty-one comparisons – three political parties each compared with seven different news media – the range of the correlations was +0.30 to a perfect 1.0. Six actually reflected the median value of +0.70, and only five of the twenty-one correlations fell below +0.70. The parties were equally successful with newspapers and television.

The 1984 American presidential campaigns did not fare as well with the news media. Comparison of the Democrats' and Republicans' emphases on six key policy issues with the news coverage on the three national television networks found no correlation exceeding +0.31, and three of the six comparisons were zero or negative.

Other evidence indicated that the parties had no better success with the newspapers.

This striking difference in the success of political campaigns as media agenda-setters is largely the result of cultural differences in American and British journalists' orientation towards elections. In other words, the final layer of our theoretical onion, the social norms and traditions of journalism, is substantially different in Britain and the US. The pattern of American election news coverage results from a normative calculus that weighs its news value each day in strict competition with the newsworthiness of all the other possible stories. In contrast, the sacerdotal normative orientation of British journalists considers election campaigns as inherently significant and important activities whose coverage cannot be determined solely by the application of news values.

This difference in how elections are covered in the two countries can be described in explicit agenda-setting terms:

> In Britain, most television news people are hesitant to define their campaign contributions in 'agenda-setting' terms. In their eyes, the phrase has 'an active' interventionist meaning, as if they are being accused of presenting issues they personally deemed significant, despite or even in contradistinction to those the parties wish to press for.... Most of the NBC journalists [in America] were less diffident about their roles. They were prepared to regard themselves as more active in the agenda-setting process than their BBC counterparts.[27]

A similar American view was reflected during the 2000 US presidential primary elections by the editor of the *New York Times* in regard to persistent press questioning of George W. Bush about the use of drugs in his youth, questions which he refused to entertain. 'There is here the question of who sets the agenda – the politicians or the press', remarked Executive Editor Joseph Lelyveld.[28] It is a central question that we explore here in considerable detail.

Although the evidence overall suggests a strong agenda-setting role for the US news media during most of the lengthy presidential election, politicians sometimes do have the edge at the outset. As we saw in chapter 6's discussion of framing, there is evidence of candidate influence on the news coverage of the 1996 Republican contenders for their party's presidential nomination in the *New York Times*, *Washington Post* and *Los Angeles Times* from 26 December (the day the *Times* began a series of in-depth candidate profiles) until 20 February (the date of the New Hampshire primary, the first primary in the lengthy US presidential election year).[29] Media depictions of the four major contenders for the Republican nomination – Lamar Alexander, Pat Buchanan, Robert Dole and Steve Forbes – were compared with the press releases on these candidates' web sites. Based on twenty-eight detailed categories, the strength and consistency of the correlations between the news coverage and each candidate's presentation of himself is striking: Alexander, +0.74; Buchanan, +0.75; Forbes, +0.78; and Dole, +0.62. Dole's status as the front runner could well explain his slightly lower, but still robust, correlation.

However, a more narrowly focused analysis of television news coverage during the New Hampshire primary itself found only a moderate degree of correspondence (+0.40) with the topics of the candidates' speeches during the primary.[30] While nearly all of the candidates' speeches included public issues, less than a third of the TV news reports even mentioned issues. The longstanding predilection of American journalists for the horserace and their lack of interest in the issues were amply apparent.

Additional evidence for the horserace's number one position on the media agenda is found in an analysis of the fall 1996 presidential campaign coverage on the four major television networks and in the *New York Times*, *Washington Post* and *Los Angeles Times*.[31] For both print and TV, horserace coverage consumed about half the media agenda. Setting aside discussion of the campaign and focusing specifically on public issues, the analysis of this news coverage indicates that the candidates' issue agendas, at best, had only modest influence on any of the media agendas during the fall campaign.

But again showing verification of candidate influence early in the election year, there is evidence from the 2000 presidential primaries that candidate issue agendas influenced network television news coverage.[32] Ten of the twelve comparisons between the four candidate agendas and the three major networks yielded significant correlations, with the median value falling between +0.64 and +0.68. Further analysis using cross-lagged correlations to examine the patterns during the early months of the presidential race found about twice as many instances of candidate influence on the media agenda of issues than the reverse.

At the second level of agenda-setting, although there is less overall evidence of influence, the strength of the significant correlations that were found compare favourably with the evidence for basic agenda-setting. Only six of the twelve comparisons of the emphasis on various audience frames – the elderly, minorities, women, etc. – by the candidates and by television news were significant. Among those comparisons, all of which involved Republicans Bush and McCain and none Democrats Gore or Bradley, the median correlation fell between +0.77 and +0.85. For a set of campaign process frames – polls, endorsements, debates, etc. – only three of the twelve comparisons were significant. All three involved Republican challenger McCain, who in the dominant media narrative played David to Bush's Goliath. For these three significant correlations, the median value was +0.69.

Three election agendas

Substantial evidence of the strong influence that journalistic norms can have on both the shaping of the media's issue agenda and the subsequent public agenda of issues comes from comprehensive national analyses of the 1992 and 2000 US presidential campaigns. At first glance, the strong correlations in 1992 of the candidates' platforms with both the media agenda (+0.76) and the public agenda (+0.78) might appear to undercut the idea of an agenda-setting role for the media and, further, to suggest that the strong correlation between the media and the public (+0.94) is overstated.[33] This is not the case. When all three elements are considered simultaneously, the strong correlation between the media and the public remains while the correlation between the candidates' platforms and the public agenda is greatly diminished. This can be observed in several ways.

When the analysis of the relationship between the media agenda and the public agenda (+0.94) also takes into account the direct influence of the candidates' platforms on both the media and the public agenda, the outcome remains an extraordinary +0.85. Alternatively, when the media agenda is viewed as the key factor intervening between the candidates and the public, that is, as the principal bridge between the candidates and the public, the resulting partial correlation – as expected – is greatly diminished. The original relationship of +0.78 between the candidates' platforms and the public agenda is reduced to +0.33 when the intervening influence of the media is removed. Of course, the media agenda is by no means constructed from whole cloth – there is significant input from media sources, as evidenced by a correlation of +0.76 – but the light emanating from presidential campaigns is refracted through the prism of journalistic norms before reaching the public.

This substantial agenda-setting influence of the news media on the issue agenda – independent of the political campaigns to a considerable degree – was replicated during the fall 2000 presidential campaign.[34] At the outset, the basic pattern of correlations was nearly identical: substantial correlations between the candidates' agenda of issues and both the media agenda (+0.79) and the public agenda (+0.76), as well as a strong correlation between the media and the public (+0.92).

Replicating the pattern found in 1992, when the analysis of this strong relationship between the media and the public takes into account the influence of the candidates on both, the correlation remains a robust +0.79. Alternatively, when the media agenda is viewed as the intervening element between the candidates and the public, the original relationship of +0.76 is reduced to +0.15. Repetition of these analyses separately for the agendas of the two major candidates, George W. Bush and Albert Gore, revealed the identical pattern. All of this is strong evidence for the agenda-setting role of the news media in focusing the public's attention on public issues.

Analysis of the 2000 presidential campaign also explored the attribute agenda-setting influence of the candidates and the news media in defining the public's perception of the social welfare issue, which ranked number one on the public agenda. Here the evidence clearly favours the primary role of the campaigns as agenda-setters for this issue during the fall 2000 campaign. The correlation of the campaign agenda for eight attributes of the social welfare issue with the news agenda is a hearty +0.76 and with the public an even stronger +0.86. Unlike the pattern found at the first level of agenda-setting in both 1992 and 2000 for the overall set of issues, at the second level of agenda-setting this latter relationship is only slightly dimmed (+0.78) when the media agenda is included in the analysis as an intervening factor. Furthermore, the relatively modest relationship between the media and the public (+0.60) for this attribute agenda disappears when the candidate agenda is introduced into the analysis.

Media agendas in local elections

At the local level in the US, there is a clear answer to the question of who set the media's issue agenda during the 1990 Texas gubernatorial election.[35] The combined issue agendas of the Democrat and Republican candidates' paid television advertising in Austin, the capital of Texas, was compared with the news coverage of those issues by the Austin newspaper and the three local television stations. The paid advertising agenda is, of course, completely controlled by the campaigns and can be regarded as a surrogate for the total campaign agenda. This campaign agenda exerted significant influence on both the local newspaper (+0.64) and the local television stations (+0.52), a pattern of influence that persisted even when other factors were taken into account.

However, the pattern of influence in the Texas gubernatorial election four years later – the election marking George W. Bush's political debut – was essentially the reverse. Comparison of the press releases from Bush and incumbent Governor Ann Richards with the coverage of the state's three major newspapers during the fall 1994 election campaign revealed that the newspapers substantially influenced the candidates' issue agendas (+0.70), the overall focus of their press releases on issues, personal images and aspects of the political campaign itself (+1.0), and the overall positive or negative tone of their press releases (+0.80).[36]

At the second level of agenda-setting, there is evidence from the 1995 local elections in the Spanish province of Navarra that political advertisements influenced the subsequent depiction of the candidates on TV news (+0.99), but only to a modest degree in the newspapers (+0.32).[37] The primary influence of the advertising was on descriptions of the candidates' qualifications. On television, the time devoted to qualifications increased more than eightfold from the early days of the campaign to the latter days. In the newspapers, mentions of this attribute doubled in the course of the campaign.

Attributes of local issues

At the local level of politics in the US, the attribute agenda-setting effects of political advertising were observed in two elections in Victoria, Texas.[38] In a 1995 local sales tax referendum in Victoria, two patterns are apparent from a pair of public opinion surveys conducted among registered voters, the first survey conducted about a month prior to the referendum, the second about a week before the voting. There was a significant increase in learning among the voters during the campaign, and political advertising played an especially strong role in shaping the pictures in voters' minds of what the proposed sales tax would do for Victoria.

From survey one to survey two, the match between the voters' pictures and the local newspaper's presentation of the sales tax increased from +0.40 to +0.65. For the political ads, the match increased from +0.80 to +0.95. When the match of these Texas voters with one source (e.g., the newspaper) controlled for the other source (e.g., advertising), the correspondence between the newspaper and the public disappeared entirely. But for political ads the correlations resulting from these controls were +0.87 (compared to the original correlation of +0.80 in survey one) and +0.94 (compared to the original correlation of +0.95 in survey two). Political advertising was the primary source of learning about this local economic issue.

In the election for mayor of Victoria that year, the voters' images of the two candidates significantly matched the agenda of attributes in local newspaper coverage (+0.60 for each candidate), but matched even more each candidate's political advertising (+0.73 and +0.85). Further analysis led to the conclusion that political ads were, by far, the major agenda-setter in this local election. When the influence of the candidates on both the media agenda and the public agenda is taken into account, the match between the newspaper and the public is reduced from +0.60 to +0.46 for one candidate, and there is essentially no correlation at all for the second candidate. However, when the relationship between the political advertising agenda and the public controlled for the media agenda, there is no evidence at all for a media role as the key bridge between the campaign and the public. The strong candidate agenda–public agenda correlations are unchanged.

Three elements of elections

These sets of evidence based on all three key elements of a political campaign – the candidates and political parties, the news media, and the public – provide the complex mix of documentation needed to examine the agenda-setting role of the news media in its full context. This rich mix addresses earlier criticisms that the evidence of agenda-setting effects by the media is fragmentary because so much of it has examined only two elements at a time, the media and the public in the opening phase of agenda-setting research and subsequently, beginning in the 1980s, news sources and the media.[39] In particular, this evidence also addresses the basic question of who are the true agenda-setters, the media or the political campaigns. If the campaigns dominate the formation of both the media agenda and the public agenda, then the media are only, at best, the proximate cause of the public agenda. In Britain, the national political parties have enjoyed considerable success in capturing the news agenda. Not so in the US, where a different set of journalistic norms has resulted in media issue agendas only weakly corresponding to the agendas put forward by the national parties during the presidential campaign. Most importantly, where the US evidence encompasses all three elements, it is these media agendas, rather than the candidates' agendas, that have by far the greatest influence on the public agenda.

All in all, across the election year in the US, the media are the agenda-setters. However, at the outset of presidential election years in the US and at the local level in both the US and Spain, the situation is more mixed. In these circumstances, political campaigns frequently succeed in capturing the media agenda. Finally, there is a normative question about the news media's role in defining an agenda that has civic utility for citizens, a question that is especially pertinent where the media are the dominant influence on the public agenda.[40] How useful are these agendas of topics and attributes – whatever their source – as the basis of the decisions that citizens in a democracy are called upon to make about public affairs?

A broader portrait

Elections offer a particularly intensive setting for examining both the influence of news sources on the media and, in turn, the influence of the media on the public. In the larger realm of history, however, elections are only tiny blips impacting the continuous rise and fall of public opinion on the topics of the day. A detailed analysis of Canadian public opinion on three issues from 1985 to 1995 offers this broader view of the flow of issue salience from a variety of news sources to the news media and from there to the public.[41] The three issues selected for analysis – inflation, the environment, and the national debt and budget deficits – also provide another look at aspects of agenda-setting theory reviewed in earlier chapters, this time in the context of a full-scale model of the agenda-setting process.

First, in terms of media effects and the concept of obtrusive and unobtrusive issues previously discussed in chapter 4, there is a clear pattern across this continuum of issues. In line with previous evidence on the obtrusive issue of inflation, there is no evidence of any agenda-setting influence by the media on public opinion. For the environment, the relationship between the media agenda and the public agenda is reciprocal – and the impact of the public on the media appears to be stronger. Finally, for the unobtrusive and abstract issue of the Canadian national debt and budget deficits, there is evidence of significant media influence on the public agenda.

This comprehensive examination also allows us to revisit the relationship between the media agenda and reality. None of the three analyses yields a significant relationship between the trend in the media agenda over these years and real-world measures of inflation, the environment and Canadian national finances. As common sense would seem to dictate, these real-world measures are linked to the trends in both the public agenda and the policy agenda for the issues of inflation and the environment. For the third issue, national finances, there is only a link with the policy agenda, which is defined in these analyses by such measures as the topics of the question period and committee reports in the Canadian parliament. Of course, elections are also an aspect of reality and a major source of news. But the occurrence of elections did not impact the media trend over time for any of these issues, and the occurrence of elections impacted the trend in public concern only for the environment.

Various manifestations of the policy agenda in the government are also potential sources of news for the media. Here the evidence is mixed. For inflation, there is evidence of a modest influence by the policy agenda on the news agenda. But for the environment and Canadian national finances there is evidence of a reciprocal relationship between the media and policy agendas – quite strong for the environment, rather modest for national finances.

A similarly mixed picture emerged from a year-long comparison of the activity of the city council in Bloomington, Indiana, and its coverage in the local daily newspaper.[42] Although there was considerable correspondence between the priorities of the council and the media agenda (+0.84), closer examination revealed major discrepancies in the rankings of seven of the nineteen categories. For four categories – arts and entertainment, nuclear freeze, utilities and elections – the newspaper's emphasis was considerably greater. For awards, animal protection and urban development, the newspaper's emphasis was considerably less. Even news coverage of formal government meetings, where almost stenographic coverage might be expected, demonstrates the interplay of news norms and news events. The reporter who covered the city council that year said that he liked 'subjects that involve controversy, debates and several actors because these characteristics make for a better story.'[43] His perspective reflects the normative influence of the narrative imperative of journalism, to tell a good story. This perspective also accounts, at least in part, for the fact that only 59 per cent of the items described in the council minutes were reported in the local newspaper.

Finally, influencing all three of the agendas just considered – the policy agenda reflected by various government activities, the media agenda, and the public agenda – is frequently the goal of a wide variety of organized interest groups.[44] Often as well financed as election campaigns, issue campaigns by interest groups share a similar record of success. A nine-year analysis of the US debate about gun control found significant links between the attention of network television news and the flood of press releases from interest groups on both sides of the issue (+0.60) as well as congressional discussion (+0.32).[45] Analysis of how this issue was framed reveals that a 'culture of violence' theme was the dominant frame in nearly half of the news stories, but in less than a quarter of the congressional statements on gun control and less than a sixth of the press releases. In short, largely independent of these news sources, the news media heeded the narrative imperative and opted for the dramatic 'culture of violence' frame. Although this may celebrate the independence of the media voice, it is simultaneously a failure to 'move the discussion beyond a simplified emotive framework to a more reasoned policy debate.'[46]

Intermedia agenda-setting

The elite news media frequently exert a substantial influence on the agenda of other news media. In the United States this role of intermedia agenda-setter is frequently played by the *New York Times*, a role now so institutionalized that the Associated Press alerts its members each day to the agenda of stories scheduled for the next morning's front page of the *Times*. It is the appearance on the front page of the *Times* that frequently legitimates a topic as newsworthy.

Despite intensive coverage by local newspapers over many months, neither serious chemical contamination at Love Canal in western New York state nor the radon threat in nearby Pennsylvania and New Jersey gained national attention until these problems appeared on the *New York Times*'s agenda.[47] Chapter 2 previously noted how the *Times*'s discovery of the drug problem in late 1985 resulted in heavy coverage during 1986 in major newspapers across the US and on national television news, a pattern that peaked with two national television specials in September of that year.[48]

Sociologist Warren Breed conceptualized this diffusion of a news story from a key news medium to a host of other media as a dendritic influence.[49] Analogous to a family tree, this arterial flow is from a progenitor to a multitude of descendants. Many times these journalistic offspring are absolute clones. In the mid-twentieth century, when the *New York Times* and the now defunct *New York Herald-Tribune* were in serious competition, the managing editors of both newspapers frequently ordered last-minute changes on their front pages in order to match their competitors' coverage.[50] Journalists frequently observe – and subsequently copy – their peers' news coverage in order to validate their own news judgement about the day's events.[51]

A classic example of this influence at work among individual journalists occurred during the 1972 US presidential campaign. The first major political event of a presidential election year in the US is the Iowa caucuses, a series of local political party meetings across that state to select delegates to the party convention. It is a highly ambiguous situation to report. Those who attend these dozens and dozens of local meetings are a self-selected group of voters who are interested enough to show up and participate. Furthermore, at this early point in the election year there is typically a large field of candidates vying for delegates. Journalists' task on the evening of these caucuses is to make sense of it all, to find the news amid all this activity.

> What happened was that Johnny Apple of the *New York Times* sat in a corner and everyone peered over his shoulder to find out what he was writing. . . . He would sit down and write a lead, and they would go write leads. . . . Finally, at midnight, the guy announced that Muskie had 32 percent and McGovern had 26 percent, and Apple sat down to write his final story. He called it something like 'a surprisingly strong showing for George McGovern.' Everyone peered over his shoulder again and picked it up. It was on the front page of every major newspaper the next day.[52]

A large-scale portrait of intermedia agenda-setting among the elite US news media is found in the natural history of global warming from 1985 to 1992.[53] As the news coverage of this issue steadily accelerated towards its peak in 1989, major newspapers – the *New York Times*, *Washington Post* and *Wall Street Journal* – significantly influenced the agenda of the three national television networks. For this complex scientific issue, a significant intermedia agenda-setting role was also played by science publications, those key specialized sources regularly scanned by mass media science writers and editors.

The role of elite news media in initiating widespread coverage of new topics and the influence of key journalists in framing the news are dramatic examples of intermedia agenda-setting. But prosaic versions of intermedia agenda-setting take place every day as local news organizations construct their daily agenda from the huge file of news sent to them by the wire services. An examination of how twenty-four Iowa daily newspapers used the Associated Press wire report found major influence on the local news agenda.[54] Although each newspaper used only a small proportion of the available AP stories, their patterns of coverage reflected essentially the same proportion for each category of news as the total AP file.

A laboratory experiment, whose subjects were experienced news-paper and television wire editors, also found a high degree of corres-pondence (+0.62) across categories between the proportion of news stories in a large wire file and the small sample selected by the editors.[55] Additional evidence about the agenda-setting influence of the wire service was found in a control condition of the experiment where there were an equal number of stories in each news category. In this situation, there was no common pattern of selection at all, either in comparison with the perfectly balanced wire file and its lack of cues about salience or among the wire editors themselves, who might be expected to share similar news values.

Early investigations of gatekeeping, the decisions by journalists editing the wire at local news outlets about which items to delete and which to pass through the gate, emphasized the psychological characteristics of the gatekeepers themselves. In contrast, agenda-setting theory calls attention to the sociological setting of this task.[56] A re-analysis[57] of the classic case study of Mr Gates[58] found substantial correspondence (+0.64) between the combined agenda of his wire services and Mr Gates's selections for his news-paper. Further examination of a replication that studied Mr Gates seventeen years later when he used only a single wire service[59] found a correlation of +0.80 between the wire agenda and his news selections.[60]

Moving to the level of local news, analysis of election coverage in Austin, Texas, during the 1990 gubernatorial campaign found that the issue agenda of the local daily newspaper influenced the issue agenda of local television news (+0.73).[61] Recall that this chapter earlier noted that the candidates' issue agenda influenced both the newspaper and the television coverage. But even when this influence is taken into account, there is still evidence of significant newspaper influence on the television coverage (+0.44).

In Spain, an examination of intermedia influence among news-papers and television during the 1995 local elections measured both first- and second-level agenda-setting effects.[62] Intermedia agenda-setting at the first level in Pamplona and in Austin was highly similar. Comparisons of the coverage on six local issues in two Pamplona newspapers yielded correlations of +0.66 and +0.70, respectively, with the subsequent television news agenda. At the second level, there was no evidence of attribute agenda-setting influence among the newspapers and local television news in the ways that they described the local political candidates. However, recall that the political advertising in the newspapers did influence subsequent depictions of the candidates in the newspapers and on television.

Journalists validate their sense of news by observing the work of their colleagues. Local newspapers and television stations note the news agenda offered each day by their direct competitors for local attention. Local outlets also note the agendas advanced by news organizations with higher status. In the US these are the major regional newspapers, the Associated Press, the national television networks, and the elite newspapers in New York and Washington. Of course, these high status outlets also observe each other.

The outcome of these routine, continuous observations and the resulting intermedia influence is a highly redundant news agenda. In the original Chapel Hill investigation of agenda-setting, the median correlation among the issue agendas of the five daily newspapers – a mix of local and elite dailies – and two television networks observed there was +0.81.[63] A similar comparison of the issue agendas for three major daily newspapers and three television stations in Taipei during the 1992 Taiwan legislative elections found a median correlation of +0.75.[64]

At the second level of agenda-setting, the framing of Japan's economic problem by two major newspapers was compared for two sets of attributes – problematic situation frames and sub-issue frames – and across two different time periods – twenty-six weeks and fifty-two weeks. The median correlation for these four comparisons fell between +0.72 and +0.73.[65] A comparison of the attributes of the economic issue in the US found a correlation of +0.80 between the newspaper and television agendas.[66] This might be termed a quasi-comparison because the two newspaper agendas and three television agendas had already been merged to create a newspaper agenda and a television agenda.

Merging the agendas of various news outlets to create a composite media agenda is commonplace in investigations of the agenda-setting role of the media because of the high degree of homogeneity among these various agendas. In the language of research methodology, these high intercorrelations among the agendas of the news media can be regarded as a measure of reliability, the extent of agreement among independent observers who are applying the same rules of observation. Applying the norms and traditions of journalism to the vast number of events and situations available each day for observation, journalists – aided, of course, by their intermedia observations – construct highly similar agendas. At the second level of agenda-setting, the homogeneity of agendas extends beyond agreement on the attribute agendas for a particular object. There is also a high degree of similarity in the attribute agendas for related objects. A comparison of the attribute agendas in the major Taipei newspapers for three mayoral candidates found a median correlation of $+0.93$.[67] The norms of journalism exert a powerful pressure towards homogeneity in telling the news of the day. While some speculate that the internet will be the source of a plethora of independent and divergent agendas, others argue that the high level of redundancy found in the current media system is likely to persist on account of the strength of journalistic norms and habits.

Summing up

Who sets the media's agenda? This question of who determines which topics are brought to public attention is especially vital. Columnist Leonard Pitts observed that, 'in a world where media set the public agenda and drive the dialogue, those things media ignore may as well not exist.'[68] The outline of an answer in this chapter to who sets the media's agenda considers three key elements: major sources who provide the information for news stories, other news organizations, and journalism's norms and traditions.

At times, national leaders do succeed in setting the news agenda. Public information officers and other public relations professionals are also significant contributors. But all of these influence streams are filtered through the ground rules established by the norms of journalism, and they are very powerful filters. The evolution of the daily and weekly news agenda is further shaped and standardized by the interactions among news organizations. In this process of intermedia agenda-setting, high status news organizations, such as the *New York Times* and Associated Press, set the agendas of other news organizations. At the city level, local newspapers and television stations influence the news agenda of their competitors.

On occasion, intermedia agenda-setting takes a very different form – entertainment media set the agenda of the news media. Extensive examination of articles about the Holocaust in major Canadian newspapers over a fifteen-year period, 1982 to 1996, found that the film *Schindler's List* had an influence – on the number of articles and the duration of the impact over time – that was more powerful than a number of Holocaust-related news events during those years.[69]

In addition to exploring the question of who sets the media's agenda, an inquiry that is of immediate interest to communication scholars and professionals, our awareness of these external agendas illustrates the expanding scope of agenda-setting theory. Although most of our knowledge about the agenda-setting process centres on the relationship between the media agenda and the public agenda, that setting is only one delimited application of the theory. Agenda-setting theory is about the transfer of salience from one agenda to another. The best developed portions of the theory focus on the link between the media agenda and the public agenda because of its theoretical roots in public opinion research and because most of the scholars whose work has built this theory were especially interested in mass media effects. Even with the shift in this chapter to the elements shaping the media agenda, the overall focus remains very media-centric. But, as we shall see, there are many other agenda-setting relationships to consider.

Historically, research into the sources of influence shaping the media agenda opened the fourth phase of agenda-setting theory and marked a significant expansion beyond the media agenda–public agenda relationship. The initial phase, inaugurated by the Chapel Hill study, was centred on the influence of the media's issue agenda on the public's issue agenda. The second phase elaborated this influence of the news media, exploring a variety of contingent conditions that enhance or constrain agenda-setting effects among the public. The third phase expanded the scope of agenda-setting influence by the media from effects on attention – agendas of objects – to effects on comprehension – attribute agendas. The fourth phase, which is introduced in this chapter, explores the origins of this media agenda. Although there is a clear historical pattern in the appearance of these four phases, they are not historical phases in the sense that, with the appearance of a new phase, the book is closed on the previous phase. All four of these phases continue to be active sites of inquiry. And there remain many additional sites to explore!

8 Consequences of Agenda-Setting

The evolutionary process typical of most social science, a process that contrasts sharply with the popular notion of dramatic scientific 'discoveries', was especially apparent for agenda-setting theory as the last century came to a close. The orderly and parsimonious canon of knowledge centred on the media agenda and the public agenda that is found in the previous chapters of this book was poised at the brink of an expansive explosion of new relationships and new settings. However, rather than the dawn of dramatic discoveries about the role of the mass media in the shaping of public opinion, these new perspectives were more the cumulative outcome of ongoing scholarship across the final three decades of the twentieth century. As a result of this scholarly perseverance, the idea of an agenda-setting role of mass communication was converging with a host of other social science concepts and interests about mass communication and human behaviour.

The intellectual history of agenda-setting theory from its origins in 1968 to the present reflects steady, albeit diffuse, progress in mapping the antecedents of object and attribute salience on the public agenda. To the initial map of agenda-setting effects first sketched in Chapel Hill were added numerous characteristics of the public and the media that enhanced or reduced these effects among the public. Also added to this theoretical map were more details about the origins of the media agenda. All of this was further explicated by the addition of attribute agenda-setting. Our theoretical map, the result of four phases of research describing and explaining the shape of the public agenda, is rich in its details.

As the twentieth century came to a close, the ideas coming to the fore in the newest versions of this theoretical map were the consequences of the agenda-setting process. This is the fifth phase of agenda-setting theory, explicating a variety of ideas about these consequences that had previously been sketched only in outline:

> Attitudes and behavior are usually governed by cognitions – what a person knows, thinks, believes. Hence, the agenda-setting function of the mass media implies a potentially massive influence whose full dimensions and consequences have yet to be investigated and appreciated.[1]

Chapter 6 ended with the observation that the combination of cognitive and affective elements in attribute agenda-setting revives the consideration of mass communication effects on attitudes and opinions. The evidence in that chapter on the salience of affective attributes in the public's descriptions of political candidates – salience acquired, at least in part, from the news media – reopens a psychological area of exploration that was largely abandoned in the mid-twentieth century in the face of strong, empirically grounded assertions about the minimal effects of mass communication.[2]

Mass communication effects can result, as many of the early scholars believed, from the sheer volume of exposure. First-level agenda-setting effects demonstrate that phenomenon. But, as attribute agenda-setting shows, closer attention to the specific content of mass media messages provides a more detailed understanding of the pictures in our heads and of the attitudes and opinions grounded in those pictures. Attribute agenda-setting and framing bring us back to the influence of the mass media on attitudes and opinions, the theoretical site where mass communication theory started in the 1940s and 1950s. This is a return to Carl Hovland's scientific rhetoric, the matching of message characteristics to attitude and opinion change.[3] However, unlike Hovland's pioneering work of the 1940s, there now exists a detailed theoretical map linking the media agenda and the public to guide our explorations.

To achieve dramatic effect, the opening scenes of some movies are in black and white or sepia tones. A sudden shift from these subdued tones to vibrant colours heightens the emotional impact. In much the same way, when the attribute agendas of the media and the public include affective tone as well as substantive attributes, these pictures of objects in the news can convey strong emotions and feelings, which is to say, opinions. In short, the concepts of public attribute agendas and personal opinions converge. However, this is not the only link or point of convergence between public agendas and personal opinions, so before we examine these relationships in detail we need to sketch some additional portions of our theoretical map for agenda-setting.

From our previous maps illustrating the first and second levels of agenda-setting, box 8.1 reproduces object salience and attribute salience. The new elements in this map are two aspects of opinion and observable behaviour. The first new element in box 8.1 is the strength of opinion, beginning with the fundamental point of whether an opinion even exists. Strength of opinion also distinguishes between weakly and strongly held opinions regardless of whether those opinions are positive or negative. The second element added to box 8.1 is very familiar, the direction of opinion, whether some object or attribute is regarded in a positive or negative light.

Linking object and attribute salience with these two aspects of opinions accounts for three major relationships. Considerable evidence exists for priming, the link between object salience on the public agenda and the direction of opinion. Exploration of the second level of agenda-setting introduced the idea of attribute priming, the link between attribute salience and the direction of opinion. The third relationship, forming an opinion, is the link between object salience and the strength of opinion. All three of these relationships, as well as their subsequent links with behaviour, are discussed in this chapter.

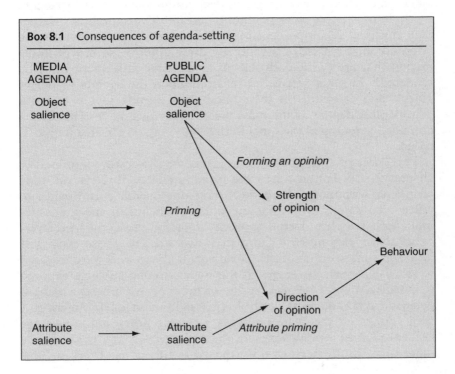

Box 8.1   Consequences of agenda-setting

MEDIA
AGENDA

PUBLIC
AGENDA

Object
salience

Object
salience

Forming an opinion

Strength
of opinion

Priming

Behaviour

Direction
of opinion

Attribute
salience

Attribute
salience

Attribute priming

Priming public opinion

Prominent among the consequences of agenda-setting effects is the priming of perspectives that subsequently guide the public's opinions about public figures, a consequence that brings the agenda-setting influence of the mass media into the very centre of the public opinion arena. The mass media do considerably more than shape the agenda of objects and attributes in our heads. 'By calling attention to some matters while ignoring others, television news [as well as the other news media] influences the standards by which governments, presidents, policies, and candidates for public office are judged', explained Shanto Iyengar and Donald Kinder in *News that Matters*.[4] This link between agenda-setting effects, which result in the salience of issues or other elements among the public, and the subsequent expression of opinions about specific public figures is called priming.

The psychological basis of priming is the selective attention of the public. People do not, indeed, cannot, pay attention to everything, a situation already demonstrated by the limited capacity of the public agenda. Moreover, in making judgements – whether in casting a ballot on election day or simply in responding to a pollster's question – people use simple rules of thumb and intuitive shortcuts.[5] Rather than engaging in comprehensive analyses based on their total store of information, most citizens routinely draw upon those bits of information that are particularly salient at the time judgement must be rendered.[6] In other words, citizens rely upon the agenda of salient objects and attributes in their minds, the agenda that is set to a considerable degree by the mass media. This agenda determines the criteria – sometimes the single criterion – on which an opinion is based.

The series of agenda-setting experiments previously described in chapter 2 also demonstrated the priming effects of television news on people's opinions about the president's overall performance in office.[7] To demonstrate that the shifting salience of specific issues influenced people's overall assessment of the president's performance, these experiments compared two groups: those who saw no news stories on a specific issue versus those who were exposed to television news coverage on the issue. Among subjects exposed to extensive news coverage on one or more of five different issues – defence, inflation, arms control, civil rights and unemployment – their ratings on the issue or issues receiving heavy news coverage influenced their overall opinion about the president's performance more than among persons not exposed to this news coverage. This influence existed whether or not the news story implied a substantial degree of presidential responsibility for the issue. In subsequent experiments where the degree of presidential responsibility for an issue was explicitly manipulated, the impact of problem performance ratings on opinions about the president's overall performance was greater when the news stories emphasized presidential responsibility.

This is strong causal evidence based on controlled laboratory experiments that the influence of the news agenda on the salience of issues among the public primes the criteria that Americans use in judging the overall performance of the president.

Additional evidence of this priming influence was found in a major American political setting, the Iran–Contra scandal.[8] On 25 November 1986, the Attorney-General of the United States announced that funds obtained by the US government from the secret sale of weapons to Iran had been improperly diverted to the Contras, a group attempting to overthrow the Sandinista government in Nicaragua. This covert operation had been carried out by members of the National Security Council, and President Reagan subsequently revealed that the director of the council and a key staff member had been dismissed. Needless to say, all these revelations received major news coverage. By a fortuitous coincidence, the National Election Study's post-1986 presidential election survey was in the field at the time of these announcements, creating a natural before–after comparison of the elements of public opinion that influenced Americans' assessments of President Reagan.

> The importance of public opinion on the question of assistance to the Contras and US intervention in Central America [in assessments of the president's overall performance] increased substantially from the pre-revelation period to the post-revelation period ... as did the importance of the public's view of the general choice between intervention and isolationism. .... Meanwhile, the public's view of the strength of the United States around the world was evidently unaffected by the revelation. This pattern of results corroborates the experimental findings noted earlier.[9]

Turning to a different political setting, public opinion about Hong Kong's last British governor was strongly influenced by news coverage on his proposals to broaden public participation in the election of the Legislative Council.[10] Tracked in fifty-two consecutive weekly polls from the fall of 1992, when the governor made his initial policy speech, public opinion about his overall performance was significantly primed by the pattern of news coverage on his reform proposals in Hong Kong's three leading newspapers.

This priming effect also occurs for political parties. Among German voters, political party preference during 1986 was influenced by the television news agenda.[11] Preference for the Christian Democrats was substantially influenced by news coverage of two issues, the energy supply and the East German situation. Preference for the SPD was influenced by three issues, East–West relations, environmental protection and pensions. Similar patterns were observed in the weekly opinion polls for other political parties. Although the overall pattern is one in which issues on the television news agenda resonated in unique ways with political partisanship, the general finding is that salient issues on the media agenda were strongly linked with shifts in political partisanship during the year.

Priming is a significant extension of agenda-setting,[12] one of the routes through which the mass media play a key role in the shaping of attitudes and opinions.[13] At times, however, these agenda-setting effects of the mass media have very direct consequences for attitudes and opinions. This is particularly the case for attribute agenda-setting, where the impact may be just as dramatic as the sudden shift in a movie from subdued tones to dynamic colour.

Attribute agendas and opinions

In mapping the mass media's impact on opinions, it is crucial to distinguish the contribution of overall media attention to an issue, the first level of agenda-setting, from the way that an issue is framed in the media, the second level of agenda-setting. More specifically, in their comprehensive examination of television's role in society, George Comstock and Erica Scharrer note, 'Conceptually, priming and framing are subspecies of agenda-setting effects that influence public evaluation and interpretation beyond the imputation of importance.'[14] These distinctions are illustrated by American public opinion regarding the Gulf War.[15] Extensive television coverage resulted in the high salience of the war on the public agenda as the most important problem facing the country, a traditional first-level agenda-setting effect. Analyses of public opinion about President Bush from 1988 to 1991 further indicated a shift in the basis of his popularity from economics to foreign policy, a priming effect. And demonstrating the effects of attribute agenda-setting on opinions, members of the public who reported higher levels of exposure to television news, which emphasized military options in its framing of the war, favoured a military rather than a diplomatic solution in the Persian Gulf.

The elements of an issue presented by the media – the attribute agenda – shape our perspective and our opinions. As chapter 5 on attribute agenda-setting noted, Cohen's classic summary must be revised to state that the media not only tell us what to think *about*, they also tell us *how* to think about it. For a local issue in a small US city, the development of a new commercial area featuring large retail stores, the salience of six aspects was compared among persons aware of the issue who varied in their exposure to the local newspaper.[16] Among those with high exposure to the local newspaper, the pattern of shifting salience for these six attributes showed a high degree of correspondence with the newspaper's attribute agenda, a match that was in sharp contrast to those with only moderate and low exposure.

Furthermore, citizens' opinions about both attributes of the issue at the top of the newspaper's agenda – increased sales tax revenue for the city and the potential for increased flooding – were significant predictors of opinions about this development issue for those with high exposure. Among those with moderate exposure, only the potential for increased flooding was a significant predictor of opinions. Among those with no exposure, neither of these attributes was a significant predictor of opinions about the development plan. The newspaper primed the attributes that citizens drew upon to form their opinions about this development issue, and the magnitude of its influence paralleled levels of exposure.

Finally, reminiscent of the concept of compelling arguments, the attribute that ranked third on the newspaper agenda, an increase in traffic, was not a significant predictor of opinions about the development among any of the groups. Apparently, it was not a compelling argument despite its relative prominence on the newspaper agenda.

Additional evidence for the influence of a newspaper's attribute agenda on how people think about an issue was found in a laboratory experiment where subjects read a newspaper article about gay rights.[17] Two different aspects of the issue, equality and morality, were systematically varied in versions of the article. After being asked 'Do you favour or oppose laws to protect homosexuals against job discrimination?', participants were also requested to describe 'exactly what things went through your mind as you were deciding whether you favoured or opposed the policy.' There were similar questions about homosexuals serving in the armed forces.

Under all experimental conditions, subjects' responses emphasized equality more than morality, but with considerable differences among the conditions both in the proportion of subjects who mentioned equality in their answers to the open-ended questions and in the difference between the proportion of subjects mentioning equality and morality. As we see in box 8.2, the proportion of subjects citing equality was only 7 per cent in the experimental condition where the newspaper article mentioned neither attribute of the issue, but 30 per cent when equality was the only attribute mentioned. When both attributes of the issue are discussed in the newspaper article, the impact of the equality frame is considerably diminished. Equality was mentioned by 19 per cent of the subjects in this experimental condition. Likewise, when the equality frame is omitted and only the morality frame is mentioned, only 15 per cent mention equality. A similar pattern across the experimental conditions is found in the differences between the proportion of subjects mentioning equality and morality.

Initial explorations of attribute agenda-setting emphasized the substantive characteristics of political candidates or public issues. Recall the discussion in chapter 5 of Jimmy Carter's and Gerald Ford's images among Chicago voters and the pictures that Minneapolis citizens held of the economic problems. However, the investigations of candidate images in a series of Spanish elections made the implications of attribute agenda-setting for attitudes and opinions explicit with the inclusion of an affective dimension for attribute agendas. Comparisons of twenty-one media and public attribute agendas, which distinguished between positive, negative and neutral mentions of each substantive attribute, yielded a median correlation of +0.66. The news media can successfully communicate both substance and tone.

Box 8.2   Percentage of subjects who used equality and morality frames to explain their opinion

	Experimental conditions			
	Neither frame	Only this frame*	Only the other frame**	Both frames
Used equality frame	7%	30%	15%	19%
Used morality frame	3%	10%	4%	15%

*30% of the subjects who saw only an equality frame used that frame to explain their opinion; 10% of the subjects who saw only a morality frame used that frame to explain their opinion.

**15% of the subjects who saw only a morality frame nevertheless used an equality frame to explain their opinion; 4% of the subjects who saw only an equality frame nevertheless used a morality frame to explain their opinion.

Source: Adapted from Paul Brewer, 'Framing, value words, and citizens' explanations of their issue opinions', Political Communication, 19 (2002), pp. 303–16.

In Germany, the tone of the news about Helmut Kohl in news magazines and major newspapers influenced public opinion between 1975 and 1984 about his political performance, first, as leader of the opposition and, later, as chancellor.[18] Shifting patterns of positive and negative tone in the media, summed across six attributes of Kohl, explained significant shifts in his level of approval among the German public. The median correlation between the affective tone of the attribute agendas for six major news media and subsequent public opinion was +0.48, with a lag time of six months.

In the US, day-by-day observation of the final three months in the 1992 and 1996 presidential elections found that the tone of television news coverage about key campaign events influenced voters' preference for the candidates.[19] Favourable coverage of Republican campaign events on national television increased support for the Republican candidate. Conversely, favourable coverage of Democrat campaign events decreased support for the Republican candidate. The strength of these media effects on voters' opinions was similar in the two years.

Further demonstrating an explicit link between the tone of people's attribute agendas and their opinions, Spanish citizens' ratings of six major political figures on a ten-point scale ranging from 'highly unfavourable' to 'highly favourable' were compared with their descriptions of these men in response to the widely used 'what would you tell a friend' question.[20] Responses to this open-ended question were coded into a descriptive matrix defined by six substantive categories and five affective categories, a finer shading of affect than found in any previous evidence. These discrete descriptions provide a richness of detail to explain the images behind the parsimony of the ratings. For the six Spanish political leaders, the range of correlations between the citizens' sets of affective descriptions and their ratings for these men was +0.78 to +0.97, with the median falling between +0.82 and +0.90. Citizens who gave a leader a low rating on the ten-point scale produced descriptions with substantially negative content. Citizens who gave high ratings produced highly positive descriptions.

Moving beyond political leaders to the broader arena of public affairs, analysis of the 1974 US National Election Study found that readers of newspapers with higher degrees of adverse criticism of politics and public affairs had higher levels of cynicism.[21] The ninety-four newspapers examined varied considerably in the proportion of critical front-page stories. Some published as few as one in ten while in others a majority of the front-page articles contained negative criticisms. The impact of this negative tone on readers' degree of cynicism was consistent across citizens varying in educational level from grade school to college as well as among persons varying in their exposure to national television news and reading about national politics in the daily newspaper.

Effects of tone are not limited to attitudes and opinions about politics. Negative newspaper headlines about the economy influence the public's perceptions about the health of the economy.[22] In turn, these opinions become self-fulfilling prophecies as people adjust their behaviour to fit their beliefs. Comparisons of economic headlines in the *New York Times*, monthly measures of consumer sentiment about the health of the economy, and major monthly statistical indicators of the actual economy from 1980 through 1993 found a series of significant agenda-setting effects:

> rising numbers of 'ailing economy' headlines appeared to dampen subsequent consumer sentiment, and positive economic headlines boosted consumer sentiment. . . . Further evidence of a strong media influence was manifested in the relationship between leading indicators and economic headlines . . . These results suggest that the amount and tone of economic news exerted a powerful influence on the economic environment and further, that the economic news agenda was generally not being set by prevailing economic conditions.[23]

This converging evidence about priming effects and about the effects of both substantive attributes and affective tone in media messages demonstrates that both the first and second levels of agenda-setting have consequences for opinions and attitudes and even public behaviour.

Forming opinions

To begin at the beginning, there is a fundamental link between the salience of objects in the mass media and the formation of opinions by the audience. With increasing salience of public figures in the news, for example, more people form an opinion about these persons. An examination of the variation in news coverage on US presidential candidates across the five elections between 1980 and 1996, a pattern of media emphasis that varied widely across these elections, found strong correspondence between this pattern and the proportion of citizens from election to election who expressed ambivalent opinions about the candidates by checking the mid-point of rating scales used in the National Election Studies.[24] Twenty of the twenty-four comparisons – six media agendas × Democrat/Republican candidates ×

strong/weak partisans – between the trends in media salience and public opinion across these years were significant, with a median value of −0.90. Note that this correlation is negative because high salience for a candidate in the media was associated with a low number of people selecting the neutral mid-point on the rating scales. Conversely, low media coverage corresponds to larger numbers of people marking the mid-point.

In the German state of Baden-Württemberg, the personal salience of two major issues, the reunification of East and West Germany and East German migrants, was strongly linked to both the strength and the direction of personal opinions.[25] For the strength of opinion on both issues, personal salience was a far stronger predictor than media exposure or demographic characteristics. For the direction of opinion, personal salience was a slightly stronger predictor than age for German reunification. For the direction of opinion about East German migrants, personal salience was equal in strength to the use of television and only a slightly weaker predictor than education.

Attitudes, opinions and behaviour

Extensive news coverage of crime and violence, including a murder and a number of rapes, on the University of Pennsylvania campus a few years ago contributed to a significant drop in applications by potential first-year students.[26] This decline in applications occurred predominantly among women. Moreover, other comparable universities experienced an increase in applications during the same period.

Another example of media influence on the behaviour of young adults is Harvard University's successful use of entertainment television programming to spread the idea of 'the designated driver', that member of a party group who abstains from drinking in order to drive his or her friends home safely afterwards.[27]

News about aeroplane crashes and skyjackings offers another example of a link between mass communication and risk avoidance behaviour.[28] Analysis explicitly grounded in agenda-setting theory hypothesized that news about crashes in which ten or more persons died or news about skyjackers' control of an airborne plane increased the salience of the danger of flying. Two complementary sets of evidence about people's behaviour were collected in a middle-sized American city, the number of passengers purchasing tickets and purchasing flight insurance over a five-year period. Box 8.3 compares high salience weeks – those weeks when there were fatal crashes or skyjackings – with low salience weeks for each of the five years. As

Box 8.3 Individual behaviour in response to news of plane crashes and skyjackings

	Average ticket sales		Average insurance sales	
	Low salience weeks	High salience weeks	Low salience weeks	High salience weeks
1969	4,493	4,030	52	56
1970	4,798	4,302	58	63
1971	5,014	4,601	60	64
1972	5,412	4,789	63	69
1973	5,667	5,021	68	74

Source: A study conducted by Alexander Bloj for McCombs's communication theory course, which was reported in Maxwell McCombs and Donald Shaw, 'A progress report on agenda-setting research', paper presented at the Association for Education in Journalism, San Diego, CA, 1974.

expected, ticket sales dipped in high salience weeks and, conversely, flight insurance sales increased. The differences in these complementary behaviours are striking. The media agenda does far more than influence the pictures in our heads. Many times the media influence our attitudes and opinions and even our behaviour.

Issue salience can be a significant predictor of citizens' actual votes on election day.[29] Beyond influencing the salience of issues on the public agenda, the media's agenda can at times also advantage a particular political party because of issue ownership, the perception among voters that one political party is more capable than another of handling certain issues. In the US, Democrats own most social welfare issues while Republicans own most defence issues.[30] Media emphasis on one of these issues will not only influence its salience, which is the traditional agenda-setting effect. That salience can also translate into behaviour, votes for the party that owns the issue.[31]

An analysis of the 1990 election for governor of Texas also found that a composite of issue positions and the images of the candidates were significant predictors of how citizens voted on election day.[32] This latter evidence amplifies a two-step model theorizing that political advertisements, mixed with elements from the news, shape voters' overall pictures of the candidates and influence their ballot decision.[33] Additional evidence about the impact of these candidate images among the public was found for a person's intention to vote during the 1998 Texas primary election.[34]

Recent investigations in the US and Japan document a variety of complementary outcomes that result from object salience on the media agenda. The details are reported in box 8.4 for three kinds of

Box 8.4 Impact on three behaviours of object salience on the media agenda		
US 2000 presidential election[a]	*Japanese experiment*[b]	
[Granger analysis of impact]	[% of subjects who changed]	
	Exposed to interpretative frame	Exposed to fragmentary frame
'Discussed the campaign' $R^2 = +0.68$[c] Impact of media $= +7\%$	*'Want to discuss the issue'* 58.3	50.2
'Thought about the campaign' $R^2 = +0.65$ Impact of media $= +7\%$	*'Want more information on the issue'* 69.5	60.6
'Paid attention to the campaign' $R^2 = +0.54$ Impact of media $= +4\%$	*'Greater interest in the issue'* 53.5	44.2

[a](US) Object = the presidential campaign
[b](Japan) Object = lowest priority issue
[c]This Granger analysis uses the squared value of r, the correlation coefficient frequently cited in this book, as a measure of how much of the dependent variable (e.g., amount of recent discussion of the campaign) is explained by previous levels of the dependent variable plus exposure to the media. Because R^2 is based on r, the range of values is the same, namely -1 to 0 to $+1$.
Source: Robert L. Stevenson, Rainer Bohme and Nico Nickel, 'The TV agenda-setting influence on campaign 2000', *Egyptian Journal of Public Opinion Research*, 2, 1 (2001), pp. 29–50, and Tsuneo Ogawa, 'Framing and agenda setting function', *Keio Communication Review*, 23 (2001), pp. 71–80.

outcomes: discussion, reflection and a desire for more information, and attention and interest. In the US, Granger analysis was used to assess the impact on each of these outcomes by the week-to-week salience of the 2000 US presidential campaign in national television news – measured by the amount of time devoted to election coverage.[35] Because a major determinant of any behaviour, such as discussing the election, is the level of that behaviour in previous weeks, the Granger analysis initially measured this impact for each of the three outcomes using national surveys across twenty-nine weeks of the campaign. The analysis then added the salience of the election on the television agenda as a predictor of the outcome. As we see in box 8.4, the media agenda significantly impacted all three outcomes.

In a Japanese experiment, the effects of object salience in the media are demonstrated in the amount of change found for three behaviours related to each subject's lowest priority issue among the four unobtrusive issues measured.[36] This evidence also adds to our previous discussion in chapter 6 about framing and compelling arguments. Half of the subjects read articles about their lowest priority issue that contained only bare facts, the typical objective and fragmentary style employed by journalists for spot news. The other half read interpretative articles about their lowest priority issue that forecast the impact of the issue on the reader. Although there is consistently greater change among subjects reading the interpretative news articles, both frames produced large amounts of change in all three outcomes. For example, more than half of the subjects (regardless of which frame they saw) wanted more information about their lowest priority issue and wanted to discuss it more.

These complementary sets of behaviours from two very different cultures and based on very different techniques of investigation are compelling evidence for the consequences of media agenda-setting.[37] These outcomes also have implications for need for orientation, the psychological concept discussed in chapter 4. Arguably, there is impact here on both components of need for orientation, the perceived personal relevance of the topic and the adequacy of one's knowledge about the topic. Perceived personal relevance also accounts for the greater impact of the interpretative frame in the Japanese experiment. In short, this evidence cantilevers from some core ideas in agenda-setting theory into new portions of our theoretical map.

A 1988 Indiana Poll brought together all these aspects of agenda-setting and its consequences.[38] Replicating a familiar pattern, the salience among the public of a major issue of that time – the US federal budget deficit – was significantly correlated with frequency of exposure to both newspapers and television news. Further, issue salience in conjunction with use of a single medium, television news, predicted the strength of people's opinions on this issue, while issue salience in combination with newspaper reading predicted actual behaviour, such as writing a letter or attending a meeting about the deficit. Here in a single setting is evidence of significant relationships between media exposure and issue salience and of subsequent effects by both on knowledge, opinions and observable behaviour.

Agenda-setting role of business news

Evidence of a link between agenda-setting effects and public behaviour was found in investor reactions to stories in *Fortune*.[39] During a three-year period when the Standard & Poor 500 stock market index increased 2.3 per cent, the stocks of fifty-four companies featured in

Fortune magazine increased 3.6 per cent. Companies receiving favourable coverage increased the most, 4.7 per cent, but any escalation in the salience of these companies resulted in some increase, 1.9 per cent with negative coverage and 1.7 per cent with neutral coverage.

This investigation was an opening gambit in a growing new arena – the agenda-setting influence of business news on the public. One well-developed specialization in this arena is corporate reputations,[40] particularly the agenda-setting influence of business coverage[41] on the images of corporations and their CEOs among the public[42] and the economic consequences of this influence.[43] Business journalism, ranging from venerable outlets such as the *Financial Times* and the *Wall Street Journal* to the proliferation of new cable channels, can have substantial attribute agenda-setting effects with major consequences for opinions and behaviour.

Another aspect of agenda-setting theory, the influence of news sources on the media agenda, is also key in this specialized arena. Chapter 7 discussed the influence of press releases in the context of public affairs – issue agendas during election campaigns, news about state government agencies, and coverage of AIDS, polio and other public health issues. Press releases and corporate web sites are also key sources of business news,[44] everything from routine reports on corporate economic performance to major shifts in business strategies.[45] The business news agenda has become a significant aspect of the agenda-setting role of mass communication.

Summing up

The agenda-setting effects of mass communication have significant implications beyond the pictures created in people's heads. In the original, traditional domain of agenda-setting, the salience of public issues, there is considerable evidence that the shifting salience of these issues is often the basis for public opinion about the overall performance in office of a public leader. In turn, the salience of a public figure in the news is also linked with whether an individual holds any opinion at all. At the second level of agenda-setting, the salience of affective attributes intertwined with the public's cognitive pictures of these leaders represents the convergence of attribute agenda-setting with opinion formation and change. Beyond attitudes and opinions, the pictures of reality created by the mass media have implications for personal behaviours, ranging from college applications to voting on election day.

9 Mass Communication and Society

Mass communication has three broad social roles: surveillance of the larger environment, achieving consensus among the segments of society, and transmission of the culture.[1] The process of agenda-setting detailed in the previous chapters is a significant part of the surveillance role, contributing substantial portions of our pictures about the greater environment. The agenda-setting process also has major implications for social consensus and transmission of culture, implications that take agenda-setting theory beyond its traditional setting in political communication.

As the roving spotlights of the media move from object to object and across the attributes of those objects in their surveillance of the environment, a variety of learning occurs among the public. Initially, through exposure to the mass media, people become aware of major elements in the environment beyond their immediate personal ken and ascribe particular importance to a select few. This aspect of learning is the core of the agenda-setting process. Within this core is the assumption – sometimes explicitly measured, but frequently not – that the degree of correspondence between the media agenda and the public agenda tends to increase with greater exposure to the media. Increased acquisition of the media agenda as a result of increased exposure to the media was explicitly documented for both the first and second levels of agenda-setting in the 1993 Japanese general election[2] and in extensive detail for the second level in the 1995 Spanish local elections.[3] As a consequence of the media's surveillance, the public forms its pictures about the important elements in that environment, the key objects and their most salient attributes.

Consideration of mass communication's role in achieving social consensus links agenda-setting effects resulting from increased exposure with the conclusion in chapter 3 that 'media agenda-setting effects are not manifested in creating different levels of salience among individuals, but are evident at driving the salience of *all* individuals up and down over time.'[4] A reasonable inference from these two outcomes taken in tandem is that the differences often found between demographic groups in public opinion polls – differences between men and women, or younger and older adults, for example – decrease with greater exposure to the mass media. Specifically, the correspondence between the agendas of various demographic groups should increase with greater exposure to the mass media.

Seminal evidence from the North Carolina Poll supports this view of agenda-setting and consensus.[5] Comparison of the issue agendas for men and for women who read a daily newspaper infrequently yielded a modest correlation of +0.55. However, for men and for women who read a daily newspaper occasionally, the degree of correspondence was +0.80 for the agenda of the most important problems facing the nation. Among men and women who read regularly, the issue agendas were identical (+1.0). Similar patterns of increased consensus about the most important issues facing the nation as a result of greater exposure to the newspaper were found in comparisons of the young and the old and of blacks and whites. Increased consensus among various demographic groups in conjunction with increased media exposure was also true for television news audiences.

Similar patterns of social consensus resulting from exposure to the news media have also been found in Taiwan and Spain.[6] These patterns of consensus among various demographic groups are summarized in box 9.1. Of course, given the considerable cultural and political diversity underlying any comparison of Spain, Taiwan and the United States, the lack of absolutely identical patterns in box 9.1 is hardly surprising.

The most frequent occurrence in these three countries of increasing consensus with greater use of the news media is found in the comparisons of men and women and of persons with high and low formal education. For men and women, there is evidence of increasing consensus in all three countries. In Spain and the US, where exposure to both newspapers and television news was measured, there is a newspaper effect but no television effect. In Taiwan, where only television was measured, there is a television effect.

Box 9.1 Patterns of social consensus with increasing use of the news media among demographic groups in Spain, Taiwan and the US

	Spain		Taiwan	US	
Demographic groups	Newspaper	TV news	TV news	Newspaper	TV news
Sex	YES*	NO	YES	YES	NO
Education	YES	YES	YES	NO	NO
Age	NO	NO		YES	YES
Income			YES	NO	NO
Race (black/white)				YES	YES

*YES means that, for demographic groups defined by this trait (e.g., men and women), the degree of correlation between the groups increases with greater use of newspapers or TV news. NO means that this pattern of increased correlation between the groups is absent.

Sources: Esteban Lopez-Escobar, Juan Pablo Llamas and Maxwell McCombs, 'Una dimension social do los efectos do los medios de difusion: agenda-setting y consenso', Comunicacion y Sociedad IX (1996), pp. 91–125; Ching-Yi Chiang, 'Bridging and closing the gap of our society: social function of media agenda setting', unpublished master's thesis, University of Texas at Austin, 1995; Donald Shaw and Shannon Martin, 'The function of mass media agenda setting', Journalism Quarterly, 69 (1992), pp. 902–20.

For the comparisons based on education, there are newspaper and television news effects in Spain, again a television effect in Taiwan, and no effects for either medium in the US. For the other demographic groups, the results vary from country to country. Overall, eleven of the nineteen comparisons in box 9.1 show a pattern of increased consensus resulting from greater exposure to the mass media.

Comparisons of demographic groups are a useful starting point in exploring the extent to which the agenda-setting role of mass communication contributes to social consensus. Everyone is familiar with these demographic comparisons that are so frequently found in the reporting on polling results. Further elaboration of mass communication's contribution to social consensus should include psychological characteristics that better tap individual differences and involvement in society. Demographics are, at best, broad-brush surrogates for people's life situation.

Transmission of culture

Aspects of mass communication's third social role, the transmission of culture, are also linked with the agenda-setting process. Media and public agendas of issues, political candidates and their attributes – all those elements that are the central focus of this book – rest on the foundations of the larger civic culture defined by a fundamental agenda of beliefs about democracy and society. Intriguing new applications of the theory explore other agenda-setting institutions that are also part of this civic culture, such as organized religion and schools.

Exploration of the media's role in the transmission of yet other cultural agendas is moving agenda-setting theory across new intellectual frontiers and far beyond its traditional realm of public affairs. These new lines of cultural inquiry extend from the historical agenda defining a society's collective memory of the past to the contemporary agenda of attributes defining the ideal physical appearance of young women and men.

Beginning with the traditional focus of agenda-setting on public issues, media issue agendas often simultaneously convey significant messages about the civic culture, that set of beliefs and activities that define the environment in which these issues arise and are acted upon. Taking the larger view, the agenda-setting influence of the media on these broad civic attitudes is far more important than any agenda-setting effects on specific issues and opinions. For example, the social health of any democracy is determined to a considerable degree by its civic culture regarding participation in elections. In the United States, where politics does not occupy a prominent position on the personal agenda of most citizens, the most significant agenda-setting role of the mass media may be to stimulate political interest every four years and position the presidential election on citizens' agendas.

An early look at this agenda-setting role during the 1976 US presidential election found that exposure to television news in the late spring stimulated political interest in the summer and fall months leading up to the November election.[7] Unfortunately, this positive contribution to the civic culture is offset by an array of evidence that the predilection of US political journalists to emphasize the negative attributes of politics has negative consequences for the civic culture. This downside of media agenda-setting is summarized by the titles of two widely cited books on political journalism and voters' responses: Joseph Cappella and Kathleen Hall Jamieson's *Spiral of Cynicism*[8] and Thomas Patterson's *Out of Order*.[9] Also recall from the previous chapter that readers of newspapers with higher degrees of adverse criticism of politics and public affairs expressed higher levels of cynicism.[10] From the perspective of agenda-setting theory, these outcomes are hardly surprising. Repetition of negative civic themes year after year makes these negative perspectives about politics highly salient.

This agenda-setting role of the mass media regarding the civic culture also defines a new approach to media criticism focused on the social consequences of journalistic practice. Traditional media criticism concentrates on the accuracy and fairness of media content. This new media criticism prompted by agenda-setting theory, especially attribute agenda-setting, considers the perspective and style of media messages in tandem with their impact on the public.[11]

New agenda-setting arenas

Another social institution with a major role in the definition of culture, as well as a major role in its transmission, is organized religion. Even within the relatively narrow civic realm of public affairs, religious agendas can exert major impact.[12]

> During the 1992 presidential election campaign, religious communication apparently kept abortion on the public agenda even though mass media attention was minimal. For a small number of subjects, all members of fundamentalist churches that encouraged their members to see a threat to their freedom, constitutional issues ranging from prayer in public schools to support for gun ownership were the most important issues even though those concerns were not part of media discourse about the presidential election.[13]

Quite apart from public affairs, religious agendas can have highly significant effects on the personal lives of adherents. The empirical evidence to date only hints at the agenda-setting influence of religious messages on people's patterns of behaviour.[14]

Sometimes overlapping the civic agenda, but occupying a broader cultural niche, is collective memory, which is a highly selective agenda of past events and situations that dominate the public's view of their historical identity.[15] These cultural myths, which are often highly salient in how a group, region or nation recalls its past, frequently bear little resemblance to factual historical reconstruction. Understanding the nature and origins of our collective memories requires examining particularly the influence of mass media narratives on personal recollections about the past.

Deep personal recollections shape the collective memory in many nations of the Great Depression, World War II and other emotionally charged times. But as new generations join the age cohort who lived through those times, the narratives of the mass media begin to move towards centre stage.[16] In a very real sense, each generation writes its own history and develops its own collective memory of the past. For millions of young Americans, their perspective on the assassination of President John F. Kennedy has been shaped largely by the agenda of filmmaker Oliver Stone. And in these young people's picture of the Watergate scandal that drove President Richard Nixon from office, actor Robert Redford is *Washington Post* journalist Bob Woodward.

As we go farther back into the historical past, the narratives of the mass media, which include popular books and school textbooks as well as films and the news media's commemoration of selected past events, hold even greater sway over the public agenda. This is true for both the first level of agenda-setting – which past events are even salient – and the second level of agenda-setting – the specific aspects and details of these events that are prominent in our memory. 'The media know how to tell stories, and they are more capable of creating legends than the traditional agents of memory', noted Israeli scholar Yoram Peri.[17]

Schools are the other great agenda-setter for our collective memories. Content analyses of school textbooks identify those aspects of the past that a society wishes to emphasize or ignore. Here again the phenomenon of interest is the transfer of salience from one agenda to another, a role at least implicitly acknowledged from time to time as educators and the public debate how the past shall be remembered in school textbooks and the curriculum. Of course, collective memories are far from the only cultural and personal agendas influenced by schools. In Spain a creative application of agenda-setting examined the agenda of professional values that is central in the education of future journalists in the university classroom.[18]

Despite the conservative orthodoxy of many academics who oppose these departures from the original domain of agenda-setting theory, inquiries of this nature will certainly continue in the future. Back in the early 1980s, in response to the question 'Who sets the media's agenda?', there were also scholars who proclaimed that area beyond the realm of agenda-setting theory. But the theory continues to thrive in new domains.

Other cultural agendas

'Our cultural sense of what is new and important – our cultural agenda – comes largely from what plays on television', observed Lawrence Wenner.[19] And today a significant portion of that televised agenda worldwide is professional sports. An example par excellence of the effects that this television agenda can produce is the ballooning popularity of professional basketball in the United States during recent decades. In *The Ultimate Assist*, John Fortunato details how the commercial partnership of the National Basketball Association and the US television networks used strategies grounded in both first- and second-level agenda-setting to build their audiences.[20] First-level effects, the increased salience of NBA games, was achieved, in part, by the careful positioning of the best teams and players on the national television schedule. Second-level effects, the enhancement of professional basketball's image, were achieved through the creative production of player and coach interviews, announcer commentary, illustrative graphics, instant replays and other elements that framed the sport in exciting ways. And it worked, both on television and at the games themselves. In the 1969–70 season, fourteen NBA teams played 574 games that drew 4.3 million fans to courtside. Thirty years later, in the 1999–2000 season, twenty-nine NBA teams played 1,198 games that drew 20.1 million fans to courtside. During this same thirty-year period, NBA revenue from television grew from less than $10 million to more than $2 billion a season. Agenda-setting, the theory, also can be agenda-setting, the business plan.

Turning to a highly personal aspect of the cultural agenda, there is growing evidence that, even more than movie stars did in the past, contemporary mass communication influences the salience of physical appearance, especially the attribute of thinness among young women and muscularity among young men. The 'tyranny of thinness' is the epithet some social critics apply to the messages of the fashion magazines, with their pencil-like models, and to their sister clones who fill many of the female roles on television. In *The Beauty Myth*, Naomi Wolf succinctly notes that these contemporary role models weigh less than 95 per cent of the population.[21]

Feeding off this norm of thinness, if not actively propagating it, is a continuous flow of books and magazine articles on dieting. Among the audience for these messages emphasizing thinness, there often is a behavioural response – sometimes to the extreme reflected in such eating disorders as anorexia nervosa. Although the precise relationship between eating disorders and the cultural agenda of the mass media is difficult to establish, a substantial increase in eating disorders among women in the Fiji Islands was observed after the introduction there of Western television programming.[22]

Another aspect of this contemporary cultural agenda is the synergy between the traditional media of mass communication and the merchandising of children's toys. The *New York Times Magazine* noted how the physiques of two popular children's toys, Barbie and GI Joe, have radically changed over the years. Barbie has become more svelte and GI Joe more muscular.[23] This focus on body image – these agendas of attributes defining ideal physiques for young females and males – shifts the phenomenon of agenda-setting far away from its traditional realm in public issues. Nevertheless, the underlying process is the same, the transfer of salience from the messages of the mass media – and mass marketed merchandise – to the public agenda.

Social roles of agenda-setting

Beyond its well-established role in the surveillance of the environment, the agenda-setting influence of the mass media is also apparent in the creation of consensus among the segments of society and in the transmission of social culture. Substantial international evidence documents the effects of media exposure on greater agreement about the major issues of the day. Other intriguing findings suggest a key media role in such disparate aspects of our culture as political participation, collective memory and personal body images.

The summary outline of agenda-setting effects and their consequences presented in box 9.2 is a greatly expanded view of the agenda-setting phenomenon that we began with in chapter 1. The imprint of the mass media that begins with its agenda-setting influence is found on many aspects of public opinion and behaviour, and there remains much more for enterprising explorers and surveyors to map. However, the basic general model underlying the diagram in box 9.2 – and the future expansions of this diagram to include many other agendas – is parsimonious:

$$\text{AGENDA} \rightarrow \text{transfer of salience} \rightarrow \text{AGENDA}$$

In the original formulation of agenda-setting, these were the media agenda and the public agenda of issues. More specifically, we now talk about the media agenda and public agenda of objects or the media agenda and public agenda of attributes. Moreover, a growing variety of specific labels can be applied to this general model. This chapter suggests studying the church and school agendas. In short, the general model can be applied in a wide variety of rather disparate settings, which is to say that a variety of operational definitions can be used in the applications of agenda-setting theory. There are many agendas in the contemporary world, and there are many different agenda-setters – family and friends, the schools and the media,

Box 9.2   A map of agenda-setting and its consequences

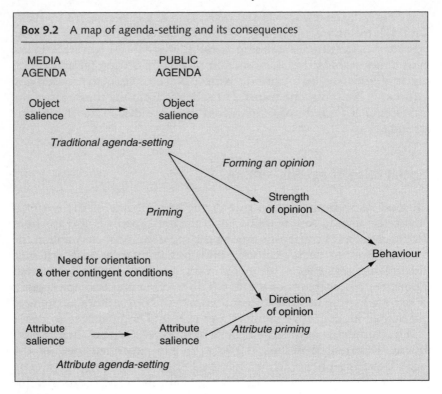

among others. However, like Julius Caesar in ancient Rome, the mass media frequently are first among equals in the shaping of contemporary life.

However, a recent addition to agenda-setting theory, the concept of agenda-melding, centres on the personal agendas of individuals vis-à-vis their community and group affiliations.[24] Individuals seek social affiliations for many reasons, and those who join a community or group, even vicariously, tend to match their own priorities to those of the group. Agenda-melding elaborates the concept of need for orientation, explaining why people may find some agendas more relevant than others, namely, because of their affiliation with certain communities or groups. In this theoretical setting, personal agendas are compared to a wide range of other agendas extending from the mass media and widely accessible web sites to other individuals.

In these new settings considered by agenda-melding, as well as in the traditional settings of agenda-setting, the core axiom of agenda-setting theory about the transfer of salience from one agenda to another provides parsimony in our theoretical vocabulary. Despite the juxtaposition from time to time in the literature of the terms agenda-setting and agenda-building, there is no fundamental difference between the two. It is a distinction without a difference. Agenda-setting theory in its fundamental form is about the transfer of salience among agendas. Most commonly, people think about the transfer of salience from the media agenda to the public agenda. But agenda-setting theory also considers many other agendas, such as the agendas of news sources and policy-makers, and some apply the term agenda-building to the process of salience transfer among a series of agendas. To be parsimonious, the process involved in the transfer of salience from one agenda to another or in the transfer of salience among many agendas is agenda-setting. There is no need for a separate term.

A horizontal model of agenda-setting might be a simple dyad grounded in two agendas – such as the traditional media and public agenda comparisons – or a more complex analysis linking a sequence of multiple agendas – such as the comparisons of the campaign, media and public agendas in chapter 7. The core theoretical proposition is the same in both settings, the transfer of salience. There also is a vertical version of agenda-setting that has sometimes been termed agenda-building. Recall the comment by Doris Graber in chapter 5:

> The media set the agenda when they are successful in riveting attention on a problem. They build the public agenda when they supply the context that determines how people think about the issue and evaluate its merits.[25]

Her distinction is between first-level and second-level agenda-setting – the distinction between attention and comprehension – and the phrase 'build the public agenda' is used descriptively rather than invoking a separate concept. Again, in the interest of parsimony, we can limit our vocabulary to the term agenda-setting and specify the setting in which we are examining the transfer of salience.

Three stages of agenda-setting theory

Our theoretical map of agenda-setting, which began in Chapel Hill over thirty-five years ago with an investigation of news media influence on the issues that voters regarded as important, has evolved into a multi-faceted theory applicable to a wide range of international settings. Here in the opening decade of a new century, the continuing evolution of this theoretical map can be described in terms of three stages:

- explication of five phases of the mass communication and public opinion process;
- expansion into new domains beyond public affairs and mass communication;
- elaboration of the basic theoretical concepts.

The first of these stages, the expansion of agenda-setting theory to five phases of the communication process, historically has been dominant. A wealth of scholarly activity has mapped – and continues to map – the influence of the news media agenda on the public agenda in regard to both attention and comprehension; the role of need for orientation and other contingent conditions in enhancing or constricting this influence; the influence of external agendas on the agenda of individual news media; and the consequences of all this agenda-setting activity for attitudes, opinions and behaviour. The major goal of this book is an orderly and systematic presentation of what we know about these five facets, a *Gray's Anatomy* of agenda-setting theory.

Creative scholars have also opened another stage of agenda-setting theory that is vastly different from the traditional concern with public affairs. At present, this stage is a loose confederation of explorations in domains as diverse as business and finance, cultural norms, professional sports and the college classroom. With the tremendous expansion of business and financial news in recent years, especially in daily newspapers and on cable television, this area may come to centre stage as a companion of public affairs. Regardless, in all of these domains, whether established or exploratory, the theoretical core remains constant: the transfer of salience from one agenda to another.

Simultaneous with these scholarly explorers venturing into new domains, theoretical surveyors have returned to examine key established concepts of agenda-setting theory and to draw new, more finely detailed maps. These new mapping ventures include the concepts of salience, need for orientation, and attributes and frames. The discussion in chapter 5 of diverse measures of salience noted, in passing, three dimensions of public salience: social salience, personal salience and emotional arousal.[26] Recent work suggests that these dimensions of public salience complement, at least in part, three recently mapped dimensions of media salience: attention, prominence and valence.[27] Merging these independent efforts at theoretical map-making seems promising. Other contemporary work further explicates the need for orientation. One approach seeks to broaden our understanding of its components, relevance and uncertainty, both in terms of their origins in personal characteristics and in terms of how people perceive and use the news media.[28] Another approach explicates three alternative components of need for orientation: personal involvement, knowledge, and the amount of effort required to acquire information.[29] Finally, chapter 6 illustrates the continuing dialogue regarding the convergence of attribute agenda-setting and framing.

Turning back to theoretical basics simultaneous with movement outwards to new domains as well as the continuing mapping of the basic five facets of traditional agenda-setting theory presents an intriguing agenda of future activity. To paraphrase Sherlock Holmes's call to adventure, 'Come, the game is afoot.'

Epilogue

New technologies, especially communication technologies, have a magical ability to create fantastic visions about a vastly changed future. In their historical turns, the telegraph, telephone, radio, television, and now the internet have spawned visionary scenarios, often utopian ones, about revolutionary changes in our society. Prominent among these changes predicted for a future with numerous and diverse sources of news and information available on the internet is the end of agenda-setting influence as we have known it during past decades.

There is no question that the internet has already greatly expanded the array of news and information sources on public issues and just about any other topic you can imagine. A vast virtual library of news and information is available with just a few keystrokes. This library includes the electronic versions of many traditional media, ranging from CNN Online to the online versions of hundreds of daily newspapers. For those who prefer to go directly to the sources of news and public affairs information, more and more public records from government at every level are available online, the electronic analogue of a vastly expanded C-Span service that allows you to sift through all the information for yourself. There are also numerous archive and reference services online that assemble virtual warehouses of information, everything from the results of public opinion polls and statistics of every variety to the back issues of newspapers and magazines over many years, even the collected works of numerous authors and scholars. Add to this the web sites of foundations, special interest groups, political parties and candidates, and even individuals offering information and commentary to advance their point of view, and the contemporary virtual equivalent of the famous library of Alexandria is now available in homes, offices and libraries around the world.

There are a lot of agendas out there readily available to the public. Some social observers predict the end of agenda-setting as audiences fragment and virtually everyone has a unique media agenda that is a highly individualized composite constructed from this vast wealth of news and information sources. The result of these idiosyncratic personal agendas will be a public agenda characterized by diversity and the scattering of attention. Perhaps, from this point of view, it is incorrect even to speak of a public agenda other than as a loose confederation of individual agendas.

This is a vision of the future grounded in a multitude of media agendas and personal agendas with little social cohesion, a vision that spells the end of agenda-setting as we have known it. This perspective on the future is the antithesis of the longstanding situation in mass communication characterized by large audiences receiving highly redundant agendas from the media. As previously noted, the initial observations in Chapel Hill of the agenda-setting influence of the news found substantial similarity – a median correlation of $+0.71$ – among the nine media agendas that were those voters' dominant sources of news and information.

Obviously, this high degree of similarity is not found across the broad array of web sites on the internet, leading to the prediction that the era of agenda-setting is coming to an end. But, like so many earlier prognostications about the magic of a new technology as the source of radical change, these predictions about the disappearance of any substantial agenda-setting influence as a potent social force may simply be wrong. That has already proved to be the case for a huge number of dot.com ventures that were going to transform the nature of commerce radically.

In any event, these predictions about the end of agenda-setting are grounded in a broad assumption that audiences will fragment and avail themselves of vastly different media agendas. Each individual – or small group of individuals – will use a different mix of these multiple sources of news and information, patterns of behaviour that will result in a large number of highly idiosyncratic personal agendas. There is also a corollary expectation that the redundancy across outlets that has characterized mass communication for many decades will be greatly reduced as niche media offer very different agendas.

At present, there is little evidence to sustain these assumptions. Most of the news sites on the internet are subsidiaries of traditional

media, the online versions of newspapers, magazines, television networks and cable TV news channels. Large media conglomerates
whose interests spread across a variety of media outlets also own
many of the most popular sites. In this setting, the popular business
buzzword 'synergy' frequently means amortizing the costs and increasing the profits of news by distributing the same basic content
through numerous channels. Within news organizations, the software
frequently used to transfer content from its original source to the
internet is referred to as 'shovelware'. It is also the case that
the audiences for all these internet sites are very small. For many
online newspapers, most of the users are also regular readers of the
traditional printed edition. In short, a high degree of redundancy in
the media agendas to which the public is exposed is likely to continue
for at least the near future.

An additional major constraint on exposure to the agendas of
multiple web sites is time and effort. Few people have the time or
wish to expend the effort to explore this virtual library in any depth
except under extraordinary circumstances. Despite the plethora of
sites that could be accessed, there is already evidence of a de facto
oligopoly of news and information where a small number of sites
command the largest proportion of the internet users:

> And the internet is a fine thing for policy wonks and news junkies –
> anyone can now read Canadian and British newspapers, or download
> policy analyses from think tanks. But most people have neither the
> time nor the inclination. Realistically, the Net does little to reduce
> the influence of the big five sources.[1]

This pattern is analogous to that found in cable television where,
despite the common availability of fifty or even a hundred channels,
most members of the audience devote the vast majority of their time
to a mere handful of channels.

Although the internet offers the possibility of a *Daily Me* tailored to
precisely my personal interests, most individuals do not have the time
to construct such a news product from the myriad sources available
to them. And, even where software allows one to specify the categories of interest in advance – with more or less precision in their
approximation to one's actual interests – most members of the public
also want to know about the day's most important events regardless
of the category in which they fall.

Under these circumstances, editors will continue to edit – that is,
select and summarize from the vast daily array of news. The front
pages of newspapers and opening segments of TV newscasts are likely

to remain largely the same. It is possible that the specialized sections of newspapers and specialized portions of other news outlets will wither because each individual may rely on a *Daily Me* for this information – albeit a *Daily Me* constructed for the most part from a few favourite internet sources. But in terms of the major news of the day, there will still be a relatively homogenous media agenda, at least until someone invents a new kind of news that eclipses the traditional news audience. If that happens, it will be the result of journalistic creativity, not technology, and it will shift the agenda-setting influence of the news media to a new source.

Notes

Preface

1   *New York Times*, 8 March 2000, p. A3.
2   Polly Toynbee, 'Press ganged', *The Guardian*, 21 May 2003.
3   *New York Times*, 26 February 2001, p. C15.
4   Max Frankel, *The Times of My Life and My Life with the Times* (New York: Random House, 1999), pp. 414–15.
5   Theodore White, *The Making of the President, 1972* (New York: Bantam, 1973), p. 327.
6   Maxwell McCombs and Donald Shaw, 'The agenda-setting function of mass media', *Public Opinion Quarterly*, 36 (1972), pp. 176–87.
7   Contrary to a statement in a recent article that the phrase 'agenda-setting' was suggested by an anonymous reviewer of the original article published in the summer 1972 issue of *Public Opinion Quarterly*, Part I of the McCombs and Shaw report to the National Association of Broadcasters in June 1969 was titled 'The agenda-setting function of the mass media'. The title of the full report was 'Acquiring political information'. A revised version of this draft report was not submitted to *Public Opinion Quarterly* until several years later. The full misstatement about the origin of the phrase 'agenda-setting' with an anonymous reviewer, appearing in Robert L. Stevenson, Rainer Bohme and Nico Nikel, 'The TV agenda-setting influence on campaign 2000', *Egyptian Journal of Public Opinion Research*, 2, 1 (2001), p. 29, is: 'The phrase itself – apparently the suggestion of an anonymous reviewer of the original journal manuscript – is at home in several languages and rarely requires translation.'
8   Maxwell McCombs and Jian-Hua Zhu, 'Capacity, diversity, and volatility of the public agenda: trends from 1954 to 1994', *Public Opinion Quarterly*, 59 (1995), pp. 495–525. Also see Tom Smith, 'America's most important problem – a trend analysis, 1946–1976', *Public Opinion Quarterly*, 44 (1980), pp. 164–80. His follow-up analysis, 'The polls: America's most

important problems', is found in *Public Opinion Quarterly*, 49 (1985), pp. 264–74.

9   My thanks to John Pavlik for this metaphoric comparison, made during a conversation about this book on 12 September 2003 in Bonn, Germany.

10   David Weaver, who came to the University of North Carolina to study for his PhD shortly after the original 1968 Chapel Hill study, quickly gained a major role in the development of agenda-setting theory. His contribution as a graduate student during the 1972 US presidential election is detailed in chapter 4 and as a faculty member at Indiana University during the 1976 US presidential election in chapter 1. Many other contributions in the subsequent years are noted in other chapters.

11   James Dearing and Everett Rogers, *Agenda-Setting* (Thousand Oaks, CA: Sage, 1996).

12   Jay G. Blumler and Dennis Kavanagh, 'The third age of political communication: influences and features', *Political Communication*, 16 (1999), p. 225.

13   Michael Gurevitch and Jay Blumler, 'Political communication systems and democratic values', in *Democracy and the Mass Media*, ed. J. Lichtenberg (Cambridge: Cambridge University Press, 1990), pp. 269–89.

14   Tom Bettag, 'What's news? Evolving definitions of news', *Harvard International Journal of Press/Politics*, 5, 3 (2000), p. 105.

15   Davis Merritt and Maxwell McCombs, *The Two W's of Journalism: The Why and What of Public Affairs Reporting* (Mahwah, NJ: Lawrence Erlbaum, 2003).

Chapter 1   Influencing Public Opinion

1   Walter Lippmann, *Public Opinion* (New York: Macmillan, 1922), p. 29.

2   Robert Park, 'News as a form of knowledge', *American Journal of Sociology*, 45 (1940), pp. 667–86.

3   Bernard Cohen, *The Press and Foreign Policy* (Princeton, NJ: Princeton University Press, 1963), p. 13.

4   Lippmann, *Public Opinion*, pp. 17–20.

5   Ibid., p. 3.

6   Ibid., p. 4.

7   Paul Lazarsfeld, Bernard Berelson and Hazel Gaudet, *The People's Choice* (New York: Columbia University Press, 1944).

8   Joseph Klapper, *The Effects of Mass Communication* (New York: Free Press, 1960).

9   Maxwell McCombs and Donald Shaw, 'The agenda-setting function of mass media', *Public Opinion Quarterly*, 36 (1972), pp. 176–87.

10   Klapper, *The Effects of Mass Communication*, chapter II.

11   James Dearing and Everett Rogers, *Agenda Setting* (Thousand Oaks, CA: Sage, 1996).

12   Donald Shaw and Maxwell McCombs, eds, *The Emergence of American Political Issues* (St Paul, MN: West, 1977).

13   David Weaver, Doris Graber, Maxwell McCombs and Chaim Eyal, *Media Agenda Setting in a Presidential Election: Issues, Images and Interest* (Westport, CT: Greenwood, 1981).

14   James Winter and Chaim Eyal, 'Agenda setting for the civil rights issue', *Public Opinion Quarterly*, 45 (1981), pp. 376–83.

15   Stuart N. Soroka, 'Media, public opinion, and foreign policy', paper presented to the American Political Science Association, San Francisco, 2001.

16   Hans-Bernd Brosius and Hans Mathias Kepplinger, 'The agenda setting function of television news: static and dynamic views', *Communication Research*, 17 (1990), pp. 183–211. The public agenda was based on fifty-three consecutive national polls. Each week 1000 randomly sampled West Germans selected as many public issues as they desired from a list of sixteen public issues. To measure the media agenda, a continuous content analysis covered all news items in the four major West German television news programmes for the year. Altogether, 16,000 news stories were examined.

17   Howard Eaton Jr, 'Agenda setting with bi-weekly data on content of three national media', *Journalism Quarterly*, 66 (1989), pp. 942–8.

18   Kim Smith, 'Newspaper coverage and public concern about community issues', *Journalism Monographs*, 101 (1987).

19   Maria Jose Canel, Juan Pablo Llamas and Federico Rey, 'El primer nivel del efecto agenda setting en la informacion local: los "problemas mas importantes" de la ciudad de Pamplona' ['The first level agenda setting effect on local information: the "most important problems" of the city of Pamplona'], *Comunicacion y Sociedad*, 9, 1 & 2 (1996), pp. 17–38.

20   Toshio Takeshita, 'Agenda-setting effects of the press in a Japanese local election', *Studies of Broadcasting*, 29 (1993), pp. 193–216.

21   Federico Rey Lennon, 'Argentina: 1997 elecciones: los diarios nacionales y la campana electoral' ['The 1997 Argentina election: the national dailies and the electoral campaign'], report by the Freedom Forum and Austral University, 1998.

22   David Weaver, 'What voters learn from media', *Annals of the American Academy of Political and Social Science*, 546 (1996), pp. 34–47.

23   Alicia Casermeiro de Pereson, 'La jerarquizacion tematica y de imagen segun los medios, y su transferencia a los habitantes de la ciudad de Buenos Aires: aplicacion de la teoria de la agenda setting al caso Argentino' ['The ranking of themes and images according to the media, and their transfer to the citizens of Buenos Aires: application of agenda-setting theory to the Argentine case'], unpublished doctoral dissertation, Austral University, Buenos Aires, 2002.

24   McCombs and Shaw, 'The agenda-setting function of mass media'.

25   Shaw and McCombs, *The Emergence of American Political Issues*.

26   Weaver, Graber, McCombs and Eyal, *Media Agenda Setting in a Presidential Election*.

27   Winter and Eyal, 'Agenda setting for the civil rights issue'.

28   Eaton, 'Agenda setting with bi-weekly data on content of three national media'.

29 Brosius and Kepplinger, 'The agenda setting function of television news'.
30 Smith, 'Newspaper coverage and public concern about community issues'.
31 Shanto Iyengar and Donald Kinder, *News that Matters: Television and American Opinion* (Chicago: University of Chicago Press, 1987).
32 Tai-Li Wang, 'Agenda-setting online: an experiment testing the effects of hyperlinks in online newspapers', *Southwestern Mass Communication Journal*, 15, 2 (2000), pp. 59–70.
33 Scott L. Althaus and David Tewksbury, 'Agenda setting and the "new" news: patterns of issue importance among readers of the paper and online versions of the *New York Times*', *Communication Research*, 29 (2002), pp. 180–207. Quote is on p. 199.
34 Gerald Kosicki, 'Problems and opportunities in agenda-setting research', *Journal of Communication*, 43, 2 (1993), p. 117. The citations included in this statement by Kosicki as examples have been omitted.
35 Maxwell McCombs and Jian-Hua Zhu, 'Capacity, diversity, and volatility of the public agenda', *Public Opinion Quarterly*, 59 (1995), pp. 495–525. See also Smith, 'America's most important problem – a trend analysis, 1946–1976', *Public Opinion Quarterly*, 44 (1980), pp. 164–80. It should be noted that some agenda-setting studies use a paraphrase of the Gallup MIP question rather than the original wording.
36 The classic discussion of this assumption is found in Bernard Berelson, *Content Analysis in Communication Research* (New York: Free Press, 1952).
37 Kosicki, 'Problems and opportunities in agenda-setting research', pp. 104–5. However, chapter 4's discussion of the psychological basis of agenda-setting will introduce an additional concept beyond frequency of exposure to the media agenda that is central in the measurement of audience salience.
38 A meta-analysis of ninety empirical investigations found a mean correlation of +0.53, with most outcomes six points above or below the mean (+0.47 to +0.59). See Wayne Wanta and Salma Ghanem, 'Effects of agenda-setting', in *Meta-Analyses of Media Effects*, ed. Jennings Bryant and Rodney Carveth (Mahwah, NJ: Lawrence Erlbaum, forthcoming).
39 William Gamson, *Talking Politics* (New York: Cambridge University Press, 1992).
40 W. G. Mayer, *The Changing American Mind: How and Why American Public Opinion Changed between 1960 and 1988* (Ann Arbor: University of Michigan Press, 1992).

Chapter 2   Reality and the News

1 Ray Funkhouser, 'The issues of the sixties', *Public Opinion Quarterly*, 37 (1973), pp. 62–75.
2 Ibid., p. 72.
3 Hans Mathias Kepplinger and Herbert Roth, 'Creating a crisis: German mass media and oil supply in 1973–74', *Public Opinion Quarterly*, 43 (1979), pp. 285–96.

4   Maxwell McCombs, Edna Einsiedel and David Weaver, *Contemporary Public Opinion: Issues and the News* (Hillsdale, NJ: Lawrence Erlbaum, 1991), pp. 43–5. Also see Pamela Shoemaker, ed., *Communication Campaigns about Drugs* (Hillsdale, NJ: Lawrence Erlbaum, 1989), especially, Stephen Reese and Lucig Danielian, 'Intermedia influence and the drug issue: converging on cocaine', pp. 29–46; Danielian and Reese, 'A closer look at intermedia influences on agenda setting: the cocaine issue of 1986', pp. 47–66; and Pamela Shoemaker, Wayne Wanta and Dawn Leggett, 'Drug coverage and public opinion, 1972–1986', pp. 67–80.

5   William Gonzenbach, *The Media, the President, and Public Opinion: A Longitudinal Analysis of the Drug Issue, 1984–1991* (Mahwah, NJ: Lawrence Erlbaum, 1996). This longitudinal study of the drug issue, which adds the policy agenda to the traditional analysis of the media agenda–public agenda, is an excellent introduction to the exploration of this larger context of public opinion formation. Although the preponderance of evidence suggests that the major transmission of salience between the media and the public is from the media to the public, there appears to be considerably more fluctuation, for example, in the flow of this influence between the policy agenda and the media agenda. James Dearing and Everett Rogers, *Agenda Setting* (Thousand Oaks, CA: Sage, 1996), among others, note that most of the research involving policy agendas has evolved in isolation from the media-centred theory of agenda-setting discussed in this book.

6   Anthony Downs, 'Up and down with ecology: the "issue-attention cycle"', *The Public Interest*, 28 (1972), pp. 38–50.

7   Salma Ghanem, 'Media coverage of crime and public opinion: an exploration of the second level of agenda setting', unpublished doctoral dissertation, University of Texas at Austin, 1996. Ghanem's study of the discrepancy in Texas between the pattern of news coverage and the reality reflected in crime statistics is a detailed microcosm of the national situation. See Richard Morin, 'Crime time: the fear, the facts: how the sensationalism got ahead of the stats', *Outlook, The Washington Post* (30 January 1994), p. C1, and Dennis Lowry, Tam Ching Josephine Nio and Dennis Leitner, 'Setting the public fear agenda: a longitudinal analysis of network TV crime reporting, public perceptions of crime, and FBI crime statistics', *Journal of Communication*, 53, 1 (2003), pp. 61–73.

8   Margaret T. Gordon and Linda Heath, 'The news business, crime and fear', in *Reactions to Crime*, ed. Dan Lewis (Beverly Hills, CA: Sage, 1981). Excerpt reprinted in *Agenda Setting: Readings on Media, Public Opinion, and Policymaking*, ed. David Protess and Maxwell McCombs (Hillsdale, NJ: Lawrence Erlbaum, 1991), pp. 71–4. Another in-depth example of the disparity between news coverage and reality, in this case, local television news and the occurrence of crime in nineteen different US communities, is presented by J. T. Hamilton, *Channeling Violence* (Princeton, NJ: Princeton University Press, 1998).

9   The newshole of a newspaper is the total amount of space left on all the pages after the advertising is inserted on the pages. In other words,

the newshole is the total amount of space available for non-advertising material in the newspaper.

10 George Gerbner, Larry Gross, Michael Morgan, Nancy Signorielli and James Shanahan, 'Growing up with television: cultivation processes', in *Media Effects: Advances in Theory and Research*, 2nd edn, ed. Jennings Bryant and Dolf Zillmann (Mahwah, NJ: Lawrence Erlbaum, 1994), pp. 43–68.

11 Kimberly Gross and Sean Aday, 'The scary world in your living room and neighborhood: using local broadcast news, neighborhood crime rates, and personal experience to test agenda setting and cultivation', *Journal of Communication*, 53 (2003), pp. 411–26. Also see Lowry, Nio and Leitner, 'Setting the public fear agenda'.

12 'The statistical shark', *New York Times*, 6 September 2001, p. A26.

13 Christine Ader, 'A longitudinal study of agenda setting for the issue of environmental pollution', *Journalism & Mass Communication Quarterly*, 72 (1995), pp. 300–11.

14 Downs, 'Up and down with ecology: the "issue-attention cycle"'.

15 Gerald Kosicki, 'Problems and opportunities in agenda-setting research', *Journal of Communication*, 43, 2 (1993), pp. 108–9.

16 Gary T. Henry and Craig S. Gordon, 'Tracking issue attention: specifying the dynamics of the public agenda', *Public Opinion Quarterly*, 65 (2001), pp. 157–77.

17 An excellent example of the research examining individual issue agendas is Jack McLeod, Lee B. Becker and J. E. Byrnes, 'Another look at the agenda-setting function of the press', *Communication Research*, 1 (1974), pp. 131–66.

18 Richard L. Merritt, *Symbols of American Community, 1735–1775* (New Haven, CT: Yale University Press, 1966).

19 David Paul Nord, 'The politics of agenda setting in late 19th century cities', *Journalism Quarterly*, 58 (1981), p. 573.

20 Ibid., p. 570.

21 Jean Lange Folkerts, 'William Allen White's anti-populist rhetoric as an agenda-setting technique', *Journalism Quarterly*, 60 (1983), p. 29.

22 Funkhouser, 'The issues of the sixties'.

23 James Winter and Chaim Eyal, 'Agenda setting for the civil rights issue', *Public Opinion Quarterly*, 45 (1981), pp. 376–83.

24 Edward Caudill, 'An agenda-setting perspective on historical public opinion', in *Communication and Democracy: Exploring the Intellectual Frontiers in Agenda-Setting Theory*, ed. Maxwell McCombs, Donald Shaw and David Weaver (Mahwah, NJ: Lawrence Erlbaum, 1997), p. 179.

25 Ibid., p. 181.

26 For a theoretical discussion of how the 'language' of television routinely refracts reality, see G. Ray Funkhouwser and Eugene F. Shaw, 'How synthetic experience shapes social reality', *Journal of Communication*, 40, 2 (1990), pp. 75–87; and Jeffrey Scheuer, *The Sound Bite Society: Television and the American Mind* (New York: Four Walls Eight Windows, 1999), chapter III.

27 Jay G. Blumler and Dennis Kavanagh, 'The third age of political communication: influences and features', *Political Communication*, 16 (1999), pp. 209–30.

28 William Safire, 'Like father, unlike son', *New York Times*, 2 September 2002, p. A17.

Chapter 3   How Agenda-Setting Works

1   Pu-Tsung King, 'The press, candidate images, and voter perceptions', in *Communication and Democracy*, ed. Maxwell McCombs, Donald Shaw and David Weaver (Mahwah, NJ: Lawrence Erlbaum, 1997), pp. 29–40.

2   George A. Miller, 'The magic number seven, plus or minus two: some limits on our capacity for processing information', *Psychological Review*, 63 (1956), pp. 81–97.

3   W. R. Neuman, 'The threshold of public attention', *Public Opinion Quarterly*, 54 (1990), pp. 159–76.

4   Jian-Hua Zhu, 'Issue competition and attention distraction: a zero-sum theory of agenda setting', *Journalism Quarterly*, 68 (1992), pp. 825–36.

5   Tom Smith, 'America's most important problems – a trend analysis, 1946–1976', *Public Opinion Quarterly*, 44 (1980), pp. 164–80.

6   Maxwell McCombs and Jian-Hua Zhu, 'Capacity, diversity and volatility of the public agenda', *Public Opinion Quarterly*, 59 (1995), pp. 495–525.

7   Samuel Popkin, *The Reasoning Voter* (Chicago: University of Chicago Press, 1991), p. 36 (emphasis in original).

8   Ibid., p. 43.

9   McCombs and Zhu, 'Capacity, diversity and volatility of the public agenda'.

10 Wayne Wanta, *The Public and the National Agenda: How People Learn about Important Issues* (Mahwah, NJ: Lawrence Erlbaum, 1997), pp. 22–4.

11 P. E. Converse, quoted by Jian-Hua Zhu with William Boroson, 'Susceptibility to agenda setting: a cross-sectional and longitudinal analysis of individual differences', in *Communication and Democracy*, ed. McCombs, Shaw and Weaver, p. 71.

12 Michael MacKuen, 'Social communication and the mass policy agenda', in *More Than News: Media Power in Public Affairs*, ed. Michael MacKuen and Steven Coombs (Beverly Hills, CA: Sage, 1981), pp. 19–144. For additional discussion and evidence about the conditions that influence individuals' involvement with specific public issues, see Lutz Erbring, Edie Goldenberg and Arthur Miller, 'Front-page news and real-world cues: a new look at agenda setting by the media', *American Journal of Political Science*, 24 (1980), pp. 16–49.

13 Zhu with Boroson, 'Susceptibility to agenda setting'.

14 Ibid., p. 82 (emphasis in original).

15 James Winter and Chaim Eyal, 'Agenda setting for the civil rights issue', *Public Opinion Quarterly*, 45 (1981), pp. 376–83.

16 Harold Zucker, 'The variable nature of news media influence', in *Communication Yearbook 2*, ed. Brent Ruben (New Brunswick, NJ: Transaction Books, 1978), pp. 225–40.

17 Michael Salwen, 'Effects of accumulation of coverage on issue salience in agenda setting', *Journalism Quarterly*, 65 (1988), pp. 100–6, 130.

18 Marilyn Roberts, Wayne Wanta and Tzong-Houng (Dustin) Dzwo, 'Agenda setting and issue salience online', *Communication Research*, 29 (2002), pp. 452–65.

19 Wayne Wanta and Y. Hu, 'Time-lag differences in the agenda setting process: an examination of five news media', *International Journal of Public Opinion Research*, 6 (1994), pp. 225–40.

20 Gerald Stone and Maxwell McCombs, 'Tracing the time lag in agenda setting', *Journalism Quarterly*, 58 (1981), pp. 151–5.

21 Similar variability in the decay of agenda-setting effects was found by James H. Watt, M. Mazza and L. B. Synder, 'Agenda-setting effects of television news coverage and the memory decay curve', *Communication Research*, 20 (1993), pp. 408–35.

22 Michael Salwen and Don Stacks, eds, *An Integrated Approach to Communication Theory and Research* (Mahwah, NJ: Lawrence Erlbaum, 1996), and Jennings Bryant and Dolf Zillmann, eds, *Media Effects: Advances in Theory and Research* (Hillsdale, NJ: Lawrence Erlbaum, 1994).

23 Chaim Eyal, James Winter and William DeGeorge, 'The concept of time frame in agenda-setting', in *Mass Communication Review Yearbook*, vol. 2, ed. G. Cleveland Wilhoit and Harold de Bock (Beverly Hills, CA: Sage, 1981), pp. 212–18.

24 Zhu, 'Issue competition and attention distraction'.

25 George Comstock and Erica Scharrer, *Television: What's On, Who's Watching, and What it Means* (San Diego, CA: Academic Press, 1999), pp. 204–5.

26 Maxwell McCombs and Donald Shaw, 'The agenda-setting function of mass media', *Public Opinion Quarterly*, 36 (1972), pp. 176–87.

27 Donald Shaw and Maxwell McCombs, eds, *The Emergence of American Political Issues* (St Paul, MN: West, 1977).

28 David Weaver, Doris Graber, Maxwell McCombs and Chaim Eyal, *Media Agenda Setting in a Presidential Election* (Westport, CT: Greenwood, 1981).

29 Wenmouth Williams, M. Shapiro and C. Cutbirth, 'The impact of campaign agendas on perception of issues in the 1980 campaign', *Journalism Quarterly*, 60 (1983), pp. 226–31.

30 Marc Benton and P. Jean Frazier, 'The agenda-setting function of the mass media at three levels of information-holding', *Communication Research*, 3 (1976), pp. 261–74.

31 Leonard Tipton, R. D. Haney and J. R. Baseheart, 'Media agenda setting in city and state election campaigns', *Journalism Quarterly*, 52 (1975), pp. 15–22.

32 Philip Palmgreen and Peter Clarke, 'Agenda setting with local and national issues', *Communication Research*, 4 (1977), pp. 435–52.

33 Wanta and Hu, 'Time-lag differences in the agenda setting process'.

34 Maxwell McCombs and Paula Poindexter, 'The duty to keep informed: news exposure and civic obligation', *Journal of Communication*, 33, 2 (1983), pp. 88–96.

35 Elsa Mohn and Maxwell McCombs, 'Who reads us and why', *The Masthead*, 32, 4 (1980–1), pp. 20–9.

36 Steven Chaffee and Donna Wilson, 'Media rich, media poor: two studies of diversity in agenda-holding', *Journalism Quarterly*, 54 (1977), pp. 466–76.

37 For additional discussion of the intense competition among issues for public visibility, see Anthony Downs, 'Up and down with ecology: the "issue-attention cycle"', *The Public Interest*, 28 (1972), pp. 38–50; S. Hilgartner and C. L. Bosk, 'The rise and fall of social problems: a public arenas model', *American Journal of Sociology*, 94, 1 (1988), pp. 53–78.

Chapter 4   Why Agenda-Setting Occurs

1 Pamela Shoemaker, 'Hardwired for news: using biological and cultural evolution to explain the surveillance function', *Journal of Communication*, 46, 3 (1996), pp. 32–47.

2 Bruce Westley and Lee Barrow, 'An investigation of news seeking behavior', *Journalism Quarterly*, 36 (1959), pp. 431–8; Maxwell McCombs, 'Editorial endorsements: a study of influence', *Journalism Quarterly*, 44 (1967), pp. 545–8; J. E. Mueller, 'Choosing among 133 candidates', *Public Opinion Quarterly*, 34 (1970), pp. 395–402; David Weaver, 'Political issues and voter need for orientation', in *The Emergence of American Political Issues*, ed. Donald Shaw and Maxwell McCombs (St Paul, MN: West, 1977), pp. 107–19; David Weaver, 'Audience need for orientation and media effects', *Communication Research*, 7 (1980), pp. 361–76.

3 Edward C. Tolman, *Purposive Behavior in Animals and Men* (New York: Appleton-Century-Crofts, 1932). Also see Tolman, 'Cognitive maps in rats and men', *Psychological Review*, 55 (1948), pp. 189–208; and W. J. McGuire, 'Psychological motives and communication gratification', in *The Uses of Mass Communication: Current Perspectives on Gratifications Research*, ed. J. G. Blumler and Elihu Katz (Beverly Hills, CA: Sage, 1974), pp. 167–96.

4 Robert E. Lane, *Political Life: Why and How People Get Involved in Politics* (New York: Free Press, 1959), p. 12.

5 Maxwell McCombs, 'Personal involvement with issues on the public agenda', *International Journal of Public Opinion Research*, 11, 2 (1999), pp. 152–68.

6 Richard F. Carter, Keith R. Stamm and Katharine Heintz-Knowles, 'Agenda-setting and consequentiality', *Journalism Quarterly*, 69 (1992), pp. 868–77. In addition to the evidence summarized here, this article generated further insights into the relevance of issues to the public with a creative methodology called 'cognigraphics'. The central question of this study, 'Why is this topic personally relevant?', is an instance of *situational relevance*, one of three aspects of psychological relevance. See Richard F. Carter, 'Communication and affective relations', *Journalism Quarterly*, 42 (1965), pp. 203–12.

7   Carter, Stamm and Heintz-Knowles, 'Agenda-setting and consequentiality', p. 872.

8   Davis Merritt and Maxwell McCombs, *The Two W's of Journalism* (Mahwah, NJ: Lawrence Erlbaum, 2003), chapter 6. Also see Michael Schudson, *The Good Citizen: A History of American Civic Life* (New York: Free Press, 1998), pp. 310–11.

9   Going beyond the concept of need for orientation to provide an in-depth explanation for this failure at agenda-setting, Julie Yioutas and Ivana Segvic draw upon two other aspects of agenda-setting theory that are the subjects of chapter 6 (the concept of compelling arguments and the convergence of attribute agenda-setting and framing). Their analysis is a rich example of the value of theory in explaining public opinion. See Julie Yioutas and Ivana Segvic, 'Revisiting the Clinton/Lewinsky scandal: the convergence of agenda setting and framing', *Journalism & Mass Communication Quarterly*, 80 (2003), pp. 567–82.

10 Weaver, 'Political issues and voter need for orientation', p. 112.

11 Paula Poindexter, Maxwell McCombs, Laura Smith and others, 'Need for orientation in the new media landscape', unpublished paper, University of Texas at Austin, 2002.

12 Weaver, 'Political issues and voter need for orientation', pp. 113, 115.

13 Toshio Takeshita, 'Agenda-setting effects of the press in a Japanese local election', *Studies of Broadcasting*, 29 (1993), pp. 193–216.

14 Maxwell McCombs and Donald Shaw, 'The agenda-setting function of mass media', *Public Opinion Quarterly*, 36 (1972), pp. 176–87.

15 David Weaver and Maxwell McCombs, 'Voters' need for orientation and choice of candidate: mass media and electoral decision making', paper presented to the American Association for Public Opinion Research, Roanoke, VA, 1978.

16 This critical combination of conditions, availability plus psychological relevance, was noted by Taik-Su Auh at the agenda-setting workshop held during the 2002 International Communication Association convention in Seoul, Korea. In turn, he cited Richard Carter's explication of psychological relevance. See Carter, 'Communication and affective relations'. For specific linkages between agenda-setting theory and Carter's concepts of salience, the closeness of an object to an individual, and situational relevance, that portion of the environment that is psychologically meaningful, see Maxwell McCombs, 'Myth and reality in scientific discovery: the case of agenda setting theory', in *Communication: A Different Kind of Horse Race*, ed. Brenda Dervin and Steven Chaffee (New York: Hampton Press, 2003), especially pp. 32–3.

17 Harold Zucker, 'The variable nature of news media influence', in *Communication Yearbook 2*, ed. Brent Ruben (New Brunswick, NJ: Transaction Books, 1978), pp. 225–40.

18 James Winter, Chaim Eyal and Ann Rogers, 'Issue-specific agenda setting: the whole as less than the sum of the parts', *Canadian Journal of Communication*, 8, 2 (1982), pp. 1–10.

19   Zucker, 'The variable nature of news influence'.

20   Kim Smith, 'Newspaper coverage and public concern about community issues: a time-series analysis', *Journalism Monographs*, 101 (1987), p. 13.

21   David Weaver, Doris Graber, Maxwell McCombs and Chaim Eyal, *Media Agenda Setting in a Presidential Election* (Westport, CT: Greenwood, 1981).

22   Warwick Blood, 'Unobtrusive issues in the agenda setting role of the press', unpublished doctoral dissertation, Syracuse University, 1981.

23   For additional evidence for the unobtrusive nature of unemployment, especially as a national issue, see Donald Shaw and John Slater, 'Press puts unemployment on agenda: Richmond community opinion, 1981–1984', *Journalism Quarterly*, 65 (1988), pp. 407–11.

24   Warwick Blood, 'Competing models of agenda-setting: issue obtrusiveness vs. media exposure', paper presented to the Association for Education in Journalism, Boston, 1980. This is a secondary analysis of data originally reported in Thomas Patterson, *The Mass Media Election: How Americans Choose their President* (New York: Praeger, 1980).

25   Edna F. Einsiedel, Kandice L. Salomone and Frederick Schneider, 'Crime: effects of media exposure and personal experience on issue salience', *Journalism Quarterly*, 61 (1984), pp. 131–6; Dominic Lasorsa and Wayne Wanta, 'Effects of personal, interpersonal and media experiences on issue saliences', *Journalism Quarterly*, 67 (1990), pp. 804–13.

26   Elisabeth Noelle-Neumann, 'The spiral of silence: a response', in *Political Communication Yearbook 1984*, ed. Keith Sanders, Lynda Lee Kaid and Dan Nimmo (Carbondale: Southern Illinois University Press, 1985), pp. 66–94. Also see Lutz Erbring, Edie Goldenberg and Arthur Miller, 'Front-page news and real-world cues', *American Journal of Political Science*, 24 (1980), pp. 16–49.

27   Lasorsa and Wanta, 'Effects of personal, interpersonal and media experiences on issue saliences'.

28   James P. Winter, 'Contingent conditions in the agenda-setting process', in *Mass Communication Review Yearbook*, ed. G. C. Wilhoit and Harold de Bock (Beverly Hills, CA: Sage, 1981), pp. 235–43; and G. Gumpert and R. Cathcart, eds, *Inter/Media: Interpersonal Communication in a Media World* (New York: Oxford University Press, 1986).

29   There is a strong example of the reinforcement role for conversation in Wayne Wanta, *The Public and the National Agenda* (Mahwah, NJ: Lawrence Erlbaum, 1997), p. 59, where the role of conversation in the agenda-setting process is significantly stronger than the role of media exposure. For a different perspective in which the news media are the prime movers, see the discussion of the French sociologist Gabriel Tarde's model of opinion formation in Susan Herbst, 'The cultivation of conversation', in *The Poll with a Human Face: The National Issues Convention Experiment in Political Communication*, ed. Maxwell McCombs and Amy Reynolds (Mahwah, NJ: Lawrence Erlbaum, 1999), esp. pp. 201–4; and Joohan Kim, Robert Wyatt and Elihu Katz, 'News, talk, opinion, participation: the part played by

conversation in deliberative democracy', *Political Communication*, 16 (1999), pp. 361–85.

30 Marilyn Roberts, Wayne Wanta and Tzong-Houng (Dustin) Dzwo, 'Agenda setting and issue salience online', *Communication Research*, 29 (2002), pp. 452–65.

31 Tony Atwater, Michael Salwen and Ronald Anderson, 'Interpersonal discussion as a potential barrier to agenda setting', *Newspaper Research Journal*, 6, 4 (1985), pp. 37–43.

32 Although need for orientation was not explicitly measured, strong positive links between the media issue agenda and the frequency of both interpersonal communication and media exposure were found by Wayne Wanta and Yi-Chen Wu, 'Interpersonal communication and the agenda setting process', *Journalism Quarterly*, 69 (1992), pp. 847–55. Also see David Weaver, Jian-Hua Zhu and Lars Willnat, 'The bridging function of interpersonal communication in agenda setting', *Journalism Quarterly*, 69 (1992), pp. 856–67.

33 Only interpersonal communication was linked with personally salient issues that lacked high salience on the media agenda, according to Wanta and Wu, 'Interpersonal communication and the agenda setting process'.

34 For discussion of the link between need for orientation and another communication theory, the spiral of silence, see Maxwell McCombs and David Weaver, 'Toward a merger of gratifications and agenda-setting research', in *Media Gratifications Research: Current Perspectives*, ed. Karl Erik Rosengren, Lawrence Wenner and Philip Palmgreen (Beverly Hills, CA: Sage, 1985), pp. 95–108.

35 Also see Jay Blumler, 'The role of theory in uses and gratifications research', *Communication Research*, 6 (1979), pp. 9–36.

36 Gerald Kosicki, 'Problems and opportunities in agenda-setting research', *Journal of Communication*, 43, 2 (1993), p. 109.

37 Donald Shaw and Maxwell McCombs, eds, *The Emergence of American Political Issues* (St Paul, MN: West, 1977).

38 Weaver, Graber, McCombs and Eyal, *Media Agenda Setting in a Presidential Election*.

39 James Winter, 'Contingent conditions in the agenda-setting process'.

40 See, for example, Tai-Li Wang, 'Agenda-setting online: an experiment testing the effects of hyperlinks in online newspapers', *Southwestern Mass Communication Journal*, 15, 2 (2000), pp. 59–70.

41 See, for example, Paula Poindexter, Maxwell McCombs and Laura Smith, 'La necesidad de orientacion: una explicacion psicologica de los efectos del agenda-setting' ['Need for orientation: a psychological explication of agenda-setting effects'], in *Agenda-Setting de los medios de comunicacion*, ed. Maxwell McCombs and Issa Luna Pla (Mexico City: Universidad Ibero Americana and Universidad de Occidente, 2003), pp. 107–19.

Chapter 5   The Pictures in our Heads

1   Walter Lippmann, *Public Opinion* (New York: Macmillan, 1922).

2   Maxwell McCombs and Donald Shaw, 'The agenda-setting function of mass media', *Public Opinion Quarterly*, 36 (1972), pp. 176–87.

3   Maxwell McCombs, 'Explorers and surveyors: expanding strategies for agenda setting research', *Journalism Quarterly*, 69 (1992), p. 815.

4   Dan Caspi, 'The agenda-setting function of the Israeli press', *Knowledge: Creation, Diffusion, Utilization*, 3 (1982), pp. 401–14.

5   William McGuire, 'Theoretical foundations of campaigns', in *Public Communication Campaigns*, 2nd edn, ed. R. E. Rice and C. K. Atkin (Newbury Park, CA: Sage, 1989), pp. 43–65.

6   *New York Times*, 1 November 2002, p. A28.

7   Bernard Cohen, *The Press and Foreign Policy* (Princeton, NJ: Princeton University Press, 1963), p. 13.

8   David Swanson and P. Mancini, eds, *Politics, Media, and Modern Democracy: An International Study of Innovations in Electoral Campaigning and their Consequences* (Westport, CT: Praeger, 1996).

9   Maxwell McCombs, 'The future agenda for agenda setting research', *Journal of Mass Communication Studies* [Japan], 45 (1994), pp. 181–171; Maxwell McCombs and Dixie Evatt, 'Los temas y los aspectos: explorando una nueva dimension de la agenda setting' ['Objects and attributes: exploring a new dimension of agenda setting'], *Comunicacion y Sociedad*, 8, 1 (1995), pp. 7–32; Maxwell McCombs and Tamara Bell, 'The agenda-setting role of mass communication', in *An Integrated Approach to Communication Theory and Research*, ed. Michael Salwen and Donald Stacks (Mahwah, NJ: Lawrence Erlbaum, 1996), pp. 93–110.

10 Lee Becker and Maxwell McCombs, 'The role of the press in determining voter reactions to presidential primaries', *Human Communication Research*, 4 (1978), pp. 301–7.

11 David Weaver, Doris Graber, Maxwell McCombs and Chaim Eyal, *Media Agenda Setting in a Presidential Election* (Westport, CT: Greenwood, 1981).

12 Maxwell McCombs, Esteban Lopez-Escobar and Juan Pablo Llamas, 'Setting the agenda of attributes in the 1996 Spanish general election', *Journal of Communication*, 50, 2 (2000), pp. 77–92.

13 Rosa Berganza and Marta Martin, 'Selective exposure to highly politicized media'; and Jose Javier Sanchez-Aranda, Maria Jose Canel and Juan Pablo Llamas, 'Framing effects of television political advertising and the selective perception process', papers presented at the World Association for Public Opinion Research regional conference, Pamplona, Spain, 1997.

14 Guy Golan and Wayne Wanta, 'Second-level agenda-setting in the New Hampshire primary: a comparison of coverage in three newspapers and public perceptions of candidates', *Journalism & Mass Communication Quarterly*, 78 (2001), pp. 247–59.

15 Pu-Tsung King, 'The press, candidate images, and voter perceptions', in *Communication and Democracy*, ed. Maxwell McCombs, Donald Shaw and David Weaver (Mahwah, NJ: Lawrence Erlbaum, 1997), pp. 29–40.

16 Esteban Lopez-Escobar, Juan Pablo Llamas and Maxwell McCombs, 'Una dimension social de los efectos de los medios de difusion: agenda-setting y consenso', *Comunicacion y Sociedad* IX (1996), pp. 91–125. Also see Maxwell McCombs, Juan Pablo Llamas, Esteban Lopez-Escobar and Federico Rey, 'Candidate images in Spanish elections: second-level agenda setting effects', *Journalism & Mass Communication Quarterly*, 74 (1997), pp. 703–17.

17 Spiro Kiousis, Philemon Bantimaroudis and Hyun Ban, 'Candidate image attributes: experiments on the substantive dimension of second-level agenda setting', *Communication Research*, 26, 4 (1999), pp. 414–28.

18 Doris Graber, *Mass Media and American Politics*, 2nd edn (Washington, DC: Congressional Quarterly Press, 1984), p. 264 (emphasis added).

19 Toshio Takeshita and Shunji Mikami, 'How did mass media influence the voters' choice in the 1993 general election in Japan?: a study of agenda setting', *Keio Communication Review*, 17 (1995), pp. 27–41.

20 Marc Benton and P. Jean Frazier, 'The agenda-setting function of the mass media', *Communication Research*, 3 (1976), pp. 261–74.

21 For both a theoretical discussion and empirical evidence on this point, see Aileen Yagade and David M. Dozier, 'The media agenda-setting effect of concrete versus abstract issues', *Journalism Quarterly*, 67 (1990), pp. 3–10. A conceptual distinction is drawn between obtrusive/unobtrusive, which was discussed in chapter 4, and concrete/abstract, which may be a useful addition to the broader idea of need for orientation that also was discussed in chapter 4.

22 Shunji Mikami, Toshio Takeshita, Makoto Nakada and Miki Kawabata, 'The media coverage and public awareness of environmental issues in Japan', paper presented to the International Association for Mass Communication Research, Seoul, Korea, 1994.

23 Michael Salwen, 'Effects of accumulation of coverage on issue salience in agenda setting', *Journalism Quarterly*, 65 (1988), pp. 100–6, 130.

24 T. Michael Maher, 'Media framing and public perception of environmental causality', *Southwestern Mass Communication Journal*, 12 (1996), pp. 61–73.

25 David Cohen, 'A report on a non-election agenda setting study', paper presented to the Association for Education in Journalism, Ottawa, Canada, 1975.

26 Alex Edelstein, 'Thinking about the criterion variable in agenda-setting research', *Journal of Communication*, 43, 2 (1993), pp. 85–99.

27 Tom Smith, 'America's most important problem – a trend analysis, 1946–1976', *Public Opinion Quarterly*, 44 (1980), pp. 164–80. Smith, 'The polls: America's most important problems', *Public Opinion Quarterly*, 49 (1985), pp. 264–74; Maxwell McCombs and Jian-Hua Zhu, 'Capacity, diversity, and volatility of the public agenda: trends from 1954 to 1994', *Public Opinion Quarterly*, 59 (1995), pp. 495–525.

28 Scott L. Althaus and David Tewksbury, 'Agenda setting and the ''new'' news', *Communication Research*, 29 (2002), pp. 180–207.
29 Tai-Li Wang, 'Agenda-setting online', *Southwestern Mass Communication Journal*, 15, 2 (2000), pp. 59–70. Similar measures of issue salience were used by Shanto Iyengar and Donald Kinder, *News that Matters* (Chicago: University of Chicago Press, 1987).
30 Dixie Evatt and Salma Ghanem, 'Building a scale to measure salience', paper presented to the World Association for Public Opinion Research, Rome, Italy, 2001. This paper has an extensive conceptual discussion of salience in addition to the data on the semantic differential scales used to develop multi-measure salience scales.
31 Edna F. Einsiedel, Kandice L. Salomone and Frederick Schneider, 'Crime: effects of media exposure and personal experience on issue salience', *Journalism Quarterly*, 61 (1984), pp. 131–6.
32 Takeshita and Mikami, 'How did mass media influence the voters' choice in the 1993 general election in Japan?' Similar measures were used by Mikami, Takeshita, Nakada and Kawabata, 'The media coverage and public awareness of environmental issues in Japan'.
33 Cohen, 'A report on a non-election agenda setting study'.
34 Benton and Frazier, 'The agenda-setting function of the mass media'.
35 Weaver, Graber, McCombs and Eyal, *Media Agenda Setting in a Presidential Election*.
36 Spiro Kiousis, 'Beyond salience: exploring the linkages between the agenda setting role of mass media and mass persuasion', unpublished doctoral dissertation, University of Texas at Austin, 2000.
37 Sei-Hill Kim, Dietram Scheufele and James Shanahan, 'Think about it this way', *Journalism and Mass Communication Quarterly*, 79 (2002), pp. 7–25.
38 McGuire, 'Theoretical foundations of campaigns'. There continues to be some debate about whether the primary *effects* of the mass media are reinforcement of prevailing perspectives or the creation of new perspectives. The distinction between the first and second levels of agenda-setting offers some intriguing implications for this debate, more so when considered in tandem with Carter's observation about media effects in terms of salience and pertinence as two aspects of psychological relevance:

> If all one is looking for is evidence of the salience aspect of value, then reinforcement of value is probably all one is going to find. On the other hand, if one looks at how the individual structures his cognitive environment in terms of the values he assigns elements, this must be accomplished through information processing of pertinence aspects of value. Thus, the apparent paradox conceivably can be dissolved by this distinction. (Richard Carter, 'Communication and affective relations', *Journalism Quarterly*, 42 (1965), p. 207.)

39 Benjamin Page and Robert Shapiro, *The Rational Public: Fifty Years of Trends in Americans' Policy Preferences* (Chicago: University of Chicago Press, 1992), chapter 2.

Chapter 6   Attribute Agenda-Setting and Framing

1 Paul F. Lazarsfeld and Robert Merton, 'Mass communication, popular taste and organized social action', in *The Communication of Ideas*, ed. Lyman Bryson (New York: Institute for Religious and Social Studies, 1948), pp. 95–118.

2 Walter Lippmann, *Public Opinion* (New York: Macmillan, 1922); Dan Nimmo and Robert L. Savage, *Candidates and their Images* (Pacific Palisades, CA: Goodyear, 1976); David Weaver, Doris Graber, Maxwell McCombs and Chaim Eyal, *Media Agenda Setting in a Presidential Election* (Westport, CT: Greenwood, 1981).

3 Pamela Shoemaker, 'Media gatekeeping'; and Maxwell McCombs and Tamara Bell, 'The agenda-setting role of mass communication', in *An Integrated Approach to Communication Theory and Research*, ed. Michael Salwen and Don Stacks (Mahwah, NJ: Lawrence Erlbaum, 1996).

4 George Gerbner, Larry Gross, Michael Morgan, Nancy Signorielli and James Shanahan, 'Growing up with television', in *Media Effects*, 2nd edn, ed. Jennings Bryant and Dolf Zillmann (Mahwah, NJ: Lawrence Erlbaum, 1994), pp. 43–68.

5 Also see Margaret T. Gordon and Linda Heath, 'The news business, crime and fear', in *Reactions to Crime*, ed. Dan Lewis (Beverly Hills, CA: Sage, 1981).

6 Elizabeth Noelle-Neumann, *The Spiral of Silence: Our Social Skin*, 2nd edn (Chicago: University of Chicago Press, 1993).

7 Maxwell McCombs and David Weaver, 'Toward a merger of gratifications and agenda-setting research', in *Media Gratifications Research*, ed. K. E. Rosengren, L. Wenner and P. Palmgreen (Beverly Hills, CA: Sage, 1985), pp. 95–108.

8 Yet another concept of framing refers to the styles of message presentation rather than message content and meaning. In Maxwell McCombs and Salma Ghanem, 'The convergence of agenda setting and framing', in *Framing Public Life*, ed. Stephen Reese, Oscar Gandy and August Grant (Mahwah, NJ: Lawrence Erlbaum, 2001), pp. 67–82, this concept is defined as attributes of presentations in order to distinguish it from the attributes of objects, which are the focus of second-level agenda-setting. This concept of framing is referred to as framing mechanisms in James Tankard, Laura Hendrickson, Jackie Silberman, Kriss Bliss and Salma Ghanem, 'Media frames: approaches to conceptualization and measurement', paper presented to the Association for Education in Journalism and Mass Communication, Boston, 1991. These concepts of stylistic framing are very close to the origins of the framing concept in photography and cinematography, where framing refers to such variables as camera angle and perspective in the styling of visual messages. By extension, stylistic framing also refers to page design and other graphic variables in print messages and to the use of metaphor and other aspects of language in verbal messages.

9   Tankard et al., 'Media frames', p. 3 (emphasis added).

10   Robert Entman, 'Framing: toward clarification of a fractured paradigm', *Journal of Communication*, 43, 3 (1993), p. 52 (emphasis in original).

11   Weaver, Graber, McCombs and Eyal, *Media Agenda Setting in a Presidential Election*.

12   Shanto Iyengar and Adam Simon, 'News coverage of the Gulf crisis and public opinion: a study of agenda-setting, priming and framing', in *Do the Media Govern? Politicians, Voters, and Reporters in America*, ed. Shanto Iyengar and Richard Reeves (Thousand Oaks, CA: Sage, 1997), pp. 248–57.

13   Jim Kuypers, *Presidential Crisis Rhetoric and the Press in the Post-Cold War World* (Westport, CT: Praeger, 1997).

14   McCombs and Ghanem, 'The convergence of agenda setting and framing'. McCombs initially outlined this view at a session, 'Agenda setting and beyond: current perspectives on media effects', at the 1991 annual meeting of the American Association for Public Opinion Research in Phoenix, Arizona.

15   Maxwell McCombs, Juan Pablo Llamas, Esteban Lopez-Escobar and Federico Rey, 'Candidate images in Spanish elections', *Journalism & Mass Communication Quarterly*, 74 (1997), pp. 703–17; Maxwell McCombs, Esteban Lopez-Escobar and Juan Pablo Llamas, 'Setting the agenda of attributes in the 1996 Spanish general election', *Journal of Communication*, 50, 2 (2000), pp. 77–92.

16   Marc Benton and P. Jean Frazier, 'The agenda-setting function of the mass media', *Communication Research*, 3 (1976), pp. 261–74.

17   Toshio Takeshita and Shunji Mikami, 'How did mass media influence the voters' choice?', *Keio Communication Review*, 17 (1995), pp. 27–41.

18   McCombs and Ghanem, 'The convergence of agenda setting and framing', p. 74.

19   In the prologue to Reese, Gandy and Grant, *Framing Public Life*, Stephen Reese offers this working definition of framing (p. 11, italics in original): 'Frames are *organizing principles* that are socially *shared* and *persistent* over time, that work *symbolically* to meaningfully *structure* the social world.'

20   Erving Goffman, *Frame Analysis* (New York: Harper & Row, 1974), p. 21.

21   Stuart Hall, 'The rediscovery of "ideology": return of the repressed in media studies', in *Culture, Society and the Media*, ed. M. Gurevitch, T. Bennett, J. Curran and J. Wollacott (London: Methuen, 1982), p. 59.

22   Entman, 'Framing', p. 52 (emphasis in original).

23   Reese, Gandy and Grant, *Framing Public Life*.

24   Douglas McLeod and B. Detenber, 'Framing effects of television news coverage of social protest', *Journal of Communication*, 49, 3 (1999), pp. 3–23.

25   L. Ashley and B. Olson, 'Constructing reality: print media's framing of the women's movement, 1966 to 1986', *Journalism & Mass Communication Quarterly*, 75 (1998), pp. 263–77.

26   Roya Akhavan-Majid and Jyotika Ramaprasad, 'Framing and ideology: a comparative analysis of U.S. and Chinese newspaper coverage of the fourth

United Nations Conference on Women and the NGO Forum', *Mass Communication & Society*, 1 (1998), pp. 131–52.

27 Mark Miller, Julie Andsager and Bonnie Riechert, 'Framing the candidates in presidential primaries: issues and images in press releases and news coverage', *Journalism & Mass Communication Quarterly*, 75 (1998), pp. 312–24. The correlations reported here were calculated by McCombs's seminar on agenda-setting theory at the University of Texas in the spring semester 2000.

28 Toshio Takeshita, 'Expanding attribute agenda setting into framing: an application of the problematic situation scheme', paper presented to the International Communication Association, Seoul, Korea, 2002.

29 Alex Edelstein, Youichi Ito and Hans Mathias Kepplinger, *Communication & Culture: A Comparative Approach* (New York: Longman, 1989). Although Edelstein, Ito and Kepplinger did not explicitly relate the concept of the problematic situation with framing, the usefulness of that link was pointed out subsequently by Salma Ghanem. See 'Filling in the tapestry: the second level of agenda-setting', in *Communication and Democracy*, ed. Maxwell McCombs, Donald Shaw and David Weaver (Mahwah, NJ: Lawrence Erlbaum, 1997), p. 13.

30 Maxwell McCombs and John Smith, 'Perceptual selection and communication', *Journalism Quarterly*, 46 (1969), pp. 352–5.

31 Ghanem, 'Filling in the tapestry', pp. 3–14.

32 Ghanem, 'Media coverage of crime and public opinion', unpublished doctoral dissertation, University of Texas at Austin, 1996.

33 A. E. Jasperson, D. V. Shah, M. Watts, R. J. Faber and David Fan, 'Framing and the public agenda: media effects on the importance of the federal budget deficit', *Political Communication*, 15 (1998), pp. 205–24. Also see David Fan, Kathy Keltner and Robert Wyatt, 'A matter of guilt or innocence: how news reports affect support for the death penalty in the United States', *International Journal of Public Opinion Research*, 14 (2002), pp. 439–52.

34 Klaus Schoenbach and Holli Semetko, 'Agenda setting, agenda reinforcing or agenda deflating? A study of the 1990 German national election', *Journalism Quarterly*, 68 (1992), pp. 837–46.

35 Wenmouth Williams Jr., Mitchell Shapiro and Craig Cutbirth, 'The impact of campaign agendas on perceptions of issues', *Journalism Quarterly*, 60 (1983), pp. 226–32.

36 Linda Jean Kensicki, 'Media construction of an elitist environmental movement: new frontiers for second level agenda setting and political activism', unpublished doctoral dissertation, University of Texas at Austin, 2001.

37 Sometimes these framing effects extend beyond the salience of a single object. Noting an exception to the general principle that agendas are zero-sum situations, Jian-Hua Zhu, 'Issue competition and attention distraction', *Journalism Quarterly*, 68 (1992), pp. 825–36, states that on occasion the high salience of an issue on the agenda results from more than straightforward agenda-setting effects. Sometimes there are complementary links

among issues due to shared attributes. Media coverage of one issue may be highly pertinent to the salience of another, seemingly independent issue. For a discussion of the theoretical link to Richard F. Carter, 'Communication and affective relations', *Journalism Quarterly*, 42 (1965), pp. 203–12, see Maxwell McCombs, 'Myth and reality in scientific discovery: the case of agenda setting theory', in *Communication, a Different Kind of Horserace: Essays Honoring Richard F. Carter*, ed. Brenda Dervin and Steven Chaffee (Cresskill, NJ: Hampton Press, 2003), pp. 25–38.

38 W. Russell Neuman, Marion Just and Ann Crigler, *Common Knowledge: News and the Construction of Political Meaning* (Chicago: University of Chicago Press, 1992).

39 Original analysis by McCombs based on data reported in Neuman, Just and Crigler, *Common Knowledge*.

40 Frank Baumgartner and Bryan Jones, *Agendas and Instability in American Politics* (Chicago: University of Chicago Press, 1993).

41 One of the best-known books presenting this perspective on highly limited media effects is Joseph Klapper's *The Effects of Mass Communication* (New York: Free Press, 1960).

Chapter 7   Shaping the Media Agenda

1 Pamela Shoemaker and Stephen Reese, *Mediating the Message: Theories of Influences on Mass Media Content* (New York: Longman, 1991). For additional analysis from Germany on this latter layer, the situation of the individual journalist, also see Wolfram Peiser, 'Setting the journalist agenda: influences from journalists' individual characteristics and from media factors', *Journalism & Mass Communication Quarterly*, 77 (2000), pp. 243–57.

2 Frequently cited classic examples from this vast literature include Warren Breed, 'Social control in the newsroom', *Social Forces* (May 1955), pp. 326–35; Gaye Tuchman, 'Telling stories', *Journal of Communication*, 26, 4 (1976), pp. 93–7; and Herbert Gans, *Deciding What's News: A Study of CBS Evening News, NBC Nightly News, Newsweek and Time* (New York: Pantheon, 1979).

3 Sheldon Gilbert, Chaim Eyal, Maxwell McCombs and David Nicholas, 'The State of the Union address and the press agenda', *Journalism Quarterly*, 57 (1980), pp. 584–8.

4 Maxwell McCombs, Sheldon Gilbert and Chaim Eyal, 'The State of the Union address and the press agenda: a replication', paper presented to the International Communication Association, Boston, 1982.

5 Thomas J. Johnson and Wayne Wanta, with John T. Byrd and Cindy Lee, 'Exploring FDR's relationship with the press: a historical agenda-setting study', *Political Communication*, 12 (1995), pp. 157–72.

6 Wayne Wanta, Mary Ann Stephenson, Judy VanSlyke Turk and Maxwell McCombs, 'How president's State of Union talk influenced news media agendas', *Journalism Quarterly*, 66 (1989), pp. 537–41. For evidence of influence on the national agenda from other presidential speeches, see

Shanto Iyengar and Donald Kinder, *News that Matters* (Chicago: University of Chicago Press, 1987), chapter 3.

7 William Gonzenbach, *The Media, the President and Public Opinion* (Mahwah, NJ: Lawrence Erlbaum, 1996); Wayne Wanta and Joe Foote, 'The president–news media relationship: a time-series analysis of agenda setting', *Journal of Broadcasting & Electronic Media*, 38 (1994), pp. 437–48. Wayne Wanta, *The Public and the National Agenda* (Mahwah, NJ: Lawrence Erlbaum, 1997), chapter 7, extends these analyses of the State of the Union address to the impact on the public agenda. An ingenious comparison of four groups of issues – those emphasized by the president but not by the news media; those emphasized only by the media; those emphasized by both; and those emphasized by neither – found that media exposure, not exposure to the actual State of the Union address on television, was the key predictor for the salience of all the issues except those emphasized only by the president. In the case of issues emphasized by both, media exposure alone was the significant predictor, suggesting that the redundancy of the media agenda outweighs the authority of the president.

8 R. W. Cobb and C. D. Elder, *Participation in American Politics: The Dynamics of Agenda-Building* (Baltimore: Johns Hopkins University Press, 1972).

9 James Dearing and Everett Rogers, *Agenda-Setting* (Thousand Oaks, CA: Sage, 1996).

10 Davis 'Buzz' Merritt, *Public Journalism and Public Life: Why Telling the News is Not Enough*, 2nd edn (Mahwah, NJ: Lawrence Erlbaum, 1998), chapter 9.

11 Barbara Nelson, *Making an Issue of Child Abuse: Political Agenda Setting for Social Problems* (Chicago: University of Chicago Press, 1984).

12 Marcus Brewer and Maxwell McCombs, 'Setting the community agenda', *Journalism & Mass Communication Quarterly*, 73 (1996), pp. 7–16.

13 David Protess, Fay Cook, Jack Doppelt, James Ettema, Margaret Gordon, Donna Leff and Peter Miller, *The Journalism of Outrage: Investigative Reporting and Agenda Building in America* (New York: Guilford, 1991). Also see David Protess and Maxwell McCombs, eds, *Agenda Setting: Readings on Media, Public Opinion, and Policymaking* (Hillsdale, NJ: Lawrence Erlbaum, 1991), esp. part IV.

14 Frank Baumgartner and Bryan Jones, *Agendas and Instability in American Politics* (Chicago: University of Chicago Press, 1993).

15 Everett Rogers, James Dearing and Soonbum Chang, 'AIDS in the 1980s: the agenda-setting process for a public issue', *Journalism Monographs*, 126 (1991).

16 Craig Trumbo, 'Longitudinal modeling of public issues: an application of the agenda-setting process to the issue of global warming', *Journalism Monographs*, 152 (1995).

17 Gonzenbach, *The Media, the President and Public Opinion*.

18 Oscar Gandy, *Beyond Agenda Setting: Information Subsidies and Public Policy* (Norwood, NJ: Ablex, 1982); Jarol B. Manheim, *Strategic Public Diplomacy and American Foreign Policy: The Evolution of Influence* (New York: Oxford

University Press, 1994), chapter 8; Judy VanSlyke Turk, 'Information subsidies and media content: a study of public relations influence on the news', *Journalism Monographs*, 100 (1986).

19 Leon Sigal, *Reporters and Officials: The Organization and Politics of Newsmaking* (Lexington, MA: D. C. Heath, 1973), p. 121.

20 Judy VanSlyke Turk, 'Public relations influence on the news', *Newspaper Research Journal*, 7 (1986), pp. 15–27; Judy VanSlyke Turk, 'Information subsidies and influence', *Public Relations Review*, 11 (1985), pp. 10–25.

21 Rogers, Dearing and Chang, 'AIDS in the 1980s'. Also see Liz Watts, 'Coverage of polio and AIDS: agenda setting in reporting cure research on polio and AIDS in newspapers, news magazines and network television', *Ohio Journalism Monograph Series* [School of Journalism, Ohio University], 4 (1993).

22 John V. Pavlik, *Public Relations: What Research Tells Us* (Newbury Park, CA: Sage, 1987), chapter 4.

23 Jarol B. Manheim and R. B. Albritton, 'Changing national images: international public relations and media agenda setting', *American Political Science Review*, 73 (1984), pp. 641–7.

24 Kathleen Hall Jamieson and Karlyn Kohrs Campbell, *The Interplay of Influence: News, Advertising, Politics and the Mass Media* (Belmont, CA: Wadsworth, 1992).

25 Nicholas O'Shaughnessy, *The Phenomenon of Political Marketing* (London: Macmillan, 1990).

26 Holli Semetko, Jay Blumler, Michael Gurevitch and David Weaver, with Steve Barkin and G. C. Wilhoit, *The Formation of Campaign Agendas: A Comparative Analysis of Party and Media Roles in Recent American and British Elections* (Hillsdale, NJ: Lawrence Erlbaum, 1991).

27 Semetko, Blumler, Gurevitch and Weaver, *The Formation of Campaign Agendas*, p. 49. The quoted material is from Michael Gurevitch and Jay Blumler, 'The construction of election news at the BBC: an observation study', in *Individuals in Mass Media Organizations: Creativity and Constraint*, ed. James Ettema and Charles Whitney (Beverly Hills, CA: Sage, 1982), pp. 179–204.

28 Joseph Lelyveld, *New York Times*, 22 August 1999, p. 18.

29 Mark Miller, Julie Andsager and Bonnie Riechert, 'Framing the candidates in presidential primaries', *Journalism & Mass Communication Quarterly*, 75 (1998), pp. 312–24. The correlations reported here and in chapter 6 were calculated by McCombs's seminar on agenda-setting theory at the University of Texas in the spring semester 2000.

30 S. R. Lichter and T. Smith, 'Why elections are bad news: media and candidate discourse in the 1996 presidential primaries', *Press/Politics*, 1, 4 (1996), pp. 15–35.

31 Thomas P. Boyle, 'Intermedia agenda setting in the 1996 presidential primaries', *Journalism & Mass Communication Quarterly*, 78 (2001), pp. 26–44.

32 John Tedesco, 'Issue and strategy agenda-setting in the 2000 presidential primaries', unpublished paper, Virginia Technological University, 2001.

33 Russell Dalton, Paul Allen Beck, Robert Huckfeldt and William Koetzle, 'A test of media-centered agenda setting: newspaper content and public interests in a presidential election', *Political Communication*, 15 (1998), pp. 463–81. The original, zero-order correlations between the various agendas are reported in this article. For this chapter, McCombs calculated the partial correlations that introduce various controls.

34 Sungtae Ha, 'The intermediary role of news media in the presidential campaign: a mediator, moderator, or political agent?', unpublished paper, University of Texas at Austin, 2001.

35 Marilyn Roberts and Maxwell McCombs, 'Agenda setting and political advertising: origins of the news agenda', *Political Communication*, 11 (1994), pp. 249–62.

36 Dixie Shipp Evatt and Tamara Bell, 'Upstream influences: the early press releases, agenda-setting and politics of a future president', *Southwestern Mass Communication Journal*, 16, 2 (2001), pp. 70–81.

37 Esteban Lopez-Escobar, Juan Pablo Llamas, Maxwell McCombs and Federico Rey Lennon, 'Two levels of agenda setting among advertising and news in the 1995 Spanish elections', *Political Communication*, 15 (1998), pp. 225–38.

38 Kenneth Bryan, 'Political communication and agenda setting in local races', unpublished doctoral dissertation, University of Texas at Austin, 1997.

39 Denis McQuail, *Mass Communication Theory: An Introduction* (London: Sage, 1987).

40 Michael Gurevitch and Jay Blumler, 'Political communication systems and democratic values', in *Democracy and the Mass Media*, ed. J. Lichtenberg (Cambridge: Cambridge University Press, 1990), pp. 269–89. Also see Davis Merritt and Maxwell McCombs, *The Two W's of Journalism* (Mahwah, NJ: Lawrence Erlbaum, 2003), chapter 6.

41 Stuart Soroka, 'Issue attributes and agenda-setting by media, the public, and policymakers in Canada', *International Journal of Public Opinion Research*, 14 (2002), pp. 264–85. For a broader, more detailed analysis of eight major Canadian issues, see Stuart Soroka, *Agenda-Setting Dynamics in Canada* (Vancouver: UBC Press, 2002).

42 David Weaver and Swanzy Nimley Elliot, 'Who sets the agenda for the media? A study of local agenda-building', *Journalism Quarterly*, 62 (1985), pp. 87–94.

43 Ibid., p. 93.

44 Also see Kyle Huckins, 'Interest-group influence on the media agenda: a case study', *Journalism & Mass Communication Quarterly*, 76 (1999), pp. 76–86.

45 Karen Callaghan and Frauke Schnell, 'Assessing the democratic debate: how the news media frame elite policy discourse', *Political Communication*, 18 (2001), pp. 183–212.

46 Ibid., p. 197.

47   Penelope Ploughman, 'The creation of newsworthy events: an analysis of newspaper coverage of the man-made disaster at Love Canal', unpublished doctoral dissertation, State University of New York at Buffalo, 1984; Allen Mazur, 'Putting radon on the public risk agenda', *Science, Technology, and Human Values*, 12, 3–4 (1987), pp. 86–93. Also see the series by media critic David Shaw on the agenda-setting role of the *New York Times* and other New York City news media in the *Los Angeles Times*, 17–19 November 1988.

48   Stephen Reese and Lucig Danielian, 'Intermedia influence and the drug issue', in *Communication Campaigns about Drugs*, ed. P. Shoemaker (Hillsdale, NJ: Lawrence Erlbaum, 1989), pp. 29–46.

49   Warren Breed, 'Newspaper opinion leaders and the process of standardization', *Journalism Quarterly*, 32 (1955), pp. 277–84, 328.

50   Richard Kluger, *The Paper: The Life and Death of the New York Herald Tribune* (New York: Alfred A. Knopf, 1986).

51   See, for example, the account of a story that was bumped from page 1A of *USA Today* until it appeared as the lead story on the 'CBS Evening News', in Peter Pritchard, 'The McPapering of America: an insider's candid account', *Washington Journalism Revue* (1987), pp. 32–7. Another example, a case study of how a specific news story about deviant behaviour by a Catholic priest triggered a flood of negative stories about clergy over a four-year period, is presented by Michael J. Breen, 'A Cook, a cardinal, his priests, and the press: deviance as a trigger for intermedia agenda setting', *Journalism & Mass Communication Quarterly*, 74 (1997), pp. 348–56.

52   Timothy Crouse, *The Boys on the Bus* (New York: Ballentine, 1973), pp. 84–5.

53   Trumbo, 'Longitudinal modeling of public issues'.

54   David Gold and Jerry Simmons, 'News selection patterns among Iowa dailies', *Public Opinion Quarterly*, 29 (1965), pp. 425–30.

55   D. Charles Whitney and Lee Becker, ' "Keeping the gates" for gatekeepers: the effects of wire news', *Journalism Quarterly*, 59 (1982), pp. 60–5.

56   Lee Becker, Maxwell McCombs and Jack McLeod, 'The development of political cognitions', in *Political Communication: Issues and Strategies for Research*, ed. Steven Chaffee (Beverly Hills, CA: Sage, 1975), p. 39.

57   Donald Shaw's calculations of the intermedia agenda-setting correlations from the classic gatekeeping studies are reported in Maxwell McCombs and Donald Shaw, 'Structuring the unseen environment', *Journal of Communication*, 26, spring (1976), pp. 18–22.

58   David Manning White, 'The gate keeper: a case study in the selection of news', *Journalism Quarterly*, 27 (1949), pp. 383–90.

59   Paul Snider, 'Mr. Gates revisited: a 1966 version of the 1949 case study', *Journalism Quarterly*, 44 (1967), pp. 419–27.

60   Shaw's calculations reported in McCombs and Shaw, 'Structuring the unseen environment'.

61   Roberts and McCombs, 'Agenda setting and political advertising'.

62 Lopez-Escobar, Llamas, McCombs and Lennon, 'Two levels of agenda setting among advertising and news in the 1995 Spanish elections'.

63 Maxwell McCombs and Donald Shaw, 'The agenda-setting function of mass media', *Public Opinion Quarterly*, 36 (1972), p. 183.

64 Pu-Tsung King, 'Issue agendas in the 1992 Taiwan legislative election', unpublished doctoral dissertation, University of Texas at Austin, 1994.

65 Toshio Takeshita, 'The results of the content analysis of the *Asahi* and the *Yomiuri*: a summary', unpublished paper, Meiji University, 2002. This research is a replication and extension of Takeshita, 'Expanding attribute agenda setting into framing', paper presented to the International Communication Association, Seoul, Korea, which was discussed in chapter 6.

66 Marc Benton and P. Jean Frazier, 'The agenda-setting function of the mass media at three levels of information-holding', *Communication Research*, 3 (1976), pp. 261–74.

67 Pu-Tsung King, 'The press, candidate images, and voter perceptions', in *Communication and Democracy*, ed. M. McCombs, D. Shaw and D. Weaver (Mahwah, NJ: Lawrence Erlbaum, 1997), pp. 29–40.

68 Leonard Pitts, 'Objectivity might be impossible, so we strive for fairness', *Austin American-Statesman*, 17 December 2001, p. A13.

69 Stuart N. Soroka, '*Schindler's List*'s intermedia influence: exploring the role of "entertainment" in media agenda-setting', *Canadian Journal of Communication*, 25 (2000), pp. 211–30.

Chapter 8   Consequences of Agenda-Setting

1 Eugene F. Shaw, 'Agenda-setting and mass communication theory', *Gazette*, 25, 2 (1979), p. 101. A creative example of a very early foray in this area is Lee Becker, 'The impact of issue saliences', in *The Emergence of American Political Issues*, ed. Donald Shaw and Maxwell McCombs (St Paul, MN: West, 1977), pp. 121–32.

2 Joseph Klapper, *The Effects of Mass Communication* (New York: Free Press, 1960).

3 Carl Hovland, Irving Janis and Harold Kelley, *Communication and Persuasion* (New Haven, CT: Yale University Press, 1953). Also see Nathan Maccoby, 'The new "scientific" rhetoric', in *The Science of Human Communication*, ed. Wilbur Schramm (New York: Basic Books, 1963), pp. 41–53.

4 Shanto Iyengar and Donald Kinder, *News that Matters* (Chicago: University of Chicago Press, 1987), p. 63. Although the evidence reported in this book concerns only television news, the bracketed words 'and the other news media' were inserted because there is substantial evidence that all the news media can prime judgements of public performance.

5 Samuel Popkin, *The Reasoning Voter* (Chicago: University of Chicago Press, 1991).

6 A classic presentation of heuristic information processing is Amos Tversky and Daniel Kahneman, 'Availability: a heuristic for judging frequency and probability', *Cognitive Psychology*, 5 (1973), pp. 207–32.

7   Iyengar and Kinder, *News that Matters*, chapters 7–11.
8   Jon Krosnick and Donald Kinder, 'Altering the foundations of support for the president through priming', *American Political Science Review*, 84 (1990), pp. 497–512.
9   Ibid., p. 505. For other evidence of priming based on various National Election Studies in the US, see Jon Krosnick and Laura Brannon, 'The impact of war on the ingredients of presidential evaluations: George Bush and the Gulf conflict', *American Political Science Review*, 87 (1993), pp. 963–75; and Shanto Iyengar and Adam Simon, 'News coverage of the Gulf crisis and public opinion', in *Do the Media Govern?*, ed. S. Iyengar and R. Reeves (Thousand Oaks, CA: Sage, 1997), pp. 248–57.
10 Lars Willnat and Jian-Hua Zhu, 'Newspaper coverage and public opinion in Hong Kong: a time-series analysis of media priming', *Political Communication*, 13 (1996), pp. 231–46.
11 Hans-Bernd Brosius and Hans Mathias Kepplinger, 'Beyond agenda setting: the influence of partisanship and television reporting on the electorate's voting intentions', *Journalism Quarterly*, 69 (1992), pp. 893–901.
12 Iyengar and Simon, 'News coverage of the Gulf crisis and public opinion', p. 250.
13 For additional discussion, see Lars Willnat, 'Agenda setting and priming: conceptual links and differences', in *Communication and Democracy*, ed. M. McCombs, D. Shaw and D. Weaver (Mahwah, NJ: Lawrence Erlbaum, 1997), pp. 51–66.
14 George Comstock and Erica Scharrer, *Television: What's On, Who's Watching, and What it Means* (San Diego, CA: Academic Press, 1999).
15 Iyengar and Simon, 'News coverage of the Gulf crisis and public opinion'.
16 Sei-Hill Kim, Dietram Scheufele and James Shanahan, 'Think about it this way', *Journalism and Mass Communication Quarterly*, 79 (2002), pp. 7–25.
17 Paul Brewer, 'Framing, value words, and citizens' explanations of their issue opinions', *Political Communication*, 19 (2002), pp. 303–16.
18 Hans Mathias Kepplinger, Wolfgang Donsbach, Hans Bernd Brosius and Joachim Friedrich Staab, 'Media tone and public opinion: a longitudinal study of media coverage and public opinion on Chancellor Kohl', *International Journal of Public Opinion Research*, 1 (1989), pp. 326–42.
19 Daron Shaw, 'The impact of news media favorability and candidate events in presidential campaigns', *Political Communication*, 16 (1999), pp. 183–202.
20 Esteban Lopez-Escobar and Maxwell McCombs, with Antonio Tolsa, Marta Martin and Juan Pablo Llamas, 'Measuring the public images of political leaders: a methodological contribution of agenda-setting theory', paper presented at the World Association for Public Opinion Research regional conference, Sydney, Australia, 1999.
21 Lutz Erbring, Edie Goldenberg and Arthur Miller, 'Front-page news and real-world cues', *American Journal of Political Science*, 24 (1980), pp. 16–49.
22 Deborah J. Blood and Peter C. B. Phillips, 'Economic headline news on the agenda: new approaches to understanding causes and effects', in *Communi-*

cation and Democracy, ed. McCombs, Shaw and Weaver, pp. 97–114. Also see Joe Bob Hester and Rhonda Gibson, 'The economy and second-level agenda setting: a time-series analysis of economic news and public opinion about the economy', *Journalism & Mass Communication Quarterly*, 80 (2003), pp. 73–90.

23 Blood and Phillips, 'Economic headline news on the agenda', p. 107.

24 Spiro Kiousis, 'Beyond salience', unpublished doctoral dissertation, University of Texas at Austin, 2000. All of his analyses are based on a minimum of five US presidential elections; those using the agendas of the news magazines are based on six elections, 1976 to 1996.

25 Patrick Rossler and Michael Schenk, 'Cognitive bonding and the German reunification: agenda-setting and persuasion effects of mass media', *International Journal of Public Opinion Research*, 12, 1 (2000), pp. 29–47.

26 *Philadelphia Inquirer*, 27 December 1996, pp. A1 & 18.

27 *New York Times*, 17 January 1989, p. 22. Internationally, Population Communications International has assisted in the production of television dramas on family planning, AIDS prevention, gender equality and a variety of other social topics in developing countries worldwide (Doris Graber, *Processing Politics: Learning from Television in the Internet Age* (Chicago: University of Chicago Press, 2001), p. 127).

28 Conducted by Alexander Bloj for McCombs's communication theory course at Syracuse University, this investigation was reported in Maxwell McCombs and Donald Shaw, 'A progress report on agenda-setting research', paper presented at the Association for Education in Journalism, San Diego, CA, 1974.

29 Marilyn Roberts, 'Predicting voter behavior via the agenda setting tradition', *Journalism Quarterly*, 69 (1992), pp. 878–92.

30 John Petrocik, 'Issue ownership in presidential elections with a 1980 case study', *American Journal of Political Science*, 40 (1996), pp. 825–50.

31 Riccardo Puglisi, 'The spin doctor meets the rational voter: a model of electoral competition and media capture with agenda setting effects', unpublished manuscript, London School of Economics, 2003.

32 Marilyn Roberts, Ronald Anderson and Maxwell McCombs, '1990 Texas gubernatorial campaign influence of issues and images', *Mass Comm Review*, 21, 1 & 2 (1994), pp. 20–35.

33 M. Sutherland and J. Galloway, 'Role of advertising: persuasion or agenda setting?', *Journal of Advertising Research*, 21, 5 (1981), pp. 25–9; Shailendra Ghorpade, 'Agenda setting: a test of advertising's neglected function', *Journal of Advertising Research*, 25 (1986), pp. 23–7.

34 Dominic L. Lasorsa and J. Robyn Goodman, 'Behavioral implications of attribute agenda-setting: news media coverage and the intention to vote', paper presented to the International Communication Association, San Francisco, 1999.

35 Robert L. Stevenson, Rainer Bohme and Nico Nickel, 'The TV agenda-setting influence on campaign 2000', *Egyptian Journal of Public Opinion Research*, 2, 1 (2001), pp. 29–50.

36 Tsuneo Ogawa, 'Framing and agenda setting function', *Keio Communication Review*, 23 (2001), pp. 71–80.

37 For additional evidence on the strong parallel between the shifting amounts of news coverage across the 2000 US presidential election year and variations in how much people talked and thought about election news, see Thomas Patterson, *The Vanishing Voter: Public Involvement in an Age of Uncertainty* (New York: Alfred A. Knopf, 2002).

38 David Weaver, 'Issue salience and public opinion: are there consequences of agenda-setting?', *International Journal of Public Opinion Research*, 3 (1991), pp. 53–68.

39 Nancy Kieffer, 'Agenda-setting and corporate communication issues: can the mass media influence corporate stock prices?', unpublished master's thesis, Syracuse University, 1983.

40 An overview of the research in this area and the programmes of the annual international conventions can be found on the web site of the Reputation Institute: <www.reputationinstitute.com>.

41 Craig Carroll and Maxwell McCombs, 'Agenda-setting effects of business news on the public's images and opinions about major corporations', *Corporate Reputation Review*, 6 (2003), pp. 36–46.

42 C. C. Chen and J. R. Meindl, 'The construction of leadership images in the popular press: the case of Donald Burr and People Express', *Administrative Science Quarterly*, 36 (1991), pp. 521–51; S. L. Wartick, 'The relationship between intense media exposure and change in corporation reputation', *Business Society*, 31 (1992), pp. 33–49; Charles J. Frombrun, 'Indices of corporate reputation: an analysis of media rankings and social monitors' ratings', *Corporate Reputation Review*, 1 (1998), pp. 327–40.

43 David L. Deephouse, 'Media reputation as a strategic resource: an integration of mass communication and resource-based theories', *Journal of Management*, 26 (2000), pp. 1091–112.

44 C. Callison, 'Media relations and the internet: how Fortune 500 company websites assist journalists in news gathering', *Public Relations Review*, 29 (2003), pp. 29–41.

45 C. Ohl, J. D. Pincus, T. Rimmer and D. Harison, 'Agenda building role of news releases in corporate takeovers', *Public Relations Review*, 21 (1995), pp. 89–101.

Chapter 9   Mass Communication and Society

 1 Harold Lasswell, 'The structure and function of communication in society', in *The Communication of Ideas*, ed. Lyman Bryson (New York: Institute for Religious and Social Studies, 1948), pp. 37–51.

 2 Toshio Takeshita and Shunji Mikami, 'How did mass media influence the voters' choice', *Keio Communication Review*, 17 (1995), pp. 27–41.

 3 Esteban Lopez-Escobar, Juan Pablo Llamas and Maxwell McCombs, 'Agenda-setting y consenso', *Comunicación y Sociedad* IX (1996), pp. 91–125.

4 Jian-Hua Zhu with William Boroson, 'Susceptibility to agenda setting', in *Communication and Democracy*, ed. M. McCombs, D. Shaw and D. Weaver (Mahwah, NJ: Lawrence Erlbaum, 1997), p. 82 (emphasis in original).

5 Donald Shaw and Shannon Martin, 'The function of mass media agenda setting', *Journalism Quarterly*, 69 (1992), pp. 902–20.

6 Ching-Yi Chiang, 'Bridging and closing the gap of our society: social function of media agenda setting', unpublished master's thesis, University of Texas at Austin, 1995; Esteban Lopez-Escobar, Juan Pablo Llamas and Maxwell McCombs, 'Agenda setting and community consensus: first and second level effects', *International Journal of Public Opinion Research*, 10 (1998), pp. 335–48; Lopez-Escobar, Llamas and McCombs, 'Agenda-setting y consenso'.

7 David Weaver, Doris Graber, Maxwell McCombs and Chaim Eyal, *Media Agenda Setting in a Presidential Election* (Westport, CT: Greenwood, 1981).

8 Joseph Cappella and Kathleen Hall Jamieson, *Spiral of Cynicism: The Press and the Public Good* (New York: Oxford University Press, 1997).

9 Thomas Patterson, *Out of Order* (New York: Random House Vintage Books, 1993).

10 Lutz Erbring, Edie Goldenberg and Arthur Miller, 'Front-page news and real-world cues', *American Journal of Political Science*, 24 (1980), pp. 16–49.

11 For additional discussion of this perspective, see Davis Merritt and Maxwell McCombs, *The Two W's of Journalism: The Why and What of Public Affairs Reporting* (Mahwah, NJ: Lawrence Erlbaum, 2003), especially chapters 4–6.

12 Recall the influence of the conservative religious organization the Christian Coalition on the agenda of the news media that was cited in chapter 7. See Kyle Huckins, 'Interest-group influence on the media agenda', *Journalism & Mass Communication Quarterly*, 76 (1999), pp. 76–86.

13 Judith Buddenbaum, 'The media, religion, and public opinion: toward a unified theory of cultural influence', in *Religion and Popular Culture: Studies in the Interaction of Worldviews*, ed. Daniel A. Stout and Judith Buddenbaum (Ames: Iowa State University Press, 2001), p. 27.

14 Jacqueline Harris and Maxwell McCombs, 'The interpersonal/mass communication interface among church leaders', *Journal of Communication*, 22 (1972), pp. 257–62.

15 See, for example, Michael Robinson, 'Collective memory: from the 20s through the 90s: the way we think we were', *Public Perspective*, 11, 1 (2000), pp. 14–19, 44–7.

16 Kurt Lang, Gladys Engel Lang, Hans Mathias Kepplinger and Simone Ehmig, 'Collective memory and political generations: a survey of German journalists', *Political Communication*, 10 (1993), pp. 211–29.

17 Yoram Peri, 'The media and collective memory of Yitzhak Rabin's remembrance', *Journal of Communication*, 49, 3 (1999), pp. 106–24.

18 Raquel Rodriguez Diaz, 'Los profesores universitarios como medios de comunicacion: la agenda-setting de los lumnos y profesores' [University professors as communication media: agenda-setting of students and profes-

sors], unpublished doctoral dissertation, Complutense University of Madrid, 2000.

19 Lawrence Wenner, quoted in John Fortunato, *The Ultimate Assist: The Relationship and Broadcasting Strategies of the NBA and Television Networks* (Cresskill, NJ: Hampton Press, 2001), p. 2.

20 Fortunato, *The Ultimate Assist.*

21 Naomi Wolf, *The Beauty Myth: How Images of Beauty Are Used Against Women* (New York: Anchor, 1991).

22 *BBC Online News*, 'TV brings eating disorders to Fiji', 20 May 1999.

23 Stephen Hall, 'The bully in the mirror', *New York Times Magazine*, 22 August 1999, pp. 31–5, 58, 62–4.

24 Donald Shaw, Maxwell McCombs, David Weaver and Bradley Hamm, 'Individuals, groups, and agenda melding', *International Journal of Public Opinion Research*, 11, 1 (1999), pp. 2–24.

25 Doris Graber, *Mass Media and American Politics*, 2nd edn (Washington, DC: Congressional Quarterly Press, 1984), p. 264.

26 Dixie Evatt and Salma Ghanem, 'Building a scale to measure salience', paper presented to the World Association for Public Opinion Research, Rome, Italy, 2001.

27 Spiro Kiousis, 'Explicating media salience: a factor analysis of *New York Times* issue coverage during the 2000 presidential election', *Journal of Communication*, 54, 1 (2004), pp. 71–87.

28 Paula Poindexter, Laura Smith and Maxwell McCombs, 'Need for orientation in the new media landscape', unpublished paper, University of Texas at Austin, 2003.

29 Chan Yun Yoo, Gunho Lee and Maxwell McCombs, 'Refining "need for orientation" as an explanation for agenda-setting effects in the digital age', unpublished paper, University of Texas at Austin, 2003.

Epilogue

1 Paul Krugman, 'In media res', *New York Times*, 29 November 2002, p. A33.

Index